WORK,
SEX,
MONEY

ALSO BY CHÖGYAM TRUNGPA

WORK, SEX, MONEY

REAL LIFE
ON THE
PATH OF
MINDFULNESS

■ ■ ■ ■ ■ ■ ■ ■ ■

Chögyam Trungpa

EDITED BY
Carolyn Rose Gimian &
Sherab Chödzin Kohn

SHAMBHALA · *Boston & London* · 2011

Shambhala Publications, Inc.
Horticultural Hall
300 Massachusetts Avenue
Boston, Massachusetts 02115
www.shambhala.com

9 8 7 6 5 4 3

Printed in the United States of America

⊗ This edition is printed on acid-free paper that meets the
American National Standards Institute z39.48 Standard.
♻ This book was printed on 30% postconsumer recycled
paper. For more information please visit www.shambhala.com.

Distributed in the United States by Random House, Inc.,
and in Canada by Random House of Canada Ltd

Designed by Lora Zorian

Library of Congress Cataloging-in-Publication Data

Trungpa, Chögyam, 1939–1987.
Work, sex, money: real life on the path of mindfulness / Chögyam Trungpa;
edited by Carolyn Rose Gimian and Sherab Chödzin Kohn.
p.   cm.
Includes index.
ISBN 978-1-59030-596-6 (pbk.: alk. paper)
1. Religious life—Buddhism. 2. Buddhism—Doctrines. I. Title.
BQ4302.T785 2011
294.3'4—dc22
2010036776

Contents

Editor's Preface

Each day, we deal with the challenges of ordinary life: mundane experiences that could be summarized by the title of this book: *Work, Sex, Money*. We all hope these aspects of life will be a source of fulfillment and pleasure, and they often are. Yet, at the same time, we all have problems with these areas of our lives, and we search for practical advice and solutions to these concerns.

There are thousands of books, articles, Web sites, radio shows, and television programs that provide advice or self-help on these topics. Concerned about work? Innumerable books and articles will give you career advice and tell you how to dress for the workplace, deal with bullies or bosses, ask for a raise, or be an effective manager. Television has a plethora of news features and shows dedicated to solving problems in your workplace and showing you how to deal with work as it relates to everyday tasks in the home—how to cook, how to dress, and how to decorate your living room. Television also makes the world of work highly entertaining, from boardroom competitions judged by Donald Trump to solving kitchen nightmares or laughing through popular comedies about life in the office.

Sex and the related areas of family and relationships in general fascinate us, preoccupy us, and cause us a great deal of trouble. Here, too, there is copious advice offered in the literature of self-help, and our obsession with sex and relationships is titillated by film, television, the press, and the Internet, whether we prefer news, fiction, the tabloids, or "reality" TV.

For many of us who live in affluent societies around the world and for many others who are aspiring to affluence, materialism has become a virtue and a goal. Money has been viewed as glamorous, greed has been extolled as virtue, and wealth has been seen as the key to success and happiness. Lately, however, with global recession looming, money has become an increasing source of anxiety. How to save, how to spend wisely, how to make more money, how to do more with less, exhilaration when the stock market rises, panic when we lose our job: we have lots of issues with money.

Generally, if we associate spirituality at all with how we deal with the challenges of everyday life, we are hoping for a magic bullet or maybe a mantra that will solve our problems and relieve our anxieties. Like Dorothy in the *Wizard of Oz*, we'd like to be carried off to a magical land where enemies can be conquered by simply throwing water on them. We'd like our everyday problems, like wicked witches, to melt through prayer and meditation. And once having vanquished the villains, we would like to be able to click our red shoes together to return home to the loving embrace of family and, we hope, a secure job and a healthy bank balance.

What are the chances for this kind of happy-ever-after solution? Not so good. A nagging feeling tells us that we are stuck with our lives and with ourselves. In fact, to cope with the anxieties and challenges of modern life, what we need is not temporary escape, because eventually we find ourselves back in the "real world." The best prescription is a dose of reality and a dose of respect for ourselves and our world of work, sex, and money. Enter Chögyam Trungpa with a book that celebrates the sacredness of life and our ability to cope with its twists and turns with dignity, humor, and even joy.

His gift to the reader is an inclusive vision of life, one that encompasses the biggest issues and the smallest details of every day. There are, in fact, few definitive answers in these pages. There is, however, lots of authentic wisdom offered, rather than pseudo words of wisdom or dogma. Instead, the author is providing us with tools to work with the toughest stuff in our lives.

If we look at the most extreme situations—such as the plight of people in a war zone or dealing with the aftermath of a disaster, as in New Orleans following Hurricane Katrina or Haiti following the devastating earthquake—it's obvious that words by themselves are not the solution. A soothing message that "everything is going to be all right" will not solve the day-to-day problems of survival faced by people whose society has collapsed. This is, in fact, also true in ordinary, everyday life— which we may often experience as a disaster on a much smaller scale.

The tools that people need to deal with their lives are also more than the things the material world can provide. We have to harness fearlessness to overcome anxiety and panic. To approach our lives sanely, we need to bring our intelligence or awareness to bear on situations. We also need a panoramic view, a way to see how the details fit into a larger pattern so that we can discover and organize order amid chaos. All of these tools are available in the pages of this book.

Here, too, you will find the key to unlock an attitude of loving-kindness or acceptance toward yourself and compassion for others, which is one of the most powerful tools that we can bring to ordinary life. Underlying all of these resources, people must have the confidence or the will to help themselves and others, the willingness to engage the tough stuff of life, and the ability to appreciate the raw and rugged qualities of life as things of beauty.

Chögyam Trungpa was not a big fan of hope, but he was a

fan of faith. By faith, he meant conviction in the sacredness of the moment, seeing that we can have faith in and commit to whatever is happening now in our lives. He contrasted this with hope, by which he referred to an attitude that looks for solutions in the future: we hope things will work out later, even if they seem hopeless now. It is faith in our direct, immediate experience that gives us the will, and the courage, to engage the most difficult moments and the most chaotic experiences.

Work, Sex, Money begins with several chapters that describe the general terrain of our discussion: problems in modern life with materialism on all levels—physical, psychological, and spiritual—and the need for formal meditation and a commitment to working with meditation in action, or applying meditative awareness to everyday life. Then Trungpa Rinpoche (Rinpoche is a title of respect that means "Precious One") gets into the juicy details of work, sex, and money, with several chapters on each topic. The chapters on work are not just about the workplace and one's career or profession. The author looks at general issues of conduct and discipline in everyday life as well as how the smallest action or everyday activity can be either an expression of simplicity and wakefulness or a source of chaos, pain, and confusion. The section on sex includes both a broad discussion on sexual energy and passion as well as discussion of relationships and relating sanely to family dynamics. In the section on money, Rinpoche looks generally at money as a form of energy. Chapters on the ethical approach to money and relating sanely to economics while being in business are included. The book concludes with two chapters on karma and panoramic awareness that tie together the whole discussion of a meditative or contemplative experience of everyday life.

Chögyam Trungpa witnessed and immersed himself in many vastly different human circumstances and lifestyles. In Tibet he was an incarnate lama and the abbot of an important monastery in eastern Tibet. He was raised in the monastic tradition, which he fully embraced in his early years. Tibet was not a culture of luxury, but within that modest society, he lived a privileged life. With the increasing presence and dominance of the Chinese communists in the 1950s, he experienced the devastation and destruction of his culture, and he was forced to leave his monastery, his family, and his country behind, forever, in 1959. He became a poor refugee in India. He led a frugal life in England, and during his early days in North America he had very little money. In the 1970s, he married and started a family, and in his later years, he led a householder's life of material comfort and relative affluence. He was an artist, a playwright, and a poet. He was the president of a university and of a large association of spiritual groups, he sat on the board of many businesses and organizations, and he helped to start a number of nonprofit and for-profit enterprises. In all of the life situations Rinpoche encountered, he harmonized and demonstrated both nonattachment and engagement. He didn't shy away from life at all, yet he wasn't trapped in life either. He made many mistakes and had many transitions in his life, and he learned from his experiences. So when he speaks in this volume of the very human challenges of working in the world, being a sexual being, engaging in intimate relationships, and relating to wealth, poverty, and money, he speaks from a broad base of experience rather than preaching from afar.

Chögyam Trungpa had an enormous effect on the standard English vocabulary now used in connection with Buddhism, and on the practice of sitting meditation in the West. *Meditation in action* was one of the phrases he coined, and it was also the title of his first book of Buddhist teachings, published in 1969. If that title had not been used then, it could have been the title or subtitle for this book. In 1973 Trungpa Rinpoche replied to a letter (from someone he had never met) with these comments about his personal life, in which he explains the meaning of meditation in action:

> With regard to your inquiry about my lifestyle, you must understand that I regard myself as an ordinary person. I am a householder, who makes mortgage payments. I have a wife and three children whom I support. At the same time, my relationship with the teachings is inseparable from my whole being. I do not try to rise above the world. My vocation is working with the world. . . . There is a fundamental idea which refuses to divide things into this or that, sacred or profane, right or wrong. That is why I write and speak of meditation in action. It is much easier to appear holy than to be sane. So the idea is to separate spirituality from spiritual materialism. This requires a practice and some courage.*

Rinpoche found life earthy, rugged, and grounding. At the same time, he found it inspiring, fascinating, and full of energy and magic. He helped others to experience life as he himself did: as totally real, not lacking in anything, and worthy of celebration. More than twenty years after his death, this book still speaks to our experience in an immediate and compelling manner. I hope that it will help many readers to find a path through life, one that blends spiritual and secular experience in a way that respects and actually enhances both. For like a bird with two wings, modern life must integrate the spiritual life with the life of every day.

In the 1970s, when the talks that form the basis of this book were given, Buddhism and the sitting practice of meditation were largely viewed, particularly in the West, as activities outside of the mainstream of everyday life. The idea of integrating

---

* Excerpt from a letter to Steven Morrow, May 10, 1973. Used by permission.

mindfulness and awareness into ordinary activities was somewhat radical. Today, the application of mindfulness is being widely accepted as a helpful discipline in the management of pain; stress reduction; the treatment of depression, post-traumatic stress disorder, and other psychological problems; and in education, developing creativity—pretty much anywhere you look. In this volume, Trungpa Rinpoche talks extensively about why and how meditation and spirituality apply to work, sex, and money. Some of this may seem commonplace now, but at the time, it was an eye-opener for many in his audience. Today, people may think of the application of mindfulness to a specific problem as important, without necessarily wanting to adopt the bigger view represented by a tradition like Buddhism. Without proselytizing whatsoever or putting labels like "Buddhist" on the insights he offers, Chögyam Trungpa nevertheless presents the big view, the vast view, a view that transforms every moment and the whole of life.

The world needs our help. But in order to help, we need to unlock and harness the spiritual wakefulness and inner resources we all possess. *Work, Sex, Money* can help us to bring the spiritual and the profane elements in our life together so that we can work with situations with cheerfulness, skill, and delight. I am personally grateful to the author for the insight he offers in this volume, and I pray that it may help many others, who in turn may help this world.

CAROLYN GIMIAN
February 2010

WORK,
SEX,
MONEY

1

■ ■ ■

THE SACRED
SOCIETY

The discussion of work, sex, and money is quite a big undertaking. Usually people see these subjects as very private. Nevertheless, we have decided to discuss them. However, the subject matter is not purely work, sex, and money but something behind those things, another dimension that is connected with how we relate with life altogether.

As Buddhist practitioners or practitioners of meditation, we are supposed to be immersed in the contemplative tradition and spiritual practice. Why would we discuss work, sex, and money? If you are involved in spirituality, you may think you should transcend work, sex, and money. Perhaps you think you should live the contemplative life, a life in which those things don't apply because you spend the whole day meditating. You should have nothing to do with those things. You shouldn't have to think about work. Nobody should be involved with sex, because people shouldn't have such lustful

thoughts at all while living the contemplative life of meditation. And money—you should be involved with that least of
all! What money? Who has any anyhow? Money—that's the
last thing we should think about. Spirituality, you may think,
is not concerned with green energy.* Forget about money—
we should have transcended that.

On the other hand, you may find that in spite of your spiritual intentions, your life is involved with work, sex, and money
anyway. In that case, maybe there is something to be said about
those subjects after all. On the whole, we are not strictly spiritual or religious at all. People have to look for work. They have
to find a j-o-b. We work for money. We may find that we are
building our lives around sex and more generally on relationships.

Then the question is, are we really working on spirituality
or not? If so, there is something that we might not have thought
about: that spirituality isn't really "spirituality" in an idealized
sense. Do you think spirituality is something purely transcendental? It's questionable. Real spirituality might have something
to do with ordinary life.

If spirituality *does* have something to do with everyday life
situations, then relating to spirituality means contributing something to society as a whole. We have to associate with society in
order to offer something to society. For some people, that is not
an easy thing to accept or do at all.

Society, as we tend to experience it in the West, functions
largely on the basis of give and take. That is to say, we tend to
think about our role in society in terms of what is demanded
of us, or what we have to give, and what we can get out of the
situation, which is the taking part. We could call this view materialism. Materialism can be physical, psychological, or spiritual.

---

* Chögyam Trungpa used the term green energy to refer to money. Today it has a
much different meaning, connected with the use of renewable resources and energy
that does not have a negative impact on the environment.—Eds.

Physical materialism is quite straightforward. You measure your life, your worth, or your experiences in terms of physical gain, or literally how much money or how many nice things you can get out of something, or how much something will cost you. Psychological materialism is more subtle. It is based on competition and psychological one-upmanship. Finally, spiritual materialism is using the spiritual path to gain spiritual self-centered power or bliss. All of these approaches are based on propping up or reinforcing the ego. If we see society purely from these materialistic viewpoints, we might conclude that it has nothing much to offer us on the spiritual path.

However, from the genuine spiritual point of view, as opposed to an idealized viewpoint, society is an extremely potent arena, full of vibrant qualities of energy. That practical approach of working with the energy of the situation is the only access point we can find. Otherwise, on an abstract level, society may seem like an autonomous process without any cracks in it, no faults in its surface, no entrances and no exits. But if we see society in terms of the practicality of work, sex, and money, we can find ways of working with it. Sex is an aspect or attribute of society. Money is an aspect of society. Work is an aspect of society. From that point of view, we can see something relevant to us in society. We can see how we might contribute something to society, or at least how we could work along with it. If we look at it in the concrete terms of work, sex, and money, society is not entirely dry and sterile; it is not insignificant for us.

The whole question boils down to whether we regard society as sacred. Society does contain profundity and sacredness. The sacredness of society is potent and powerful. I'm sure many ordinary people would not accept such an idea. They would think that we are trying to infiltrate; we are trying to sneak something into the idea of society, to impose some foreign element or idea on it. However, it seems genuinely important to see the spiritual aspect, the visionary, almost psychedelic, aspect of society.* We have to see not only the basic happenings but also their basic quality of energy, the energy that they contain. That is what we are looking into here.

Work, sex, and money are actually the energy outlet of society, its energy radiation, the expression of its sacredness. So we should try to see the spiritual implications of society, the spirituality even within Madison Avenue or Wall Street. What is the spirituality of a place like Wall Street? What is its healthier aspect? For that matter, what does America altogether mean? What does landing on the moon mean?** What does producing supersonic aircraft mean? What does all this mean in terms of spirituality?

You might feel that if we are discussing a spiritual approach to society, the discussion should be peaceful and have a lovely sense of equilibrium. You might think we should approach the subject matter in a detached, spiritual way, according to the picture that many people have of the Eastern tradition of spirituality as peaceful, nonviolent, gentle, genteel.

Should we approach it from that point of view, where everything is good and everybody loves each other, all is peaceful, and everything is going to be okay? Or should we take another approach, where there is energy happening, there is something to work on, and things are dynamic and provocative? There are flashes of negative energy, flashes of positive energy, flashes of destruction, flashes of hatred and love. All of this is happening within the big perspective of a mandala, a sense of totality or wholeness, a pattern and a structure that unify and contain all the parts. Can we approach our discussion from that angle as well? Can we approach spirituality and our relationship to society from that engaged perspective?

---

* In today's parlance, the term *psychedelic* implies distorted perception and hallucination. At the time, however, Rinpoche was using this term to refer to genuine visionary insight into the energy of a situation.—Eds.

** The first manned moon landing (Apollo 11, July 1969) was still a fresh and hot topic at the time of this seminar.—Eds.

You are part of society. Otherwise you wouldn't be here reading this, and we couldn't communicate. If you were not included in society, you wouldn't breathe the same air as others; you wouldn't eat the same food. The main issue is whether you are genuinely open to relating with society as part of your personal journey of spirituality. Does society mean anything to you in your personal search, or do you purely want to attain liberation by yourself, without society? Do you really want to abandon all the others? Do you care how society suffers or how it might gain bliss?

Some of us find it almost impossible to appreciate the sacred aspect of living in a big urban center. We might want to escape and live in the country, where we can just laugh at the whole city phenomenon. How funny life is in the city, we think, how terrible, how ironical, but at the same time funny. We would like to step out of city life, have nothing to do with it.

In that situation, the whole city could become your guinea pig colony. Your guinea pigs are living everywhere, running around the city. Your relationship to the city is the same as that of scientists relating to their guinea pigs. They inject things into the guinea pigs and the guinea pigs have some reaction. That's the kind of attitude that some people involved in the spiritual scene have toward the city dwellers.

That's a very uncompassionate attitude. The city just reminds us of a big display of irony—irony in the negative sense rather than in the sense of natural self-irony. We are laughing at other people rather than seeing the contradictory and humorous aspects of our own lives. If that approach becomes part of a spiritual view, it's rather sickening, because that view regards normal citizens as terrible, as a failure of humanity, as embarrassing. That approach comes from preconceived ideas about life in the city, and we are not willing to communicate with those preconceptions.

More generally, preconceptions come up in people's relationship to money, their relationship to work, their relationship to sex, even their relationship to their parents. We find it difficult to relate to these things, especially as they manifest in urban life. That doesn't mean, however, that we should run away from these issues. Because there is something difficult and destructive involved, there must be something creative involved as well. Relating to that creative aspect is the point here. You don't have to abandon things because there is something destructive in them.

There is the Buddhist story of the arhat, one of the Buddha's disciples with self-realization, who goes to the charnel ground, a burial ground in India. There he picks up one human bone, and he ponders that. He sees that a bone comes from death, and death comes from birth, and birth comes from desire, and so on and so on. Finally he works out the whole chain of causality from this one bone. He realizes that desire comes from grasping, and eventually everything comes from ignorance. Just from this one bone, he is able to see the chain reaction of the twelve links of interdependent causality, known as the *nidanas*. *Nidana* is a Sanskrit word that means "cause" or "source." The twelve nidanas refer to twelve aspects of *samsara,* or the cycle of birth and death, often compared to twelve spokes of a wheel. In *thangkas,* or traditional Tibetan paintings, or the wheel of life, the twelve nidanas are shown as the outer circle of the wheel. Here in this story, the arhat is able to see the whole chain of causality of the twelve nidanas by just contemplating one bone. We could work in the same way in our own situation. We don't have to reject or abandon anything. We could work on the creative aspect of situations.

New York City might represent death to you, at times. I can see that. People on the street might look to you like walking corpses with no expressions on their faces. And there are urban jackals, which might manifest as cars with sirens blaring and policemen inside. The dry air of death is in your nose all the time and in your mouth. As an occasional way of cheering up, you come back to the deathlike displays in store windows with their lifeless mannequins. Gigantic buildings have been built; people are blocked off in boxes without any air—a further expression of death. The whole city could really be seen as an expression of death.

When I first came to America with my wife, Diana, and we visited New York City, the first impression I got was the smell of the city as a corpse—the smell of human bodies, of corpses. The first impact was that. But that's okay! It's perfectly okay. That could be the continuous starting point of your inspiration. Dharma teachings are not going to be romantic or beautiful— oh no! The teachings are going to be painful, even invoking paranoia. At the same time, we can work with the situation and find something creative in it. We can include all of these urban jackals, lying corpses, and expressionless faces as part of the inspiration. There's nothing wrong with that scene in the city at all, absolutely nothing. It's just a demonstration of life. The whole thing is based on work, sex, and money.

On the other hand, perhaps you find the city entertaining. We try to entertain ourselves all the time, particularly in the Western world. There are hundreds of books and hundreds of pictures, and we have hundreds of different types of friends, friends who are eccentrics and into all sorts of exotic things. Then there's the telephone—you can always make a call. And there's the news.*   All sorts of things are happening for our entertainment. Right now we are being entertained. Entertainment constantly occupies our time. Visiting a big city like New York, that quality becomes obvious. Entertainment proclaims itself—to the extent that we find it too irritating. That kind of self-deception is too obvious; it's too painful, because it's too true to be true. So we have to crawl back to our suburban home, to our own familiar deceptions. That way we can be entertained in a more genteel or spiritual way rather than a gaudy and flashy way.

* Today, of course, there's also the Internet.—Eds.

We don't have to completely eliminate entertainment. The problem is a tremendous lack of sense of humor throughout the whole thing. We are *so* serious about our entertainment. We are entertained seriously even by comedy. But if you are no longer self-seriously looking for results, you see the ironical qualities of situations as they are, as they come and go. If you watch a whole television show beginning to end, including the ads, without changing the channel, and you have a sense of humor, you can enjoy it. This doesn't have to be a cynical sense of humor. You can enjoy everything as play. Whereas if you impose your own likes and dislikes, then you laugh occasionally, but you also turn things off when you don't like them. When you begin to select things like that, the whole situation becomes very tiring, because you're seriously selecting all the time.

We should look into all kinds of life situations. Take the case of people whose goal in society is to become rich and have color television sets, plush carpeted rooms, central heating and cooling in their houses, and lots of cars. They hope to become more powerful and happier by having those things. Or let's consider people whose politics are extremely conservative, who support America's being involved in foreign wars and all sorts of conservative causes. Some of them are almost fascists, from a liberal point of view. In the West, you might find ranchers and cowboys, who are supposed to enjoy the natural life, living in contact with cows and horses, but at the same time their political mentality might be totally reactionary. How would you relate with that scene? If you are a liberal, you probably would want to raise yourself above the whole thing. You don't want to be like one of them. However, we should look more closely at that scene, evaluate it without immediately dismissing or judging it.

From your point of view, you may observe that many people with conservative social values don't want to get into the nitty-gritty of work, sex, and money. Their approach to their life is very sterile. It's not potent. It's largely based on the reproduction of concepts, and it's a very serious view—but so is the view of those who reject life in the mainstream.

For many of us, regardless of our politics or our status in society, money is a private thing, sex is a private thing, and so is work. We don't want to discuss them with others at all. We would like to find something transcendental that raises us above those situations. People don't want anything to do with death either. Most of us still have the dualistic notion of death as bad and birth as good. That kind of notion is pervasive, and that is precisely why we need to talk about these subjects.

As practitioners, we have to work with the karmic situation of America, to start with. A certain reformation can take place by natural force —not through carrying placards or staging demonstrations or anything like that. On the other hand, change is not going to happen in an easy or luxurious way. To begin with, we don't know what the reformation is going to look like. We have to work on our own inspiration.

The city could re-form. The whole world could reform. Our duty is to help. You might try to get away from the city, to create your own ideal city, so to speak, your own alternative living place in the country. But you'll still have to relate with society there, in any case. There will be the conflicts of how to get your food supplied, how your mail is delivered, problems with your milkman, and all kinds of details like that.

On the other hand, you might find it necessary to have a certain separation from society at large at times, in order to gain perspective. Without a comparative point of view to see society from, there's no working basis. When you step back for a little while, you gain perspective on your life. However, engaging with society is also necessary, so that you have the perspective from that side also. So the process of stepping back and then reengaging should alternate or be joined side by side—like the idea of wisdom and compassion being side by side. Meditation can provide that nondual perspective.

Once a person is involved with meditation practice and with working on the spiritual path, then the problems encountered in engaging with society are not hang-ups anymore. They are creative opportunities. Those everyday-life situations become part of meditation practice. The situation slows you down, or the situation pushes you. It depends on how much you engage. If you are too engaged, then something will slow you down. If you are not involved enough, there will be some reminder that pushes you to get more involved.

We have to work on our own attitude, to develop an attitude of openness. That will create an entirely new approach to working with situations such as life in the city. Then the city will reform in its own way. We can't really think that we are going to do this and that thing, and then the city will reform according to our wishes. We have to relate with a much bigger world that includes everyone, including the cowboys and cops. They are a source of inspiration, definitely. They are beautiful people, unique. We should work with them. In fact, at a certain stage, we won't be able to escape working with them. They will appear on our path, definitely so.

We don't want to undermine the culture. Cultural situations provide a focal point, a focus for us to relate with. Therefore, we will work with them. We may begin to realize that both we and others make inaccurate evaluations of situations. However, the inaccuracy or the accuracy doesn't really matter. If you work along with situations, things become clear. The initial evaluation doesn't have to be the ultimate landmark. Any evaluation, any conceptual view, is just a relative landmark. We can use it and work with it as we go along.

The more you involve yourself with society, the more experiences you have, the more workable situations will become. The intensity of your engagement brings space. The more intensity there is, that brings out more space. When you involve yourself with situations such as the overpopulation and

the overpowering experience of being in the city, your involvement acts as a guardian. It helps others. It helps to protect them,
because you refuse to abandon them. You can find inspiration
within work, within sex, within money. Within those things,
you can find a connection to the sacredness of society.

2

■ ■ ■

MEDITATION AND DAILY LIFE

S houldn't the basic point of spiritual practice be to inspire an understanding that permits us to relate with life in the fullest way? From that point of view, work, sex, and money could be said to be the highlights of the spiritual experience of everyday life. Further discussion may be necessary for you to accept that the daily living situation should be regarded as a main means of practicing spiritual discipline. So we should look into what we actually mean by spiritual practice.

A prominent idea of spirituality is that the point is to surrender, give away, or renounce the world. Relating with the world, accepting it rather than renouncing it, goes against that view. In almost all spiritual traditions, renouncing the world is regarded as one of the first steps in spiritual practice. Spiritual practice is often regarded as a means of salvation. According to that conception, spirituality should provide a permanent shelter where we can be happy and free; and since our daily living situation does not provide permanent shelter, we have to look for something higher or safer. The idea here is that spiritual practice should lead us to some form of eternity—eternal happiness or eternal youth.

This popular and, we might say, rather primitive notion of spirituality is based on searching for happiness, a sense of security. It tells us we should practice meditation in order to attain enlightened mind or union with God, or something of that nature. All the developments in our practice are regarded as steps toward that permanent happiness, which will lift us above misery, pain, and suffering. We will find a final home or nest to dwell in. The attitude of maintaining oneself in permanent happiness is actually the expression of ego or confused, neurotic mind. It is the neurotic desire to maintain myself, me, my whole being, as a solid entity, as ego. This approach could be called spiritual materialism.

Spiritual materialism is a further step on top of physical and psychological materialism. This materialistic attitude comes about because there is uncertainty about oneself: Am I a definite person? Am I a complete person the way I always wanted to be—do I have power and security? This wishful thinking invites unhappiness, confusion, and dissatisfaction with our way of handling ourselves. We feel that there is something not quite solid about our life, and because it does not seem solid, the possibility arises that *me* and *myself* do not exist in a long-term way. This doubt as to whether we exist or don't exist as an individual entity is a big threat to us.

We are constantly baffled, bewildered, and confused about this. When this confusion crops up, the only way to prove to ourselves that we do exist as an individual entity—as myself, with such and such a name—is to act something out, to make an emergency or extreme move. Such a move may take the form of defending ourselves by means of aggression against what is threatening us, which is a repelling technique. On the other hand, we may defend ourselves by grasping whatever can be used to maintain us, to prove that our existence is a reality. So our choices are either repelling or grasping. Repelling is aggression, hatred. Grasping is passion, desire. Those emotional principles are the main mechanisms ego uses to maintain itself. On the basis of those two mechanisms, we develop all sorts of other emotions, such as fear, hope, pride, jealousy, and so on. Those further means of maintaining ego are accessories on top of the basic hatred or desire.*

However, these tactics might not work. In fact, there are constant failures, because maintaining the continual awareness of ego is such a big task. There are constant gaps where we slip up, we forget to relate to our ego, we forget to defend ourselves, or we forget to control ourselves. This is not entirely bad news, because in fact these gaps, which occur continually in our mental state, are the only way to see the nonexistence of ego. They expose us to the fickleness of ego. Seeing this, we can say that though the ego does exist in some sense, it does not exist as a solid entity. Its nature is transparent. We see the transparent quality of ego through these continual gaps, which again and again brings fear of losing our identity, which automatically provokes further fear and paranoia.

This fear and paranoia result in psychological materialism. There is the constant attempt to maintain ourselves by using external pretexts, ideas, and concepts to prove that I do exist, that the functions of ego are right, that they are a definite thing. I constantly have to prove that to both myself and others, and this produces a particular competitive attitude, which is psycho-

---

* Here, Chögyam Trungpa explains ego's activity of maintaining its ground, referring to its use of passion and aggression (or desire and hatred) as the basis for developing all the emotional states. In most traditional accounts, three principles—passion, aggression, and ignorance—are given as the fundamental mechanisms that power ego and our confusion. They are known as the three poisons. However, it is not rare, as in this talk, to mention only passion and aggression, since these are the active and obvious ones out of the three.—Eds.

logical materialism. By constantly looking for external sources of praise and blame, we hope to reinforce a solid sense of existence.

Spiritual materialism, which uses a similar logic, comes into play when ego feels that psychological materialism has failed to prove ego's existence adequately. At that point ego looks beyond or above—it looks for a higher level of proof. One might try to meditate, to develop mental power, a greater level of concentration. But this approach to meditation is based on securing ego's territory rather than going beyond it. The hope is that in this way ego can become a more intense and continuous ego rather than just the ego in the form of patches of consciousness that we have been experiencing, which is not really satisfying. Such a patchy ego is not really foolproof in terms of defending itself, so a person looks for all kinds of spiritual ways of maintaining or strengthening the awareness of me, myself, ego. That is spiritual materialism.

The whole problem with these materialistic approaches is too much centralization. There is too much concern with the nature of one's own games as opposed to concern with the external projections of the world around us. One is preoccupied with *here*—wrapped up in the self-consciousness of "What is the best way for me? How should I do it? How should I overcome? How should I achieve thus and such? How should I defend myself?" So one tends to reject the messages from the projections of the world outside. To overcome this self-centered situation, we need to gain an understanding of egolessness, centerlessness, the nonexistence of ego. We cannot just start on ego itself. We cannot rely on ego to discover the folly of ego. We need to recognize our actual experience of egolessness.

Ego is dependent on the confirmation from the relative situation outside. When external phenomena become problematic, as the paranoia of ego begins to rise up, gaps begin to appear in ego's game. So the best way to see the absence of ego is to use the confusion that arises when ego relates to the daily living situation—the projections of the world outside. "Projections" in this case refers to the output of ego, which constitutes or makes up our seemingly solid, everyday, bodily situations. These interchanges are made up of all kinds of interactions with people and physical situations, which automatically include the sources where ego's passion and aggression begin. Now, if we are fully in touch with the phenomenal world and see its play completely and thoroughly, then the self-consciousness of ego ceases to be our focus and to play such an important role. By being fully in touch with external situations, we are no longer totally preoccupied with ego's centralized games. We begin to realize that security is not all that important. So relating with our living world, our daily living situations, becomes a way of transcending psychological materialism.

Therefore, the meditative disciplines that have been recommended to us by great teachers should be accompanied by interaction with the world. Meditation practice could be described as the training ground, and the actual application of those training-ground exercises occurs in working with the situations of daily life. That is why the topics of work, sex, and money become our immediate concern. Spirituality is all about how to handle the situations of daily life.

If you look methodically through the history of the Buddhist tradition, you see that hermits don't stay in retreat their whole lives. This is true even though they may take vows to remain in retreat. It has been said that retreat doesn't end completely until you come back into your old life situations. Then your retreat is completed. For instance, Milarepa, a great Tibetan Buddhist practitioner and teacher, took a vow to regard his retreat cave as his tomb. He went into retreat with that attitude, but in the end he couldn't avoid the world altogether. There were huntsmen passing through collecting feathers for their arrows, and other people occasionally dropped in to ask him questions. Finally he had to move on, leave his retreat and walk out into the world. He had to step out of that retreat situation.

There is also the story of Anathapindika, who was a disciple of the Buddha and a great supporter of the community of monks. He provided meditation centers for the monks and food for them, and he created environments in which the Buddha could teach. Without him, there would have been no possibility of propagating the teachings on such a wide scale at the time of the Buddha. Anathapindika asked the Buddha if he should give up his work serving the *sangha* and devote himself purely to meditation practice. If he did, it might be good for him, he thought, but on the other hand it might not be a good thing on the whole because he would no longer be providing situations for other people. The Buddha's answer was that he should remain a householder. The best way that he could serve the Buddha, the dharma, and the sangha—and follow his own path to enlightenment—would be to practice within the householder's life.

For each of us, the answer to this question depends on our individual situations. Your choices depend on what you have gotten yourself into already. There is a Tibetan saying that it is better not to begin things, but once you begin, you should finish properly. So once you have gotten into the householder's life, you may not be able to undo that, and there is a way to practice within it. However, there are other possibilities: if a person is free to do anything he wants in life, he might choose to respect the sacredness of that freedom by putting restrictions on himself and living the contemplative life of a retreatant or a monastic for a period of time. In the Buddhist tradition, retreat seems to be approached quite differently from some Christian traditions of monastic enclosure, where you take a vow to lock yourself behind a grill for the rest of your life. In the Buddhist tradition, there is respect for the principle of retreat and the contemplative life, but still there is some allegiance to samsara, to the ordinary confused world we inhabit. It's almost like an allegiance to paying back the world's kindness.

As it stands now, we have a lack of clarity about relating

with our ordinary life situations. Should we abandon everyday life as a bad job? Should we try to do our best with it? Should we just muddle through? None of these questions is based on a firm and clear understanding at the beginning. It's just guess-work. We think there must be some real and right way of doing things, but we don't know what it is, so we just push ourselves into situations and hope for the best. This haphazard approach lacks the basic discipline of meditation practice, which is the only way to develop a continuity of insight and clarity.

Meditation practice, in this case, is not at all a matter of building something up, which is the approach of spiritual mate-rialism. Rather, meditation is allowing ourselves simply to be and to open by using certain techniques that take away the self-conscious preoccupation with tactics and strategy. Through meditation we develop a way of doing nothing, absolutely noth-ing—physically nothing and psychologically nothing. The only way to do nothing is to pick some focus and treat it as though it were nothing. This is the technique that meditation has tradi-tionally developed. We pick something like breathing or walk-ing to meditate on. But these are transparent things. They have no individuality. Everybody breathes. Everybody walks. So we choose breathing and walking techniques as ordinary and trans-parent techniques.

Through relating fully with such techniques, we reach a point where psychological upheavals will arise in our prac-tice. Subconscious hidden emotions begin to come through, to come up to the surface. In other words, meditation practice using transparent techniques such as working with the breath becomes the practice of doing nothing, and that provides a clear place in which whatever comes up will be noticed and recog-nized.

This is a way of relating with phenomena in the internal sense. In meditation, you don't have interactions with people or the world outside verbally or physically, but still the practice is a way of relating with phenomena directly, rather than being caught in the centralized games of ego. Meditation is not a matter of withdrawing—you are not drawing in, retreating from the world. In fact, you are getting into the world. Until now the world hasn't been able to show us its fullest expressions, because we never let it happen. We were constantly seduced by this or that. In the meantime, we were missing the boat all the time. Whenever there is an upheaval or uproar—all kinds of energies coming up—our minds are preoccupied with something else. We never become conscious of those things properly. But in meditation there is a sense of forthcoming, opening. Meditation allows us to see the hidden things, so we don't miss one moment of energy or upheaval. We see them clearly, precisely because we don't evaluate them in a self-conscious way. Evaluation requires more self-consciousness, and in the meantime, while we are evaluating, we miss something else. We miss the implications that happen around those energies that arise in our minds.

So in this case, meditation is a way of developing clarity, which allows us to see the precision of daily life situations as well as our thought process so that we can relate with both of them fully and completely.

From this viewpoint, meditation is also associated with how we approach work. A person should be able to carry out his or her job without interruption, and meditation supports this approach. In this way, the meaning of work becomes part of our spiritual practice rather than purely a part of our daily struggle. Work in this case is actual physical involvement with objects, people, and the energies around that involvement. In this sense, working is a constant tutorial. The teacher, in the form of the work situation, is always there: if you do something badly, it shows; if you do something well, it shows. There's no way of fooling this process.

There is no need here to get involved with the self-conscious rigidity of a deliberate artistic approach to work or to dealing with objects. At the same time, one has to have respect for the importance of life situations. Things around us always have an association with us, whether they belong to us or not. Once we begin to feel that association, we begin to feel things and relate to them directly, properly, and fully.

With this approach, if you are making a cup of tea, you are in complete contact with the process: with what kind of tea you are going to brew and what kind of kettle and teapot you are going to use. It is a matter of relating with those little things, which is not a big deal particularly. It's not a matter of life and death if you make a bad cup of tea. At the same time, in some sense it *is* a matter of life and death, because relating with each individual thing is important. This is what I mean by work. It doesn't particularly have to relate to a job, although this same style of relating fully to things could be used in the job situation as well.

The little things we do in life may not seem to have a direct bearing on spirituality; maybe they seem quite unspiritual. Nevertheless, it is your world you are dealing with; it is your environment. So the things you are doing should be felt fully rather than rushed through.

That doesn't mean doing everything slowly and deliberately. Rushing doesn't necessarily mean doing things quickly. You can rush slowly—no matter how slow you go, you are missing the point all the time. However fast or slow you rush, there is a sense that your mind is preoccupied with something, constantly preoccupied with hopes or fear or passion or aggression, or something of that nature. Because of that, you fail to relate directly with objects, as in making a cup of tea.

If you're going fast, just trying to go slow doesn't help; nor the other way around. You see, the point is not particularly to change your pace. The main thing is to become aware that you are not in contact with what is happening, because you are so concerned with getting ahead. Whether you do something slow or fast, there's a sense of absentmindedness. So what is necessary is to learn to relate with what you are doing completely. If you relate completely with what you are doing, then you can't rush. You don't have to think about the future particularly; you are content with what is there at that very moment. Not rushing is having complete contact with what is happening at that very moment. In other words, a sense of nowness is necessary. Some humor or light touch is also helpful. Then you begin to see the present situation fully and completely, because the rushing process is a very serious one, very earnest and honest, in some sense quite solemn.

When you relate to situations directly and simply, you realize that body and mind have a very close relationship. Mind and body are one thing rather than separate. Body is mind, mind is body. The expressions of body are also constantly the expressions of mind. Work, which is an expression of everyday life, brings the body and mind into play equally. We do not have to develop a special philosophical attitude in order to make our work spiritual, even if our activity appears to have nothing to do with spirituality. We do not have to try to interpret it in a special way. We do not have to find appropriate ideas or ideologies to fit a particular job.

On the other hand, many people's work is largely intellectual. This is not a problem. You can appreciate the ordinariness of life in any situation. However, I think some physical discipline is also necessary in a person's life. Without that, you could become totally wrapped up in your ideas, like an absentminded professor. There's always a need for some grounded perspective like physical work or doing artwork—something where you can use your hands as well as your intellect. Once you get in the habit of using the intellect constantly as a means to understand things, there is a tendency to become completely lost in ideas. One might tend to become aggressive, feeling that all the scientific ideas one has are right and foolproof. One fails then to pay attention to ordinary life. So there's an incompleteness to working entirely with the intellect.

There's no need to philosophize work in order to make it

spiritual. It has spiritual bearing anyway. If you regard your-self as a person on the spiritual path, then whatever you do is part of the path, an expression of the path. Decentralization, the absence of ego, the lack of searching for happiness and not avoiding pain—all of that brings us into the reality of dealing with things directly and thoroughly. Dealing with things in this decentralized, egoless manner is known in the Buddhist tradition as *upaya,* skillful means. Without that, there is no means of discovering the inner guru, or inner teacher, as one might call it, which is the constant instruction that you begin to receive on the path. The daily living situation becomes the teaching; it becomes a constant learning process. There's no way of developing that sense of inner teacher if you fail to relate with daily living situations directly, because without that there's no interchange with your world.

The experiences that are part of the learning process in everyday life do not have to be particularly mystical. They do not have to be anything like a voice telling you to do this or do that. They are not like seeing spiritual symbolism everywhere. It's not as literal as that. The spiritual path is profound in itself—it's just a matter of things being seen as real and direct and simple, but that means a lot. Because of the simplicity, we are able to work with whatever comes up. Because situations are simple, they are pure. There are no alternatives involved at all. It's a direct situation.

Dealing with the physical situations of the world also means dealing with emotions at the same time. The emotional expressions of body, of physical engagement, are obvious, and we can work with them in a direct and simple fashion. The point is that we cannot reject the situation we are in now. We won't necessarily achieve spiritual advancement by changing our lifestyle. In fact, we could almost expect the opposite. We should have continuity in our lifestyle, a continuity of experience, and we should get into that and try to find the follow-up, the next step, within that, rather than trying to get into a prefabricated environment that is supposedly conducive to spiritual advancement. Such an environment might be conducive temporarily, but at some point we become weak because that situation is ideal and softens us up. Then, when a problematic situation finally arises, we won't be able to deal with it. We will find ourselves trying to re-create that ideal, beautiful situation. We will end up with a constant yearning for the future and an inability to relate with the present situation of nowness. So transcending spiritual materialism has to be based on working with the daily living situation. That is the basic point.

3

. . .

THE MYTH
OF HAPPINESS

We all want to discover the meaning of life. Some people say the meaning of life is to be found only in spiritual practice. Others say the meaning of life is to be found in the human dignity that comes from dealing with the world successfully. Still, the meaning of life remains under dispute. It is the subject of philosophical struggles and metaphysical doubts. Those go on and on; the question is still there, and the answer remains uncertain.

I myself do not expect to fully answer this question. As far as the meaning of life is concerned, I think we could say I am no further advanced than you are. So we have something in common, myself the author, and you the readers. We are baffled about the real meaning of life. We do not know. We are completely uncertain. A lot of people would like to hear definite answers, and I could make up some things to say. I could say that the meaning of life is only found in spirituality, or the meaning of life is getting down to earth and being a good citizen. However, I feel that producing answers is not particularly a kind thing to do. Quite possibly, it is not necessary to solve the problem as such.

However, since we have to start somewhere, let's start with this thing that we have in common—our confusion. We are bewildered, baffled, so let us start with this. Maybe the language of confusion can be understood. In this inquiry, the author does not regard himself as superior to the readers. Let us consider that we are relating on an eye-to-eye level. There is a Sanskrit term, *kalyanamitra,* which means "spiritual friend." This term seems appropriate here. We can relate to each other as friends rather than as student and master. We are equals, and the rest of the world is also on an equal level with us.

The physical living situation is the only way we can relate with our lives. I do not believe in a mystical or etheric world— the world of the unseen, the unknown. There's no reason to believe in that, because we don't perceive it. Belief comes from perception, so if we don't perceive something, we don't believe in it. Belief does not come from manufacturing ideas, although millions of arguments and logics have been set forth to that effect. For example, it is said that there is an unseen world that operates on the higher levels of consciousness. Supposedly this higher world fulfills human concerns, and it punishes those who don't believe. But from the point of view of physics, that world is unreal. I'm afraid I'm not brave enough to say there's another world. This world that we live in is the only world. Of course, we have the psychological world too. This world where we are, which has these two aspects, the psychological world and the physical world, is the only world we live in.

We have problems in dealing with this physical world. Fundamentally, we become too centralized in relating to it. When we see things in physical terms, we feel we must prove ourselves in that physical realm. We take a materialistic approach, trying to gain something from the world. We want our activity to produce a good end result; thus our relationship to the physical world becomes one of materialism.

There are two types of materialism here: indulgence in physical materialism and indulgence in psychological materialism. Both are concerned with the achievement of comfort and happiness. However, we want to achieve not only momentary happiness but ultimate happiness. People feel that physical materialism concerned merely with temporary happiness is not sufficient. They feel that if they indulge themselves purely in immediate pleasure, they won't end up with complete, ultimate comfort. Therefore they feel they must work and sacrifice their partial, momentary pleasure in order to achieve greater pleasure. To achieve this, we must all go to our jobs, earn money, have a good roof over our heads, the best food to eat, and close friends around us.

A certain number of people want to go beyond mere happiness, and they seek fame. They feel that they are special people. They wish to become famous actors, famous musicians, famous artists. If you are such a person, you feel that your life is a work of art, and that it is worth a great deal. Your life brings a lot of pleasure for yourself as well as others, and you feel that your intellect and manipulative mind cannot be rivaled by anybody. You possess a high IQ. In business ventures, you are successful. As a successful businessperson, you have more money, comfort, and power than others do. You are respected in your neighborhood or even in the nation as a whole—if your dream goes beyond the level of the neighborhood. Some day you hope to become an internationally recognized person.

Physical materialism at this level is believing in physics on a literal level, in terms of literal gain. Initially, seeking to become a bigger, more powerful, more highly successful person is physical materialism. This becomes psychological materialism at some point, because you plan all of these projects of becoming famous on a psychological level. In fact, psychological one-upmanship is always an important factor here. You are constantly seeking to outwit your competitors. Physical materialism and psychological materialism in this sense amount to the same thing. The physical situation comes along with the psychological attitude toward it.

Then we have the third type of materialism, which we've already discussed somewhat, which is spiritual materialism. Spiritual materialism always has the same logic. In order to achieve a higher level of spirituality, an elevated spiritual goal, in order to attain enlightenment, union with God, and so on, we feel we should become better persons spiritually. We should become conscientious and willing to put up with problems and discomforts of all kinds. We should be willing to give up this and that and become a hardworking and genuine person who is reaching for spiritual attainment. The object, from a spiritual materialist's point of view, is to achieve a permanent spiritual home. We want to reach heaven. You want to reach a permanent place where you don't have to maintain yourself anymore at all. You want permanent happiness, to be happy ever after. You hope to achieve this by means of all sorts of sacrifices. You're willing to sacrifice this and sacrifice that, inflicting pain on yourself; you are willing to submit to discipline, as you call it by way of euphemism. You give up this and give up that, thinking in this way to gain this and get that. You inflict the pain of sacrifice on yourself because you think your present volume of pain will be equal to your volume of happiness in the future. When the time comes, you will be rewarded by heavenly beings, or whatever.

In aid of this kind of process, new techniques are continually being introduced in our society; new books are constantly brought out. You think the books might tell you how to become a better person, a happier person. The whole time, you are looking for a happy, permanent relationship to something. You want to be happy forever, permanently and independently.

This also seems to be the idea that many people have of freedom, but this is a misunderstanding of what genuine freedom is. You are being entertained by the idea of freedom rather than truly becoming spiritually free. This idea of freedom actually means bondage, in this case. In your mind, your happiness becomes tied to the idea that sometime in the future you will be free. Once you are free, you think, you will be able to indulge in your spiritual achievement. You will be able to see the future; you will be able to see the past. You will have telepathic powers and be able to read people's minds. You will have power over others. You will be able to wipe out their pain, regardless of karmic situations. Something in you thinks you might take over the whole world. Becoming a spiritual emperor is the essential idea of spiritual materialism.

In short, from the materialistic point of view, spirituality is another dream of happiness. You have the idea that you won't have to pay your electricity bills or your phone bills. You will be able to take off into the mountains and live in a cave. Life will be much simpler and more pleasurable. You will live on natural food and be healthy. You will not be bound by any kind of obligations whatsoever. You won't have to answer the phone; you won't have to maintain a household. You will be perfectly "free." Living in a cave in the mountains amid the beauties of nature and the fresh air, meditation will come naturally because there will be no disturbances. Everything will be quiet. Silence will reign. There will be no one to irritate you, because you've left the nasty associations of your past history behind. You've forgotten your past, you've given it up. You don't care who you were, you think; you only care who you are now. Live in the mountains, enjoy nature, fresh air, fantastic vibrations . . . blah, blah, blah.

There is something uncertain about this whole vision. There may be some wisdom in it, but it has been said that it is not only wisdom that is important but also compassion. If we take the need for compassion into account, the scenario above doesn't completely address the problem. It is in connection with compassion that the difference between the materialistic approach to spirituality and the natural, genuine quality of spirituality begins to break through. The spiritual approach without spiritual materialism is based on compassion. Compassion tells you that finally you have to return to the world. Not only just finally, but the whole time you have to work with the world, relate with the world, because enlightened mind contains wisdom and compassion simultaneously. You have an obligation to the world you were brought up in. This is the world you belong to; you can't give it up altogether. You can't dissociate yourself from the past or whatever irritates you.

In fact, compassion brings us back to dealing with the world as the only way. We have to work with people. We have to work with our fathers, our mothers, our sisters and brothers, our neighbors, and our friends. We have to do that because the people with whom we are associated in our lives provide the only situation that drives us to the spiritual search. Without those people, we would not be able to look into such possibilities at all. They provide irritations, negativities, and demands. They provide us with everything. Because their energy, possibly even their kindness, inspires us, we should feel indebted for the opportunity to work with them.

So, after all, our spiritual journey is not such a romantic thing at all. It has nothing to do with a vacation or a holiday whatsoever. It is connected with our ordinary, sometimes irritating, everyday life. From that point of view, the spiritual search is a very sober thing. It has nothing to do with special pleasure or transcendent happiness.

Of course, this does not mean that you should seek out pain. Basically, spiritual practice means coming back to the world, working with the existing, living world. If you were brought up in the suburbs, come back to the suburbs and work with the people. If you were brought up in the city, come back to the city and work with the people. Come back. Come back. That is the only inspiration there is. You might read scriptures, the sacred writings of great teachers, but those writings can become no more than a myth. They tell the story of somebody who lived in the past, who lived a particular kind of life back then and wrote about those things. The true scripture, the true text, lies in the living situation in which we were brought up. It lies in this living situation of dealing with the world we are familiar with, our irritating world. It might be quite uncomfortable, but nevertheless that's where the inspiration lies.

This is where compassion leads us. Compassion is not trying to feel charitable, as many people think. Compassion is the basic generosity that means that you don't have to hold anything back. You relate to the living situation around you generously, without defending yourself.

Sometimes there are problems with how we try to apply compassion and how we try to help others. There's subtle one-upmanship involved when you are *trying* to be skillful and compassionate to others. Let's say I would like to see you become a very together person. I have an idea of what it means to be a together person, and I want to mold you into that. So I lay my trips on you, rather than letting you be as you are. That's often the problem in the relationship of parents and children. Your father is a lawyer and you have a family history of famous lawyers, so automatically the idea is that you should be a lawyer too. Your great-grandfather was president of this country, so you should be a prominent politician as well.

The real idea of skillful means, or upaya, is to have a direct, almost scientific or detached understanding of things as they are at this very moment without projecting the past or the future onto the situation. Your understanding is almost at the level of a mechanic repairing a car. It's not a question of what used to be wrong with your car or what might go wrong with your car in the future. In order to fix the car now, you have to know what is wrong at this very point. Certain parts are defective, certain parts have deteriorated—or whatever the circumstance is. Just relate with that actual situation. That is skillful means. The situation speaks for you, rather than your having to strategize anything. It's what is there at that very moment.

The popular, confused notion of compassion suggests a certain idea of charity, which is trying to be kind because you feel that you are well off and therefore you should be kind to others who are not well off. You might go off to underdeveloped nations or join the Peace Corps. Your country is wealthy, but those other countries are not. The people are illiterate, so you will teach them how to read and write and how to manage things. In this approach, you actually look down on those people.

Or you might think in terms of psychological volunteer work. You are supposed to be psychologically well balanced, so you can work with those who are mentally unbalanced. You can function as the model of sanity. Perhaps we like the idea of improving the world. But when we manage to turn an underdeveloped village into a highly sophisticated industrial town, we expect to be rewarded. We expect something in return. We could play all kinds of games of charity, but those are not real charity at all. They are one-upmanship games.

Real compassion is not a matter of "I would like to make this person happy by making the person fit into my idea of happiness"; rather, it is a matter of actually seeing that a certain person needs help. You put yourself at the disposal of that person. You just get into a relationship with that person and see where that leads. That is a more demanding and a more generous approach than following your expectation that the person should end up thus and such a way.

This is the genuine approach to compassion, which is very powerful. This is what we are going to examine further in this book: compassion beyond psychological and spiritual materialism. It is the genuine approach to things, the true approach to our living situation. We have to distinguish between the ordinary approach to spiritual practice, which is spiritual materialism, and true spiritual practice. We have to see this difference clearly.

The notion of spiritual practice can easily be misleading.

People think they are embarking on the spiritual path, but they soon find themselves into spiritual materialism. It is much easier to get into the spiritual materialism that is associated with the competitive world than to get into true spirituality, which means giving up our ambitions and aggression. This is much harder and not particularly appealing. I would say it is not particularly colorful either. Unfortunately, or perhaps fortunately, it is not particularly entertaining.

In working with others, the approach of genuine spirituality is to just do it, just help. If you're doing it unskillfully, you'll be pushed back. A direct message is there always, unless you are dreaming, in which case you don't receive any messages. But if you are relating with things directly, even with ambition, that's okay. There will be messages coming toward you automatically. It happens on the spot. This could be called genuine mystical experience.

Mystical experience lies in our actual living situation. It's a question of relating with the body, the physical situation. If you put your hand on a hot burner on the stove, you get burned. That's a very direct message that you're being absentminded. If you lose your temper and slam the door after a quarrel, you may catch your finger in the door. You get a very direct message— you hurt your finger. In that situation, you are in direct contact with things, with the energies that are alive in the situation. You are in direct contact rather than strategizing a result or thinking in terms of molding or remolding your experience. Then the situation automatically provides you with your next move. Life becomes like music. You dance in accordance with life. You don't have to struggle to remold anything. That is precisely the idea of the absence of aggression, which is one of the key ideas of the Buddhist teaching. Dancing to the music of life is not an aggressive situation at all. It is living with the four seasons, to use the metaphor of how a plant grows throughout the year. This is the idea of *lalita,* a Sanskrit term that means "dance." We might also translate *lalita* as "dancing with the situation." Situations inspire you, rather than you create situations.

Again, this approach is not based on strategizing how to help someone. Instead: just do it. If you throw a puppy in the river, it automatically swims. Basically, the underlying intelligence is always there, but we tend to dismiss it and look for something else that is more profound and accurate. As long as we relate with our underlying primordial intelligence and as long as we push ourselves a little, by jumping into the middle of situations, then intelligence arises automatically. When you're in the middle of a situation, you automatically pick up on what is needed. It's not a question of how to do it—you just do it. And you find yourself doing it perfectly, even surprising yourself. That can happen. If, on the other hand, we fixate on *how* to do it, that automatically makes us more self-conscious. The approach of "how to do it" automatically contains two ideas: how not to do it and how to do it. Your mind is already split into two sides, involved with possibly making mistakes and possibly accomplishing your result. So taking the approach of "how to do it" can be negative, whereas just doing it is very positive.

The technique of meditation is the way to just do it. In meditation, life exposes itself to you, so you find yourself in the middle of a living situation. This definitely requires an intuitive approach. Using your intuition in this way requires a positive attitude, a conviction that you are a basically healthy person, you are not condemned, and you are not regarded as a sinner. You are already a healthy person, fundamentally. Despite the projections that may be cast on you, despite the shadow that may be cast on you, the point is to see through the shadow and just do it and live it. That is intuition.

Confusion is a split, a kind of schizophrenic attitude, confused between this and that. You can't get confused unless you have two sides to get confused about. When you are confused, reasoning just clouds things even more so. Sometimes people confuse the application of skillful means based on intuition with impulsiveness. Impulse is frivolous. You think of something that you want to do, and then immediately you do it. Impulsiveness is mindless. It's based on fear and confusion rather than the direct style of "just doing it" that we are discussing. In the case of intuition, you feel out the situation completely before you do something, but you don't create a split. There's a very big difference between applying intuition versus fixating on "how" or "what" to do in a situation.

The whole point is that you can't get directions in advance for specific first-aid techniques to apply in *every* situation you will encounter. That is why we speak of applying your intuition. There are no directions to tell you how to deal with every specific situation. The question is how to deal with situations *altogether,* before the particular highlight you're involved in has occurred. So if your ongoing daily living situations are related to with intuition rather than impulse, then any particular challenge can be accommodated. There are no set guidelines for how to handle yourself at cocktail parties, for example. If such guidelines were provided and you tried to follow them, you would have to switch on the spot to being a different person, which is not possible. Skillful means and intuition are a matter of your continual process of working with life, even when the cocktail party is not happening. You have to relate with a continual process of intuition and try to sort out the difference between the qualities of frivolous impulse and intuition. If you're able to relate with that during the day, when the party begins in the evening, you'll already be well equipped. There's no quick programmed answer at all. The whole endeavor has to be seen as a long-term process. We have to meet ourselves for the first time completely and properly. We have to make friends with ourselves. I have to get to know who I am, what I am, and what the world is in relation to me.

Intuition is trusting yourself. You feel that you can *afford* to trust yourself, which is making friends with yourself. Then you feel that you are not a dangerous person, as you might have believed. You may have been told that you are a dangerous person, that you have to watch out for yourself, but now finally you can relax, you can work with yourself. The very existence of yourself is not all that outrageous or dangerous or suicidal.

You are good; fundamentally, you are healthy. Moreover, that particular health is capable of accommodating your badness as well as your goodness. When you're good, you're not particularly bashful about your goodness, and when you're bad, you're not particularly shocked by that either. These are simply your attributes. When you begin to accept both aspects of your being as energy, as part of the perspective of your view of yourself, then you are connecting with the fundamental goodness, which can accommodate all of these energies as part of one basic being. This is very solid and earthy. It is invincible in fact. That is the basic idea of good: that good can accommodate both wrong and right at the same time. Because of that, it is good. It is solid soil, solid ground.

You have nothing to transcend, in the final sense, when you begin to relate with both good and bad. You do that on the basis of the nonexistence of the solidity of good and bad. When you looked at them as solidly existing, you saw good as being finally hopeful and bad being finally hopeless. You don't see it that way anymore at all. Now, when you find yourself bad, that doesn't mean hopelessness; when you find yourself good, that isn't definitively hopeful either. You can accommodate the energies of both light and dark on this basic ground. This is not exactly transcending, but it is accommodating—acknowledging that there is good and bad at the same time. The basic ground is not infected or influenced by either one of them.

From ego's point of view, solidity means that you do not allow any space for flowing qualities to develop. The whole space is concretized. In other words, space becomes antispace. There's no room at all to move about. But there is another idea of solidity. In the positive sense, it means being fully in contact with nature. You know how to relate with things directly. You know the laws of nature directly. You are not likely to be influenced by frivolousness of any kind, because your ground is definite. You have no doubt about yourself.

The genuine spiritual search is not purely looking for happiness. However, this limited approach is still very prevalent. In this prevailing idea of spirituality, a person who attains realization looks very happy. He is smiling all the time and saying nice things about everybody. When people follow this approach to the spiritual path, they say "I love you" and they kiss you, throw flowers, wear white, and everything is beautiful and smooth and happy. Their point of view is that spirituality is ultimate happiness, and the idea presented is that once you join their club, you will be happy forever, because they don't believe in badness or unhappiness. Everything's going to be beautiful and full of flowers. Spiritual life is colorful, happy, and bright.

That's the "trip" of spirituality, and the important thing is to get off that trip. Once you do that, your compassionate attitude might still be somewhat fake to begin with. Practitioners have to learn to push themselves overboard to communicate with other people. In the beginning, you may not feel like communicating, so you might have to push yourself to communicate, communicate with the world, communicate with pain and pleasure and all the rest. After all, the spiritual world is not all that happy a world; it also contains tremendous pain, suffering, and misery—along with happiness and inspiration, of course. But relating with the real world is not a matter of pure happiness alone. So the practitioner might need some stepping-stone to begin with. He or she might have to do some playacting, which is not perfect. It could be said to be ego activity, but that doesn't really matter at all. If a person is able to proceed in that way, then she will gradually develop conviction and confidence. Her way of working with situations will eventually become real. She will be dealing with the real world.

At the beginning, even your meditation is not real medita-

tion in the complete sense. You are imagining yourself meditating. Initially, whatever spiritual disciplines you may be practicing are not real at all. You are just imagining yourself doing
them. But that kind of limited deception and that kind of acting
out have to be accepted as a stepping-stone. We have no other
way of doing it. We cannot start perfectly, not at all. We have to
use imperfection as a way toward the perfect. That's all we can
do. We have to use poverty in order to become rich. There's no
other way.

Mysticism usually involves the mysteriousness of something hidden that you can't approach. But a true approach to
mysticism would involve appreciating the mysteriousness of
the play of phenomena, which is not really hidden from you.
Mystical experience in this second sense is often playful and
contains a great deal of humor. There is something that is not
quite solemn and solid but rather operates on the level of the
delight of experiencing things as they are. In the Sufi tradition,
for example, there are hundreds of stories about the great mystic Mullah Nasruddin. Nasruddin's approach to the world was
very humorous. He discovered humor in every situation. Real
spirituality has that same quality, because it realizes that the
world is a spiritual world already. You communicate with life as
it is rather than trying to invent some new spiritual approach to
it. Taking delight in things as they are is genuine humor.

Real spirituality is an acceptance of the world as spiritual
already. So you don't have to remold the world. For those who
believe in a traditional view of mysticism, the world is mysterious. They can't experience mysticism in its fullest sense because
they expect too much. They become deaf and dumb to the
teaching. It is highly mysterious for them. But it isn't mysterious for those who actually relate to mysticism in its fullest sense.
The reality of the world could be called self-secret. Something
spiritual or mystical in this sense means something that strikes
the truth. True spirituality is an absence of frivolity, an absence
of belief in good and bad in the religious sense, an absence of

religiosity. So spirituality seems to transcend the religion of an established church. It is that which is contained in the living situation, which speaks truth, which reminds you of the natural situation of things as they are.

4

• • •

SIMPLICITY AND
AWARENESS

We have two quite common approaches to
work: filling the space so there is no room
for the creative process, or being afraid of the creative process
and therefore being unwilling to embark on it. These are two
examples of ego's approach to work. By filling the space instead
of letting be and letting a creative process develop, ego automatically imposes the next clue on our awareness about what is
taking place. This is because we are afraid of a gap, which would
allow us to look back and see our basic origin. It is very disturb-
ing for ego to see its own nakedness, which brings the sense of
a defeat for the ego. Therefore, when you see this open space,
you become afraid of embarking on any further creative process
that might reveal the space again.

Understanding this process could help us go beyond the
usual commonsense approach that we apply to work. Generally, if we feel that we have to work to make money, then we

just work in a mechanical fashion. If we no longer feel that we need to work, then we do something else. With this mechanical approach, we do not have a proper relationship to the work itself. Work doesn't just mean earning money and doing a job or purely getting something done efficiently. Work is a creative process.

Resistance to creativity also comes from being unwilling to relate to the earth. Not allowing yourself to associate with the earth means not being able to appreciate things properly as they are, not being able to really feel the relationship between you and the objects you are dealing with. If you feel the relation between yourself and a flower in the wild, you might bend down and smell it. You don't feel lazy about it.

If there is that kind of fluid communication going on between yourself and the object, then ego doesn't get a chance to digest anything; it doesn't get a report back from you and your work. When your work becomes natural and spontaneous communication, ego doesn't get a chance to act as a middleman. Generally what happens, however, is that ego has messengers that bring information back to its switchboard. Then ego accepts or rejects. Everything depends on the pleasure of ego. On the other hand, if you have good, fluid communication with the work, then you are working without ego's authority, which is very humiliating for the ego.

Ego comes from our confusion, and confusion comes from panic and fear. There is no such thing as a definite ego as such; rather, ego is made up of different ingredients. Therefore, I wouldn't say ego is particularly bad, but it is not a very healthy thing, because starting with confusion, ignorance, and fear is like trying to plant cement dust as a seed. It is a feeling of being totally separate from the rest of things. That's why there is panic. You feel apart from everything else, and therefore you feel tremendously insecure. It's like you are alone in the middle of the Sahara Desert. You begin to be threatened by everything. Then the panic starts, and once panic starts, confusion comes as well—because when you panic, you don't know what you're doing. Ignorance takes over, to put it very crudely. So ego is not creative.

Wanting to fill space is a common neurotic response to panic. Work then becomes a means of escape. If you are experiencing depression or fear, or life is simply not going smoothly, then immediately you start polishing your table or weeding your garden. You immediately try to find something to do. This is a way of physically acting out the mental pattern of ego. In this case, the worker has no real communication with the actual work at all. The work is a way of escaping, or on the mental level, it is a way of avoiding looking into the basic problem. Here the person is involved with the process of momentum. He or she is seeking a kind of pleasure in the moment. In one way, she is living in the now, living in the moment. But this is the wrong way of living in the moment, because she doesn't feel able to cope with analyzing the basic problem, with looking back and learning from it. Automatically she tries to fill the space—the physical space as well as the mental or spiritual space. Space—any empty corner—seems to frighten her.

Often this approach can be seen in the way a person decorates his house. Wherever there is an empty wall, he puts something up on it. If a space becomes empty, he puts up another picture or fills it with furniture. Every time there is a feeling of space, he fills up the gap. So his style of interior decoration becomes one of completely filling up the rooms. The space becomes crowded with more and more things. The more crowded his place is, the more comfortable he feels, because he doesn't have to deal with any unknown, undetermined areas.

Another aspect of this kind of ego manifestation is that whenever a person sees a bit of dust somewhere, he feels that bit of dust represents so much that he has to clean it away immediately. Every speck of dust becomes an intrusion into his space, and he has to clean that space up and put his things in it. He is busy trying to fill the gaps all the time.

Many people have this filling-space kind of neurosis. If their job has come to an end and they are living on an old-age pension, then they immediately try to find another job to keep themselves occupied. Without that, they are afraid of losing their speed, their sense of constantly going forward. Just moving forward, going on with something, becomes their occupation, which is a very neurotic process.

The other approach, based on the fear of creativity, is that of a person who resists taking a job or working. That approach shows a kind of blindness, not using one's intelligence. In the 1960s and '70s, many young people reacted against having to get a job. That protest is a way of refusing to associate with the practicality of life, refusing to associate with the earth itself. This refusal is very significant. Any human being, young or old, has tremendous intelligence. And because of this intelligence, they see the problems that would be involved if they embarked upon any creative process. The main problem they see is: once you start, you can't stop. You have to go on and on being involved. One kind of work leads to the next kind of work, and that would mean continually having to work on oneself.

The whole point of discussing these approaches to work is to realize that whatever we do physically also happens in our state of mind. Every move that we make on the physical level has spiritual significance. That may sound airy-fairy, but it is so. When I speak about spirituality here, I am not referring to anything pious or religious. Here spirituality means the truth, the is-ness of the natural facts of life. Every situation has bearing on one's psychology, on one's true psychology, the absolute aspect of mind.

A person could be very, very intelligent and refuse to work. He is too lazy to apply himself to anything. He would rather daydream or think about something. This is, I suppose, a kind of anarchistic approach. If you do something constructive and practical, it is connected with society. It means taking care of something. That seems to be very threatening for this type of person, because he does not want to help maintain or develop society.

Even if you are against the materialism of society and you do not want to support it, refusing to work is still grasping the wrong end of the stick. Not taking part in work and practical activity is not going to achieve anything. More than anything else, it will simply magnify your own negativity. By not doing anything to help, you will merely feel the sense of being useless in society. If you really take this kind of nonparticipation to its logical conclusion, it means that you shouldn't eat, you shouldn't even breathe, because the air you breathe also belongs to the world or society. This approach could become quite extreme. If you take it all the way, it means you shouldn't exist at all.

There's a great deal of confusion about materialism and society. Just taking care of one's business or even running a business doesn't amount to materialism. There's nothing wrong with that at all. What really produces the materialistic outlook toward society is *psychological* materialism. Materialism has a pervasive kind of philosophy connected with it that is passed from one person to another orally and taught to everyone through examples. One person catches it from another. This is how psychological materialism works. However, trying to reject that contagion by purely not doing anything, not caring for anything at all, simply doesn't work.

Not doing anything takes the form of laziness, and in order to be lazy we have to develop a certain kind of intelligence. Laziness has tremendous intelligence in it, in fact. When you are lazy, as soon as you have the urge to do anything, immediately a kind of answer comes to you that you can present about why you don't have to do it. Later you can say: "I didn't do it because I didn't have time. Thus and such happened and I didn't have a chance to do it. It was because of this and that." This automatic answer that comes to you is very convenient. One has to be very intelligent to find these kinds of excuses. There is tremendous intelligence in laziness, but it is misused intelligence.

The best way of using our intelligence is to learn to feel what the skillful action in a situation is. To do that, we have to relate to the earth as directly as possible. Interestingly, we call this being "grounded." In this approach, we do not regard work as just a job but as a way of expressing ourselves. It could be work in the garden or work around the house—cooking food, washing the dishes—whatever. These are not really jobs, but they are what has to be done because nature demands attention. It is very interesting that if you leave something undone or do not relate to even a small matter like, for instance, cooking with full and proper attention and clear thinking, then some kind of chaos is going to come up. This will happen because you are not relating properly; you are not expressing your love properly toward the earth. Either you're going to break a dish or you're going to spill something, or the food you're cooking is going to turn out badly, or something else will go wrong. Nature tends to react very sensitively this way. If you don't feel the relationship between the work and yourself, then chaos is going to arise.

A balanced state of mind depends on the way you do things, the way you pour a cup of tea and the way you put sugar and milk in it. It may seem to be a really insignificant thing, but it means everything. You can always tell whether a person feels the activity she is engaged in as dealing with the earth or whether she feels it as just some casual thing or something she is doing because she *has* to. If the person is not relating to the earth, then you can always feel a certain clumsiness, even if the person's action appears to be smooth. This is very evident and easy to sense.

This also applies to how to deal with your life in general. Every situation has spiritual significance. If you do not feel every step you take, then your pattern of mind becomes full of chaos and you begin to wonder where these problems are coming

from. They just spring out of nowhere, because they are a signal
that attention is needed. They are saying, "Something's wrong,
and we want attention." Situations demand attention because
you refuse to see the subtlety of life. But if you are able to see
the subtlety, if you pay attention, then they do not demand
attention. Here it is impossible to cheat. You can't pretend that
you can pour a cup of tea beautifully. You can't fake it. You
can't cheat; rather, you actually have to feel it; you have to feel
the earth and your relationship to it. Then, having started this
way, you also have to finish everything else in the given work
process. I've just been talking here about the domestic situation,
but this relates to other situations as well.

It is very interesting to watch a Japanese tea ceremony. It
begins with bringing together the necessary elements, the bowl
and napkin, the whisk, the boiling water, and so on. Everything
is deliberately and properly done. Then the tea is served, and
the guests drink the tea deliberately and with the feeling of
dealing with things properly. The ceremony also includes the
proper way of cleaning the bowls, putting them away, clearing
everything away. Clearing away is just as important as setting
up at the beginning. Generally when we first get an impulse to
do something—let's talk about cooking again—we tend to collect a lot of ingredients, and we chop them and cook them with
a lot of enthusiasm. Then, having chopped and cooked, having churned out the dish, we often just leave everything lying
around. We don't think in terms of cleaning up. We hope that
perhaps some other wise person will come and help us clear
everything away. If he's wise, he doesn't say anything at all. He
just quietly washes our dishes and puts everything away before
we even know he is there. Don't we wish!

In the materialistic round of life, there are endless adver-
tisements for things to buy, and endless things are produced,
but nobody explains how to clear everything away—how to dis-
pose of the garbage. That seems to be the biggest problem that
we have. This is another take on the Tibetan saying we already

used: "It's better not to begin anything, but if you begin, don't leave a mess behind." So the challenge is not just the work itself but also how to end the work properly.

Our approach to a job in the world outside, beyond our domestic situation, is also extremely important. As long as you don't use the job as an escape or as a way of ignoring your basic existence, then it is good to work. Whether you run your own business or work for somebody else, work is important. It is tremendously important if you are interested in spiritual development, because the difficulties in working with yourself always come up in your relationship with other people and in your relationship with the mess associated with your relationship with other people, objects, and things. If one is able to deal with these things, that is one of the most subtle ways of bringing discipline into yourself. If you work in a factory, you shouldn't look down on the others as merely factory workers or as merely producers of material things. You can learn a tremendous amount from your factory job and your coworkers.

Many of the problems people have in relating with work come from a pseudosophistication of analytical mind: you don't want to engage physically at all; you purely want to work intellectually or mentally. This is a spiritual problem. The problem occurs when anyone interested in spiritual development thinks in terms of the importance of mind. We would like to have a deep understanding or higher understanding, that mysterious, highest, and deepest understanding of things, whatever it may be. In fact, the highest and deepest, most profound transcendental things exist in the kitchen sink or at the factory. Those situations might not be particularly blissful. They might not be as fascinating as reading about spiritual experiences, but the actual reality exists there. Working with people and encountering their simplicity as well as dealing with all the problems that come your way brings tremendous depth of experience. If you're actually working in a factory or running your own business, then you encounter all sorts of people and things that resonate with your own state of being. There is a subtle simplicity in dealing with ordinary working situations. Spirituality of the earthbound, and we might almost say peasant-kind, is something we are often very much lacking. That sort of tribal quality, or peasant quality, is one of the most beautiful, sane, and balanced qualities there is.

If you have this earthbound quality of simplicity, then, in fact, you won't have problems dealing with your mind at all. Everything will work in a balanced, earthbound way. Everything will be dealt with properly, thoroughly, and simply. When we encounter, say, the native peoples of India or Mexico, or Native Americans, we find they have an earthbound sanity. There is something sane about them, because they have worked with situations with their own hands. They have a rough and rugged and powerful quality. If you look at their faces, it is almost impossible to imagine that they might freak out. There is something solid and practical about them. People of the past such as Buddha or Christ were that type of people. They spent a long time with peasants and simple people. The people who wrote and gathered the Vedas and the Dhammapada and all the great scriptures were not high-strung intellectuals.* They were simple people. They lived a very simple life. They fetched their own water and chopped their own wood so they could boil the water to make their tea and soup. They learned to deal with domestic matters and to live in an earthy way.

To truly develop spiritually and become capable of skillful action, we have to simplify our approach to life a great deal. If we are able to do so on a bodily or physical level, we will be able

---

* The Vedas are the most ancient sacred writings of Hinduism, written in early Sanskrit. Traditionally, they are believed to comprise four collections: the Samhitas, the Brahmanas, the Aranyakas, and the Upanishads. The term *Veda* is from the Sanskrit word for knowledge. The Dhammapada consists of a collection of 423 verses in Pali believed to be spoken by the Buddha for the benefit of a wide range of human beings. These sayings were selected and compiled into one book because of their beauty and relevance.—Eds.

to work with our psychological aspect as well, because this simplicity also makes a tremendous difference in our state of mind.
Our whole pattern of thinking will change. The internal game
that goes on will become much less of a game; it will turn into a
practical way of thinking in situations.

So work and our relationship with work are based both on
our state of mind and on how we relate to the earth. Meditative
awareness is very important to this. We can describe meditation in terms of taking a leap. Taking a leap means experiencing
the openness of space. You can take this kind of meditative leap
while you are working. It is connected with bringing air and
earth together. You can't feel the earth unless you feel the air.
The more you feel the air, the more you feel the earth. Feeling
the air and the earth together is feeling the space between you
and the objects you are working with. This becomes a natural
awareness of openness. You automatically begin to feel peace
and lightness. The way to practice this is not to try to concen-
trate or try to be aware of yourself while managing the task you
are doing at the same time. Rather, you should have a general
feeling of acknowledging existence with openness while you
work. Then you feel that there is more room to do things, more
room to work. By cultivating a continual meditative state, you
are acknowledging the existence of the openness. You don't
have to try to hold on to this or try to bring it about deliberately. Just the pure acknowledgment of that state is enough.
Acknowledge the vast energy of openness. Just flash on it; just
acknowledge it. Flash on it for a second. A flash of acknowledgment is all it takes. Having acknowledged it, don't try to hold
on. You almost ignore it after that. Continue with your work.
The feeling of openness will also continue, and you will begin
to develop the actual feel of the situation, the feel of the things
you're working with.

So the awareness we are talking about here is not constant
awareness as an object of mind. Instead of taking awareness as
an object, you become one with awareness, one with the open

space, which of course also means becoming one with the actual things you're working with. Then the whole process becomes a very easy one-way process, rather than a situation in which you're trying to split yourself into different levels of awareness, with one level minding the other. With this easy one-way, one-step process, you begin to make a real relationship with objects and with the beauty of objects as well.

Don't try to possess the openness, but just acknowledge it and then turn away from it. It is important to turn away, because if you try to possess the openness, you have to chase after it. You try to follow it, which you can't actually do. You can't actually possess it at all. If you let go of it and disown it, and then continue working, this feeling stays with you all the way along.

Openness here refers to a meditative state of simplicity or lack of complication. The absence of complications becomes simplicity. Within simplicity there is room to do things, to move about. This is true of everyday actions as well as formal meditation itself.

Psychological materialism is also related to openness and complication. It is the opposite of the spaciousness of meditative awareness. In general, psychological materialism is a tremendous feeling in the background, behind your activities, that you want to fulfill something. You relate to situations through grasping and possessiveness. In other words, you take your logic of what's happening too seriously and you try to follow up on it with deliberate grasping. It is an ongoing painful state of wanting to fulfill certain goals. You are caught up in a competitive state of mind. There is a general heaviness in your way of pursuing things. This heaviness of mind feels almost like your mind is filled with heavy metal. It is almost a metallic state of mind. You might try to get away from this by rejecting it, but then the alternative becomes pure fascination with objects, with things. Rather than feeling them in an earthy way, you are fascinated by them. This produces a kind of plastic world.

So the materialistic mind can have these two qualities:

heaviness or fascination. To put it in terms of the modern world, we might compare these two qualities to metal—one might say ironlike metal—and plastic. The plastic approach is fascinated with colors rather than the actual qualities of things as they are. The heavy or metallic approach pursues things very seriously, almost demonically. In this state of mind of heaviness, there's no room at all for a sense of humor; there's no room to create fresh thinking. Everything has to be numbered and worked out. The mind here has a powerful demanding aspect to it. This may lead to action, but that action is a product of the mind that is caught up in the heaviness. In fact, such action is less horrific and less demonic than the state of mind, which is so heavy and so solid.

With the materialistic approach, it is as though the whole of space were filled with cement, with metal, or with plastic! This is the reason people feel such tremendous claustrophobia about materialism. It is not only because of all the material things that surround them. It is much more because they feel their whole psychology has turned into aluminum and plastic. There's no room to move, no room to do things. Instead of open space, their space has become solid space.

I am describing the heaviness of the state of mind of psychological materialism as almost demonic because there is something terribly cruel and self-destructive about not allowing space. We could almost describe this state of mind as evil, because that state of mind is so self-destructive. It never allows any kind of freedom at all. When you are in this state of mind, the more you feel there's something to work on, the more you are driven to put energy into it. This becomes an endless chain reaction. It feels demonic in the sense of being without air, which is connected with a feeling of death, really. It's as though there were no windows in a room at all. It's completely suffocating. This is deathlike because there's nothing thriving, nothing growing, nothing developing further. Everything's purely being drawn in and collected, and you never let anything develop at all. Although the space has already been totally filled, one collects more and more stuff until situations completely break down. So psychological materialism is the suicidal process that results from ego's hunger. It doesn't have any sense of humor or any exuberant quality. It is mean and possessive.

The whole point of discussing this is that while we may not have to run the world exactly, we do have to run ourselves, whether we like it or not. We are the world. So that simplifies things a lot. The notion of evil isn't that something exists outside us that is fundamentally all that bad, as we know, but evil is that state of mind which destroys our capacity to develop or grow. Evil is solidity, with no room to develop anything at all. The confused mind, which we all have, tends to be self-destructive, collecting things and not digesting them. Simply by continuing the process of collecting things, we are not letting ourselves digest them. We could destroy ourselves if we keep that up. You might end up in a kind of eternal mental hospital, which would be called the confused state of hell. I don't mean a physical mental hospital on this earth. Rather, I am referring to what is known in the Tibetan Buddhist tradition as *vajra* hell. It's the personal hell that perpetuates the hallucinations of confusion all the time. At this level, there seems to be no way of getting out of this confusion. It could be called the ultimate egohood.

However, even at the level of the greatest intensity of this psychological materialism, our primordial intelligence does not cease; it does not give in. Ultimately, we begin to find something wrong with materialism. This is happening now in the Western world—we are looking for something beyond the materialistic outlook. The heaviness and crowdedness we all feel automatically brings doubt. The doubt inspires people to search beyond this heaviness, and they begin to discover something beyond materialistic thinking. This is happening now, but the result is that people tend to condemn this world as a complete failure, as completely bad. Here, they go too far, because buddha nature, or spiritual intelligence, thrives all along the way. That is never going to leave, never going to abandon us; it is never going to give out or give in. Whenever we find something that takes the form of an answer, then automatically our intelligence works and sees that this answer is not the real answer—which means that you have found the answer, in the form of a question.

Similarly, life continues, or the consciousness continues. I'm not referring here to actual reincarnation, physical birth and death. That's actually a very crude example of rebirth. Rebirth occurs in every moment. Every moment you die and you are born again. This birth and death takes place all the time on and on and on. So as long as there's consciousness, which dies and gives birth to the next moment, then that is continual reincarnation, continual rebirth. The next moment depends on one's state of consciousness in this moment; then you give birth to a similar next moment as well. The next moment depends on whether this moment of consciousness has a negative quality or a positive quality. That quality continues as you give birth to the next moment. The minutes and seconds of the hour continue as minutes and seconds in the night as well as during the day.

You may not remember your past life. There's nothing to prove or disprove it, particularly. However, you can't stop your consciousness; you can't kill your consciousness or stop the consciousness of this moment. This exists continuously.

Many ordinary people have had experiences that they feel confirm the existence of reincarnation. In England I knew a Catholic family whose daughter died in an accident. They had another daughter a few years later. One day the second daughter was crossing the road with her father, and suddenly she said: "I don't want to cross this road. This is where the accident happened last time, isn't it, Daddy?" And indeed it was where the accident had occurred. Similar things have happened to a lot of people, but I don't want to speculate about that or try to make people believe this. The main point is that consciousness continues all the time. It can't be destroyed. Whether we are asleep or we are unconscious, consciousness continues, all the time.

As long as we feel some sense of empty space and openness, there is something to work with. It's not so very difficult
to find this sense of space. It just requires taking a leap into the
empty space by not questioning or second-guessing ourselves.
This feeling of empty space might be unpleasant to start with,
but just leap into it. See what happens.

Meditation, in particular, provides us with the inspiration to
relate to the spaciousness of life. To begin with, this comes from
working with our thoughts. In your meditation practice, you
might find that thoughts are constantly rushing through your
mind. If you see them as purely thoughts rather than focusing
on the subject of your thinking, then there is more space. When
you think of your thoughts purely as a thinking *process,* rather
than focusing on the contents of the thoughts, that will make
your attitude toward thoughts very impersonal. If you were
watching a cloud, and within this cloud you saw your friends and
relatives walking around, then immediately you would associate yourself with those people and you would name them and
fixate on them, apart from the cloud. Then you are caught up
with the whole thing, and it becomes very crowded. Whereas if
you just notice the people, and don't try to identify with them,
it's more impersonal. It's the same thing with your thoughts.
In meditation you develop this impersonal way of looking at
thoughts.

In our modern approach to work, I think we use too many
automatic devices, which makes it more difficult to appreciate
space. Once when I was living in Scotland, some of us were trying to scrape the old paint off a wall. We were using manual
paint scrapers and making quite good progress. There was a
person working with us who didn't particularly like doing this
kind of work. Nevertheless, I had asked him to work with us,
and he joined us. After about half an hour he said, "Let's buy an
electric tool and get it done faster." So we bought one, and we
tried to use it. Then he said there was something wrong with

the sandpaper we were using. He convinced us we needed to buy a coarser kind. So we bought some very rough sandpaper, but the result was that we ended up with a kind of dimpling in the wall.

So at times we are spoiled by using too many gadgets. This is why I am suggesting that we cultivate the kind of peasant quality of just working, disregarding whether you are making good progress or not. If you only think in terms of finishing a job, you don't actually make a good worker. If you are enjoying the process, then you make a good worker.

I wouldn't say that human society is going downhill, but human beings have created more and more substitutes for all kinds of real things. All of these tools that human beings have created can be overwhelming. The tools become bigger and bigger, until finally you find yourself in a house filled with gigantic gadgets. All the factories and machinery must have started from a few simple tools: a sickle, a knife, a spoon, and maybe some chopsticks as well. Now instead of using simple things, we use complex, gigantic tools. Instead of our using the tools, the tools are using us. I think we are missing the point. We have to come back to simplicity.

However, if you tried to go back and imitate the life of the Stone Age, that wouldn't cure the problem at all—because then leading the Stone Age life would become a new form of chic luxury that would have to be overcome. Instead, we have to work with the situation we have and try to develop the peasant quality in the midst of working with all the machines. I think we can do this. There may be very few examples of this type of earthy mentality in America, but we could be among them. If we're able to overcome psychological materialism, then we'll be able to work properly with the machines. Because materialism isn't the machines; it isn't things. It is the psychological aspect, our materialistic mentality. We have one of the greatest chances ever to discover simplicity amid the complications.

That is the greatest discovery we could make. That would be a wonderful achievement for human beings, and we are just about to do it.

There could well come a time when the heart of spirituality will be discovered in more advanced countries. One day, instead of students going to India, Tibet, or Japan to study under great spiritual teachers there, the Indian, Tibetan, and Japanese students will come to America to study here under great wisdom teachers. The cycle works like that.

5

■ ■ ■

OVERCOMING
OBSTACLES
TO WORK

FRIVOLITY

When you begin something haphazardly, frivolously, the whole process is going to end up as half-finished work. Before you begin, if you don't approach the situation properly, you get into it in a frivolous way. I don't mean to say that you should be solemn, but there should be respect for the sacredness, the perpetual sacredness, of the situations you are in. Those situations are sacred because of the unique fact that you are there. The situations you are in are part of your reminders, part of your way of expressing yourself. If you ignore the tremendous opportunity they provide to express your true nature, then your whole approach to life becomes frivolous.

There could be confusion between frivolity and a genuine sense of humor. A real sense of humor without frivolousness is a state of confidence, fearlessness, because you know the situation as it is. You leap into it and you take part in it. Because you know what you are doing, it is a joyful situation, rather than being solemn or too serious. In the case of frivolousness, that whole area of confidence has been obscured. Instead, there is a facade of impulsiveness. Partly embarrassed and partly lacking in confidence, you get into something. Then you become like an amateur comedian trying to please the audience. In such cases, it is better not to begin.

Frivolity is secondary rather than your inborn nature. It would be hard to find someone who developed his whole personality around being frivolous all the time. Everybody has a dignified style, which is inborn and available to us. When a person's behavior is based on expressing something genuine and human, there is always dignity involved. It doesn't matter what you are doing, even if the activity is sleeping or defecating. Again, frivolity is a secondary thing. That is why it is possible for a person to tune in to the primordial state of his whole being, whatever he may be doing. That is always possible.

Frivolousness is obvious. It is a sort of semidetached state of being. There's a fundamental self-conscious and self-apologetic quality present in frivolity. That's why you have to bring a serious element into any frivolous situation. That need should be obvious to you when it is happening. There will be a point in the frivolity where there's room for temporary seriousness. This seems to be the only occasion where seriousness or solemnity could act as an entryway for a genuine sense of humor. That moment, where you can replace the frivolity with real humor, will be obvious.

You don't have to conceal your frivolousness and pretend it's not there. First there's the act of being frivolous. Then a sudden awareness, a double take about being frivolous, brings you back to seriousness. Then that leads to developing the real, ultimate sense of humor.

Frivolity doesn't become irrelevant. What happens is that you realize it is taking place. When the frivolity has been caught, spotted, then it can transform into something else. The alternative, of trying to rule out frivolousness altogether, could lead to a very static attitude—like very orthodox parents who don't allow their children to enjoy themselves or play at all. Anything frivolous, any excitement the children try to express, is regarded as childish. The parents try to push the children into an adult state, which ends up being quite negative, because then the children have no chance to become aware of the frivolous state as it is. Also, apparent frivolousness could be purely an expression of enjoyment or spontaneity. So there's no point in trying to suppress frivolousness. Rather, frivolousness can ignite a sudden understanding of the situation, and that could lead to a sense of humor.

SPEED

Another obstacle to work comes from speed, which prevents you from developing a relationship with the actual work. There is often a misunderstanding or confusion between accomplishment and speed. They are very closely related. The genuine energy of accomplishment tries to go along with the patterns of that moment in the work, so that you don't miss an inch. You are dealing all the time with every corner and every detail that occurs, so what you do is very efficient. In the case of speed, there is also a tendency toward accomplishment, but accomplishment without relating with the situation—just purely speeding along for the sake of action alone. Quite possibly that will cause inefficiency, because you don't see the details of the work when you are more involved in your speed than in accomplishing something. It is difficult to generalize, but in this situation you have to experiment and try to examine your whole approach: whether your approach is based on communication with the work or whether it is based on speeding. Speed has a lot to do with expectations. You set your mind to accomplish things to the level of what you expect, and when things don't meet that level of expectation, you speed up further. Speed is also connected with a territorial feeling, a feeling that you are involved with your speed; therefore anybody around you should clear out of your way; they should draw back into their own territory.

DAYDREAMS

Another obstacle is purely thinking about the things you need to do rather than actually doing them. You can almost convince yourself that you've accomplished things just by thinking about them. In that case, the alternative is to be more realistic. At some point, as a Buddhist practitioner, you might do visualization practice. In the beginning, when you first do such a practice, you might start at the wrong end of the stick. You might visualize yourself as the Buddha, already enlightened, and you are sending out your emanations to help other sentient beings and save them, and in your mind, you become a great world figure. But when you wake up from your daydream and return to your practice, you find yourself in the same old situation. You don't necessarily regard the dreaming process as bad or an obstacle, but you have to realize that it's not realistic enough. Action speaks louder than words. You should regard the daydreams as pure thought patterns.

In this situation of fantasizing, you need to relate with earth, the physical situations of life. Usually daydreams and imagination come up when you are in a seemingly comfortable situation, a secure situation. Then you get a chance to extend your tentacles, stretch your legs, and dream about a lot of things.

You don't have to torture yourself to overcome this problem, but at the same time, you should include physical activity, actual manual work of some kind, in your daily life. You might even dig trenches or direct traffic. In Calcutta in the 1960s, after I left Tibet, for the first time I saw women directing traffic on construction crews. They had to be right on the point, directing which car could pass next. There was no chance to dream.

I have a friend who is an outstanding Buddhist scholar, and he invited me for tea one day in Oxford. I went to his place, and he had hired another friend to make tea for the two of us. She made the tea, and then she put the teapot, the cookies, and all the tea things there on the table. Then she left, because she had to go somewhere. So my friend had to pour tea for both of us, and he was actually shaking as he did this, so that he couldn't pour the tea properly. He was spilling the tea all over the table. He is a great thinker, supposedly.

When I finished my cup of tea, he was hesitant to offer me another cup of tea. I let him pour another cup! While we were having tea, he was giving me a long talk about how Tibetans roll up thangkas, Tibetan paintings, and he seemed completely oblivious to the fact that I was a Tibetan. It was as though he were talking to some unknown nobody without any idea where Tibet is. He was showing me, actually demonstrating: "This is what Tibetans do! They roll up thangkas this way. This is a Tibetan thing they do." He was telling me all about it. This is an example of what happens when there is no earth or grounded-ness in the situation.

INTERPERSONAL CONFLICTS

There is another problem that arises when people work or live together and they are in conflict about how something should be done. For example, some people may want a place kept tidy, but others don't mind if it's a mess. In that situation, it's not really a question of what you mind or don't mind, but it's a question of what's applicable to the actual situation as it is.

Such conflicts can be a tremendous opportunity for us to realize that we can't hold on to our concepts of the situation. You may have all kinds of conversations with yourself: "I don't mind having an untidy place, but at the same time, it may be necessary for me to put my effort into doing something about it. Maybe I am getting too relaxed, partly because I don't want to clean the place, and partly because I like being untidy. It's more casual and spontaneous that way." You bring up all sorts of discussions in your mind. The real question is: are you putting your view, your particular idea, out there for the sake of contributing something to the situation or not? One has to step out of one's own comforting situation, one's comfort zone. You have to learn to step out further, to feel the panoramic view of the whole situation, the whole community, the whole group of people. You should try to work accordingly, rather than purely sticking to your view. Your view is this way, their view is that way, and therefore, there is no meeting point. But others can step out of their point of view as much as you can step out. If they're not willing to step out, then you should set the example of stepping out into the general aerial view of the situation. Then something can come from the mutual meeting of the two views of the situation.

In fact, you could point out to the person who is dogmatically involved with keeping the house completely, absolutely clean that there's something not very healthy about that approach. That person might respond that your style of being messy is not healthy either. At that point, you might say, "Okay, that's true; both situations are not very healthy. So let's find a new ground to work on this." It's not quite compromising in the sense of reaching a happy medium alone, but it's realizing that there is a great chance to relate with each other.

If the relationship between two people is absolutely simple and direct, then you can reach such an understanding. If the relationship entails more fundamental problems, and if the other person is approaching you and raising an objection to your behavior or style on the basis of other subtle aspects of the relationship, then you have to deal with that subtle relationship as well. You can't just act stupidly or simplemindedly. That would not be creative or honest.

In many situations, people know that they have subtle conflicts in their relationships with each other. But in order to approach each other, they pick on mundane things, small details, on the pretense that the relationship exists purely in those mundane situations. Since the other person doesn't want to relate with the subtleties either, he or she will also approach the relationship from that mundane point of view. That small disagreement over who takes out the trash or cleans the pots in the sink may be solved by common sense, but something greater is still not solved. Even saying something like "Good morning, how are you today?" could have all sorts of implications behind it. Once you begin to focus solely on the simple situation as the problem, without acknowledging the larger disagreements, this situation becomes more and more complicated. I'm not acting as a psychiatrist here or trying to solve people's problems for them. You have to respect the situation and use your intelligence. Everything we've discussed already is a rough guideline.

VIEWING PROBLEMS AS UNIVERSAL

Sometimes people try to look at the issue of conflict from some view of universal consciousness. You say to yourself that your problems are everybody's problems, and your happiness is everybody's happiness. Actually, when you have to think about it in this fashion, the problem or the promise ceases to be universal. It becomes very personal. On the one hand, I'm sure everybody's problem is everybody's problem. The pleasure is everybody's as well, but that approach to problems actually makes them harder to solve. It might seem easier to understand things this way, but practically speaking, how are we going to put our understanding into practice? You have to find somebody—one person—to make the first move, not everybody. As we said earlier, action speaks louder than words. One person has to make the first move; it's not everybody acting together because it's a universal problem. The whole problem must be reduced to a single stepping-stone by somebody. Somebody finds the stepping-stone, one particular person. It would be very difficult to divide things up so that everybody could do the same thing at the same time, like everybody trying to pass the salt at once. From the practical point of view, it's impossible.

CONCEPTUALIZING GOOD AND BAD

Once we become involved with a spiritual path and spiritual teachings, there's often a fundamental problem of conceptualizing good and bad. This can be our biggest problem in relationship to work or activity: immediately, when a situation presents itself, we think in terms of the Teaching, with a capital T, which makes us self-conscious. Then we act in accordance with that self-consciousness. We act in terms of what will feel better or feel worse or will make us feel we've behaved clumsily or beautifully, from the viewpoint of a conceptualized and reified view of the Teachings. Then nothing real happens in the way of a genuine human relationship. This is one of the biggest of all problems throughout history: trying to act according to the capital T Teaching, according to ideas rather than the actual teaching contained in our experience. The clumsiness or self-consciousness connected with conceptualizing situations can only be freed if a person breaks through the barrier of self-consciousness, the watcher. Then a person can act truly and properly—as it is. Then our action becomes like buddha activity. A person doesn't do things a certain way because he's a buddha, but he acts as the situation calls for.

There is no simple solution to any problem until conceptual evaluation drops away, which requires tremendous loosening up. A person might feel that he or she is absolutely self-conscious about everything. This person might have studied all the teachings about being spontaneous. However, the more information about spontaneity that is presented to him or her, the more self-consciousness develops. Finally the tension becomes unbearable. The only thing to do is just to give up the whole attempt and be an ordinary human being.

When you begin to give up your concepts about how things should be, you may begin to question your obligations and commitment to the teachings altogether. However, giving up your conceptualizations doesn't mean you have to be disrespectful toward the teachings. You could still respect the teachings while giving up your personal concept about them. That would help each of us to become a true person, a real person, as opposed to a person according to the books. I've been talking here about giving up preconceived ideas about the Buddhist teachings, in relationship to how you conduct yourself in everyday life. But this can apply to any system of thought or ethics that you try to apply in a narrow way, if it takes you away from the immediacy of your life and prevents spontaneity in your response to situations.

That doesn't mean that you give up basic sanity. In fact, that is what you embrace. You have to give up your limited personal views on it. Your basic sanity is a part of you anyway. If a person is in a state of mind where he is brave enough to give up the conceptualization of the teachings, that person has an earth-grounded quality already, which allows him or her to give up the hang-ups of the teaching. At that point, he or she becomes a teacher. This is true whether we're talking about a teacher of meditation or a master gardener or a chef.

Although some people feel that the trip, the concept, of the teachings should be given up, they feel it is far from a possibility for them. You never know. One should never underestimate oneself. That might be your big step. It was for Gautama Buddha. He gave up the teaching that he received from other great Hindu yogis, and that caused him to attain enlightenment. The ability to take that step is as available to us as it was to the Buddha. In any case, when you are working with yourself and come to that kind of crossroads, you can't really step back; you can't regress. What you are giving up is the concept. Since you are on the path anyway, you can't really give up your whole journey at all. You just give up the concepts. On the other hand, it would be dangerous to be too sure of yourself: "I have the confidence to give up the trip. I can do without the concepts. I can stop now." That could be ego double-crossing you.

The point is that you don't have to be 100 percent faithful all the time, like a professional following the formula expressed in the teaching. If that profession begins to be a hang-up, then you give it up. That's why we have levels of spiritual development like the ten *bhumis,* or stages, of the bodhisattva path. The bodhisattvas move from one bhumi to the next by seeing that their previous involvement was a trip and then stepping out of it. Then they get involved in another trip, and they step out of that one as well. And so it goes, on and on.

The attitude we are discussing here is quite different from the hinayana approach of following very specific, concrete precepts, like always being friendly and generous and never killing anything. The ordination in Tibetan monasteries into the monastic discipline is called *dompa* [*sdom pa*], which means binding. The discipline binds you constantly. You feel that you are permanently bound by the precepts. You are bound by the discipline and bounded by it; you don't have a chance to act spontaneously and then push yourself over the line, because the whole thing is set and completely patterned. That is a necessary part of monastic discipline and very important to follow in that situation.

The hinayana precepts are very much based on rules to deal with whatever physical situations arise. Once a monk lost his begging bowl washing it in a rushing river, and that resulted in a new rule: in the future monks shouldn't wash their begging bowls in rushing rivers. When you take monastic ordination, you have to get into all the little details, all those little rules that developed throughout the life of the Buddha. You're not supposed to sleep on a mattress filled with black wool; you're not supposed to sleep on somebody's roof; you can't have a pointed post on your bed.

Bodhisattva precepts are different from these hinayana

precepts. Bodhisattva precepts are based on working with human psychology, and beyond that, there are the *vajrayana* or tantric precepts, which are connected with a highly sophisticated psychological state of being. All three approaches to precepts are valid, but we should understand that there are differences between them. We are not all going to live like monks or yogis; in fact, very few of us will do either. The mahayana or the bodhisattva approach to working with daily life may be particularly helpful and applicable for lay practitioners at this time.

OBSTACLES TO GENEROSITY

Continuing with the discussion of how to go beyond our concepts of good and bad, we could look at the approach to generosity, which is the first *paramita,* or transcendent action, of a bodhisattva. Real generosity is generosity without expectation. Usually when you're being generous, you expect something in return, some expression of gratitude or some gesture in return. If you don't expect anything in return, you could be transcendentally generous. Real generosity is like being rich and poor at the same time. You are rich: you can afford to give lots of things; but you are poor at the same time: you appreciate whatever you receive without feeling entitled to it. The sutras mention practicing generosity just by stretching out one's arm and bringing it back again. Give, receive, give, receive, give, receive. It is worthwhile to practice being generous even though there might be a conceptual component in it. The first step is sometimes painful for people to take. It seems ridiculous to give in such a simpleminded fashion, because one is afraid to be a fool. What possible reason could you give yourself for trying to be generous? It could allow you to realize that you are a fool. It says in the Dhammapada that a person who realizes he is a fool is a wise man indeed.

If you're being generous for a reason instead of being genuinely generous for no reason, when you realize that, you can go ahead and still be generous. You work from where you are; you don't have to stop being generous. If you stop, it's another double cross from ego. Instead, you go along with whatever happens. You are just following the pattern of the path. You pass tigers and poisonous snakes on your way. You don't stop for them, you just go along. When your impulse is to hold back, maybe because you feel that your generosity is purely conceptual, you should push ahead, as though you were an actor. That doesn't mean that you forget the impulse to retreat; that could still be there. However, you push ahead and take a generous action nevertheless.

Maybe inside your circle of comfort, generosity feels very natural. Then when you step outside that zone of comfort, generosity may feel unnatural. As you step out, you feel uncomfortable, and it feels as if you were playing a game or acting out a part. Just go ahead and do it—push a little bit. You don't have to go as far as to make your activity into a complete game. Actually, at the moment you're about to step out, the idea that there is a game going on doesn't come into your mind—because you actually see precisely at that very point of stepping out. After that point, the idea of generosity as a game and all sorts of conceptualized notions might come along, but they are of a secondary nature. You begin to realize that real generosity is possible. In fact, you are doing it!

Pushing yourself overboard in this way is very powerful. Often, because you are so involved with maintaining your territory and your resentment, you don't want to step out, and doing so may seem like a big deal. In fact, it has a tremendous impact on you to step out even a little bit. In certain situations, the best way to loosen up is to step out of the psychological situation into the physical situation of actions, which is very concrete.

A further obstacle to developing generosity is our preoccupation with so-called personal dignity, of the sort that comes from being brought up as self-centered people. This is sometimes reinforced in our experience in school, through the course of our education. Nobody likes to give up that game of self-importance, because it is something we can hold on to; it's our handle. So the first time you try to be generous, you give up just a little bit of that space. Then, the next time, you can give much more, and then more and more. The process develops over time, but eventually fundamental honesty begins to develop from those gestures of generosity.

The first time you try to give up, try to open, you may know there's no reality there. You're just acting. Then quite possibly the thought might come up: "This is just acting, this is not a serious thing; this is not real." Thoughts like that might close you in and make you feel that you shouldn't try to open to others. Analyzing yourself at the point when you are about to open is not important; in fact it becomes destructive. Just go ahead and give. If they arise, step over those doubts and second thoughts. Being generous in a concrete, physical way is very healthy and opportune. That doesn't necessarily mean that a person has to start with a full smile, but she could. She might find that she's smiling at her own full smile. Then the next smile becomes a more spontaneous one.

ACKNOWLEDGING THINGS AS THEY ARE

There are many ways to overcome the obstacles to work. What you need to do depends on the basic pattern you have. Easing up or slowing down becomes useful in some situations because that's the only way to keep your speedometer related to the earth. In other situations, it's less useful because your downtime becomes fantasizing, a dream of nonexistence, where you spend your time anticipating how your dreams will come true. That doesn't really help.

On the whole, it is difficult to give definite prescriptions about how to relate with situations of the moment. A person simply has to be awake and open to her situation and work along with it one way or another. You have to relate with situations as they are, absolutely. Then the whole situation of work becomes more friendly, because you can relate to work in terms of your own state of being, where you really are. If you can't relate directly with the situation, all your efforts become a waste of energy. Then the direct feedback from the situation may actually seem uncompassionate, and it can sometimes even seem cruel. The feedback can definitely be very sharp and heavy, but it is definitely true.

You can't fundamentally improve things by thinking that last time you did badly; therefore this time you should do better. If you're comparing now to last time, you can't improve at all. Things have to be measured on the merits of the present given situation, and that situation can actually seem very cruel to you. If you're out of touch, the situation rejects you. If you're right there, it accepts you infinitely, beautifully. However, if you are disconnected from what's happening, the situation rejects you painfully. It may even destroy you. Dealing with the chemistry of a situation is like that. If it's the right medicine, it cures you. If it's the wrong medicine, it poisons you. Relating directly is very sharp, pointed. However, it is helping us, in the fundamental sense, because we can't con situations. We can't change them at all by trying to work around them or approaching them by the back door. Things don't work that way. Our approach has to be honest, direct, and very precise.

A lot of people complain about the feedback from the world. Some people may think: "If God is love, why should I have such bad luck? I have had such a succession of mishaps, and yet I haven't killed a fly. I'm honest, a good citizen, a good person, a religious person; how could this happen to me?" They may go on thinking: "Sometimes I have to question whether God exists at all. I wonder about that, but that's an evil thought." People do question themselves like that. There were a lot of questions like that after the two World Wars, because so many misfortunes befell seemingly good, faithful people. People began to complain about the injustice of it. However, somehow justice isn't based on maintaining such general concepts of good and bad. It's much more intelligent and finely tuned than that. Justice is based on the minute details of your approach to things. In some sense, people deserve their painful or pleasurable situations, as difficult as this may be to accept.*

Buddha was criticized by one of his attendants as being wise but lacking in compassion. This attendant, Lekpe Karma, spent twenty-four years with the Buddha. After serving him for so long, the attendant said to himself, "I could be a buddha myself if he is the so-called Buddha. Except for his calmness and methodical way of approaching things, there's no difference between us." Those were the only differences he could see between himself and the Buddha. At one point the Buddha told him, "You are going to die in seven days." The attendant felt very apprehensive, saying to himself, "Sometimes what this devil says is true." He fasted for seven days to avoid any cause for illness and death. On the seventh day, he was on his way to see the Buddha to show him that he wasn't dead. He was very happy, but as he was going along, he suddenly felt a powerful thirst and drank some water, which turned out to be poisonous. He died on his way to see the Buddha to prove to him that what the Awakened One had said was not true.

As a Buddhist teacher, you can't always present things gently, because situations are not gentle. You may have to say, "You're going to die, and that's a fact." There's no point in saying, "Oh, I'm very sorry and upset about it, but you're going to die in seven days." I'm sure the Buddha didn't go to the trouble of manufacturing such apologetic language. Instead he acted

* According to the Buddhist view of karma, or the law of cause and effect, situations do not arise randomly in one's life, but they come about because of our former actions, or the karmic causes and conditions that lead to a situation. In a later chapter, Chögyam Trungpa talks about how one can step out of this perpetual creation of good and bad karma. For most of us most of the time, however, we are reaping the results of past actions and creating the seeds for future conditions to arise.—Eds.

as a reflection, as a complete mirror. He spoke from his true psychological state rather than trying to provide a cozy home, which he couldn't have done anyway. On account of that bluntness, the Buddha was accused by his attendant of having wisdom without compassion, knowing everything but being without emotion.

The softness in the situation has to come from you rather than someone else adding it in. If someone falls in love with you, it doesn't help if you aren't in love with that person. Nothing can be manufactured from the outside. You have to be in a state of softness or openness to the situation; the outside situation can only act as a reminder. Outside situations can only act as landmarks. That is true of your relationship to a spiritual teacher as well. The teacher can only tell you where you're at. She doesn't say, "This is where you are at; therefore you're a beautiful person," or "This is where you're at; therefore you're a terrible person." That extra phrase doesn't help. The message is purely: "This is where you're at."

6

. . .

THE NOWNESS
OF WORK

E go is very goal oriented. With ego you have
somebody *here* on this end who is going *there*—
to the goal. If you are fixated on an aim, an object or a target,
then your search becomes a battle. Then the whole spiritual
journey becomes a battle, a matter of hope and fear. The problem with having a goal is figuring out what to do after you get
to the goal. As long as there is a goal, that means there's a dead
end. It's like receiving your PhD. After you receive your degree,
you have to look for a job. All roads lead to a dead end, even if
the road is a highway. No matter how big the road is, there's
always an end to it. At last you come to the ocean, and you can't
drive any farther. You have to turn back.

The spiritual search should be aimless. Otherwise it ceases
to be spirituality, because spirituality is limitless. For that matter, this applies to anything in life, not just the spiritual journey

as such. Bodhisattva activity is a model of action without ego's goal orientation, at least theoretically. Ideally, bodhisattvas—mahayana practitioners who have vowed to help all sentient beings—would say: "I surrender myself, and I see a glimpse of egolessness. Egolessness has a much greater territory than I ever imagined. It extends to all sentient beings, as far as space reaches. I'm going to help them all." As a bodhisattva, you have to have this greater vision, an absolute vision that goes along with infinite feeling. That infinite feeling—that you're going to save all sentient beings—has no end because you have seen the infiniteness of the inwardness as well. There's no end out there, and there's no end at this end either. In that sense, both sides are equal.

You might think this means the bodhisattva is just working on himself or herself. But no, the bodhisattva is just working *there*. He's fulfilling needs everywhere. Wherever help is needed, he is providing help. There's actual infinite space. The bodhisattva is identifying with the person who needs help, not with himself. That's the whole point. If you are helping others just to make yourself feel good—"I want to help people because I want to see those people happy"—that is just entertaining yourself. Instead, you help others because help is needed.

The bodhisattva vows to save all sentient beings, but that is not a goal in the relative sense. The bodhisattva realizes that what she is saying in that vow is completely impractical. You can't really do it. We see this from the mythical story of the great bodhisattva Avalokiteshvara. He had a literal mind in the beginning. He took that vow, "Until I save all six realms of existence, I will not attain enlightenment." He worked and he worked and he worked to fulfill his vow. He helped beings, and he thought he'd saved hundreds of millions of them. Then he turned around and saw that an even greater number than he had saved were still suffering, and he had flickers of doubts at that point.

At the beginning, when he took the vow, he had said, "If

I have any doubts about my path, may my head split into a thousand pieces." This vow came true at this time. His head began to fall apart. He was in tremendous pain of confusion, not knowing what he was doing. Then, according to the myth, Amitabha—a great buddha of compassion—came to him and said, "Now you're being foolish. That vow you took shouldn't be taken literally. What you took was a vow of limitless compassion." Avalokiteshvara realized that and understood it. Through that recognition, he became a thousand times more powerful. That's why the iconographical image of Avalokiteshvara often has twelve heads and a thousand arms. You see, once you take the meaning of saving all others literally, you lose the sacredness of it. If you're able to see that compassion applies to every situation, then compassion becomes limitless. You don't try to attain enlightenment at all, but you find yourself enlightened at a certain stage, because you continuously put in such a concentrated effort.

You realize that the path is also the goal. The bodhisattva is quite happy with the path he is treading on. The path is what there is to work with, and that work is there eternally, because sentient beings are numberless, and we have to work with them eternally. That realization manifests as vast energy. The bodhisattva vow is really an acceptance of the energy. It is saying, "I take a vow to commit myself to work with this limitless energy." It is a commitment to work twenty-four hours a day without time off. You can't have part-time bodhisattvas.

When we say that spirituality has to be aimless, this is saying that spirituality is recognizing that unlimited energy. From that, you begin to develop a clear and precise understanding of nowness. Now is everything. Whatever you do in this very moment is everything; it's the past, it's the future, it's now. So you develop tremendous confidence that what you are doing is true and honest and absolutely realistic.

For example, you can't hear a piece of music in advance. When you listen to music, you are hearing the present music at that time. You also can't undo the past, the music that you've heard already. You can't do that; you hear the music of the moment. Now is a vast thing. Past and future can't exist without now. Otherwise, without the criterion of now, they cease to be past and future.

Now is all the time, and it is choiceless. There is always now, always now. The forms and memories of the past are always in relation to now. The future also is a situation relative to now. There's always this precision of now, which is there all the time and which helps us to relate with the past and the future. With now, we know where we are, and therefore how we relate with other things. Of course, by the time you're trying to relate with a situation, the actual experience has gone past. Still, there is some anchor somewhere, of now, now, now, which goes on all the time. From this point of view, the choices we make depend on how much we are accurately in the now.

Conceptions come from either future or past. Somehow they don't apply now. The absence of conceptions is very helpful, and the absence of conceptions also becomes the source of learning, which is now. The minute when you begin to speculate, that moment is past already. You perceive now rather than think it. Now can only be perceived, rather than thought of. The minute when you think of now, that's a double take. It's useless already. So you may think that conceptions from the past are helpful, since they provide helpful reference points for what we are doing now, but also their absence helps, not only their existence. In the present moment, you may feel that you are going back and forth into the past and the future. However, the present moment is really the only thing. It's the one thing, the choiceless choice.

Work takes place now. Now is never careless. If you perceive now as it is, it's always right on the spot. If you have to make a choice, you can only make a choice of whatever is now, at that moment. In some sense, you may feel you make a choice, but actually you don't really make the choice; it just happens that way because you see the situation precisely. Precision comes from now. Any possibilities of a careless choice come from past and future. They are purely dreams.

Let's talk more practically about work. The point of view of nowness provides a very good ground for our discussion of work. First let's look at some of the ordinary attitudes toward work. There's the impulsive approach, as for instance, when you feel like being helpful to someone, and you get up and do their dishes. At that moment, you're keen to help. More often, you see the work in front of you as something you must do. It's a chore, a drag. Once again, it may be better not to begin something in the first place, but if you do begin, then accomplish it properly. However, a lot of people, after already having become involved in a work situation, start to question it, asking themselves whether they should really be involved in this project or not. That undermines the present situation they are in already. As long as we are working and being of potential service, we have to face the situation as it is. Unless we pack our bags and escape, we have to deal with circumstances directly. Even if we do escape from one situation, then we will have to find another. Circumstances are perpetually arising where we have to deal with work of some kind.

You might have to run a household, or you might be working with an organization. When you are doing any kind of work, there is a need to open up and relate with it. There are often relationship problems to be faced. There may be uncertainties as to who the authority in the household is or who your boss in the organization is. You might find yourself waiting for an authority to tell you what to do, or you might find you are trying to avoid the boss's eyes so you can work less. In any case, you have a sense of "them and me."

You can't escape those situations. At home or at work or in any community you join, you will find that effort and help are needed. Even though you may not have been approached by anyone to pitch in, you are right there at that very moment. You are present in that space. You are breathing the same air as the other people in the office or your home, and you're sharing the same roof. At that point you have the choice of being a nuisance or being open. That choice is always there, in any situation.

Suppose you decide to be a nuisance. You want to have a good time in that place without working. Okay, you go ahead and take that approach. Soon you find that your approach does not provide a very luxurious result. The moment you say, "I'm just going to have a good time and not do any work," every corner of the place begins to haunt you. You continually have imaginary housewives coming at you, or imaginary bosses, wardens, or trustees of the community. They're continually coming at you with horns and tails. You are not having a good time at all, unless you have developed tremendously skillful insensitivity, the absolute insensitivity of just camping out by yourself as an independent unit.

Even being totally insensitive requires a certain amount of inspiration and intelligence, which basically means that you are not a blunt and insensitive person at all. There has to be some intelligence there to maintain that insensitivity. As long as there is intelligence, that means there will be paranoia. So it seems that being a nuisance is not particularly fun, even though you think it might be fun to do nothing, just breathe the air and be there, just present yourself as a lump sum.

Of course, the other alternative is trying to communicate, trying to be of service. However, trying to be useful may not be that inspiring either. You walk up to somebody and say, "What can I do for you?" For some people, this comes naturally. But for some people it's incredibly awkward to extend themselves. You feel so heady; you feel like a gigantic head on two feet. In spite of this awkwardness, you should try to help.

Another situation you encounter in the work environment is the innuendos of who's playing a game with whom. All sorts of little suggestions of games going on might come up, but at the same time, there is a way of adapting oneself to all of that. On the whole, working with others is based on relationships. It's not so much a matter of producing useful work all the time as it is a matter of communicating.

It doesn't really matter whether you are working in an office or as a housekeeper, whether you are a secretary or a manager, or even whether you are a guest in a house or living in a community somewhere. All of those situations involve communication. They all present the same challenges in relating to others.

When you are looking for work, all kinds of questions arise, such as, "Will I be accepted or not when I have my interview?" If you have a job interview, you try to present yourself as very respectable; maybe you cut your hair and shave your beard. Still, the right haircut, a clean shave, a decent suit, and polished shoes do not address the whole question. The interview presents a deeper challenge than that. The challenge is how to have actual communication with others and with the situation as a whole. Indeed, in any aspect of the work environment, the challenge is how much communication we can actually have.

There might be patterns of behavior or activities in the workplace that you don't agree with. You might find that you do not agree with the basic philosophy, the end product, or the whole atmosphere of the place. In spite of those things, there is still room to communicate, room to associate yourself with that scene, since you are karmically already involved with the situation.

There is constant checking back and forth with ourselves when we are newcomers to the workplace. Bewilderment plays a very important part—not knowing who you are, why you are here. We are constantly asking ourselves, "Why am I here at all?" Then we try to go beyond bewilderment and make a move. That move often becomes fraught with paranoia—we are eager but anxious about being accepted, eager to be included in the conversations of the in-group in that place. Or if we have been newly accepted as a manager in a firm, we want to be sure we have all the information about what is going on. A lot depends on fellow managers or maybe even shareholders—how much do they trust and accept us? How many dinner invitations and cocktail-party invitations have we had? The more of those we have had, the more our confidence builds that we are being accepted. Still, the whole approach is based on distrust or paranoia.

At a certain stage, a person may finally begin to relax a little bit more, make friends with people, begin to smile a little bit, exchange occasional jokes. "Here I am," you think, "exchanging jokes with people." After you begin to relax, you might become more daring. You feel braver; you might begin to make little decisions—in a diplomatic fashion, if you are a diplomatic person at all. You try to present your ideas. You associate yourself more with the whole work situation. You try to do everything following the basic principle of faith in the firm, and all of your decisions are based on good intentions. You make decisions very seriously, of course. These little decisions you make are appropriate and pleasing to the boss. All the while you are becoming more relaxed, less self-conscious.

You are becoming more fundamentally ingratiating, but this requires subtlety. If you are too ingratiating, that might also be fishy from the point of view of your employers. They might suspect your motives; think you are up to no good. Nevertheless, you go on being more daring. You make small moves. You begin to stretch and yawn in front of people. At this point, you are still wondering if you are really communicating at all. Some people can extend this phase of relationship on and on, even for twenty years—if they spend that long at a corporation. They continue to take the same approach: They remain officially paranoid persons. They try to keep up the same image, exactly the same as when they had their first interviews. They try to maintain this same continuity, which is stale and plastic in nature.

On the other hand, more adventurous people will try to get into new areas. They will try to drop the mask that they originally presented. They will try to get into the nitty-gritty of the job, try to get into the aim and object of what they really want to achieve. They begin very officially, but then they relax after they finally learn to identify with their particular organization. However, even if they reach that point, there is still something wrong, something missing. Real work has still not begun at all. The whole situation is a stage prop. What is the actual work that hasn't begun?

You seem to have the whole realm or situation of relationship happening in your job, and you are so involved in the games you are playing. However, suppose you want to relate to somebody in another department. You need to get some information from someone, but it's not going to be easy to find out what you need to know. You can't just send the person a memo. It won't work. You need some human contact with the person. But that is very awkward. You invite the person for a meal or for a walk. Somehow it doesn't happen smoothly. It's obvious to him or to her—and to you—that you have an ulterior motive. Some basic thing is still lacking there. Where's the magic? What is missing? If you knew that, you could become the heart of the whole organization. You could become the very much needed missing person.

What is lacking is a sense of humor, which means getting along with yourself. Once you have that, you begin to see the joy of working in a situation. When I talk about sense of humor, it sometimes seems complicated for people. In the West, people usually don't laugh unless you're being rude or cynical. People don't laugh just from seeing the natural humor of a situation. When you laugh, people can get very paranoid and think they are being laughed at or that you are making fun of them. I am not talking about that kind of humor or humor used to bring comic relief to a situation that is too intense. I'm talking about basic delight.

The whole play of the scene you are involved in is delightful. Whatever scene it might be, it has its own qualities and characteristics. In fact, the situation you are in is unique. If you had to create that situation deliberately, nobody could do it. Spontaneous humor can only come about through appreciation of a situation as a unique work of art. The situation really is beautiful. When you are genuinely enjoying working somewhere, you see the uniqueness there that brings out your sense of humor. At that point, your work is going to become creative, and you are going to be very helpful to the firm, the organization, the society, or whatever it is—maybe even a meditation center. You see the irony in situations. That very healthy interplay within the environment is self-enlightening.

That is why we need work. It seems that such a rich situation cannot come about for us at all unless we put ourselves into the discipline of the work process. Discipline means getting into what is happening. In the Buddhist scriptures an analogy for our affinity to discipline is that a swan is automatically drawn to water and vultures are automatically drawn to the charnel ground. That is just saying that you have to involve yourself in the situations you encounter in life. We have to go through the process of being part of a situation; otherwise we will not be exposed to this richness. In order to see the delight in a situation, we have to become involved in it. We have to really feel it; we have to touch the whole texture of the complete situation. Then we will be able to relate properly with the actual work involved. Then, automatically, the efficiency of dealing with all the little details will happen naturally.

Again, this requires a certain amount of humor, which is related to having a certain amount of openness, of seeing the whole situation as it is. Unless whoever is taking part in the situation has an aerial view of the whole thing, a real connection to the details does not take place. Even though a particular person may only be standing at the gate checking the visitors coming into the building, even in such an uninspiring position, that person needs to take a panoramic view. He has to have the whole feeling of inspiration for the entire environment of that institution. The more a person is able to relate to that whole feeling from as far away from the center as the entry gate, the better he will be able to see what is necessary to fulfill his job. He will become very efficient. Not that he will be trying to impress other people; it is just that he will see what is needed. You could be the gatekeeper, or your activity could be as small a thing as emptying the ashtrays or cleaning up a little bit of dirt; nevertheless, that simple occupation becomes everything. As long as a person has that panoramic view, the paranoia we have been talking about will be absent.

Once you have a sense of humor in the work situation as it is, you will be able to relate with all the human situations around that. Each person is unique. I don't mean by that that there is only one John Brown who was born in 1967 and that's why he's unique. Each person has his own characteristics and his own way of handling his style, which is beautiful and inspiring in its own way. It doesn't have to be your style alone that inspires you; any style of being can be inspiring. If you are involved with a community, appreciating other people's styles could lead to a very beautiful sangha sort of feeling, a feeling of group connectedness. We all enter into a learning process with our own styles, our own habitual patterns, our own points of view, and all of that provides spice in the life situation we are sharing. If we are not able to work with situations in this way, then we are missing valuable training.

7

...

CREATIVITY
AND CHAOS

O nce a person is able to connect with the basic creative environment of work, then the rest of the process becomes less of a struggle. Creativity is the key to work. Strangely enough, it seems to be the key to sex as well, which we will discuss later. Both are a process of communication as opposed to purely relating with material objects or people as objects. Once you have understood the basic philosophy of work as we discussed it earlier, then somehow work becomes very simple. It's not a matter of tit for tat but a continual process of open exchange.

When work is based purely on ambition, it's as though you have a target that you want to destroy, or else you want to build something very big with your ambition. There's a Tibetan story about a local landlord who wanted to cut off the peak of a certain high mountain because it prevented him from getting sunlight in his residence in winter. He ordered his people to do the work. Then halfway through the job, they had a realization and rushed down to his residence and chopped off his head. They said they had realized that it was much easier to chop off the landlord's head than to chop off the head of the mountain. So ambition can backfire on you. If your whole approach is based on ambition, then you may lose your connection to the real meaning of work.

A lot of people find work negative, particularly if they have uninspiring work, regular day-to-day work to which they have no personal commitment or link. The trouble is that somebody has to do the routine work. Not everybody can be a craftsman or an artist. That would leave nobody to do the routine jobs. The public wouldn't get its regular services. Somebody has to be willing to be a milkman and deliver the milk; somebody has to be willing to be a security guard and hang around a huge building all day. There is always that need.

However, as we discussed in the last chapter, even routine, uninspiring work can be approached from the point of view of humor and communication. Otherwise we end up with a division in society where talented people feel extremely proud, and so-called untalented people feel useless and purely functional. That's like applying a distinction among humans as though it were a division between human beings and animals. There is a big problem when people are unable to relate to all kinds of work with a sense of communication. If you really communicate, if you are able to see the creative process in an apparently uncreative situation, you are constantly inspired. In that way, everybody can be a talented artist—in fact, much more of a talented artist than the kind of official artist who has the very limited scope of purely awakening her own potential. Those who are not artists as such, who are doing manual labor and ordinary jobs—repetitive jobs—are extremely skillful artists indeed when they are able to see and use the pattern of creativity in their work. We have to look into all kinds of work situations. The Buddhist teachings are not intended for genteel society or intellectual society alone at all. The teachings are presented to anyone, everyone. There should be a universal quality to the teaching. Of course, we can't achieve anything purely by talking about it. We have to apply the teachings; people actually have to do it.

If a person had been a manager and then he took a job as a simple office worker, he might take days and months to get used to being in his new position. As long as he is open to the situation of being an office worker, he can express the same kind of individual style there as in his previous managerial work. There's no doubt about that—you can express your work of art in any situation. This is true as long as you are not offended by being put in a lower situation, as long as you don't resent that, thinking, "I belong to a higher class of people. I should have a higher position, because I am more artistic or more intelligent." That kind of thinking creates a tremendous barrier.

When the Communist invasion took place in Tibet, many great teachers were put in labor camps. They had never swept a floor or carried bricks before. It took them a long time to get used to manual labor, but apparently once they did, they remained great teachers because they were good workers. They were often made leaders of ten groups of workers. They were shifted to that kind of post because they were ordinary about their work and kept their equilibrium. That kept the work going, so they automatically became leaders.

I'm envisaging something more creative here than purely getting into the meaninglessness of the situation. Things are not really as bad as that, although we might think so. Things could be bad, they could be the epitome of bad, the worst, but what we are trying to point out here is that there will still be some stepping-stone in the situation, in any situation.

There's a big advantage if you are dealing with people, even repetitively. Then it's always a creative situation. People often ask me how I find giving interviews all day long, hearing the same thing over and over again. People have their own individual style, and each style is distinct, so it's quite creative. The greater problem seems to be when we are talking about a repetitive, mechanical job where you don't see people, where it's purely a matter of pressing buttons or dealing with the constant repetition of objects coming through on an assembly line. Even then, there should be a creative way of relating. A person could explore even a situation like that. One should not seal it off completely and give up all hope. Look into the situation and find some way of working with it.

Your basic attitude toward work is very important. If you feel that you are completely trapped in a job, then you fail to see the interesting aspect of it. People in boring, repetitive situations who don't expect to stay in those jobs forever don't feel so trapped. They feel that they could get out at any moment; it's purely a temporary measure. Therefore, their minds are open, and they can see their job as a creative situation. Your attitude may come down to how much you fear that you are trapped in something, or how much you feel that the present moment provides freedom to you. Again, it's a question of the future and the past. If you view the future as a closed future, then there's no room for inspiration at all. If you realize that the future is an open future, then there is room for inspiration. It is a matter of opinion, from that point of view.

A person might find it inspiring to spend the rest of her life doing some particularly simple work. She's purely living on simplicity. She could find it extremely rewarding and secure in some sense. She doesn't have to step out into another territory and explore any wholly strange situations anymore. On the other hand, if she wants to explore other territories and she hasn't had enough excitement yet, she might feel completely trapped. Our attitude depends on some sort of acceptance.

The same thing happens in monasteries. Monks or nuns feel that the rest of their life is committed to doing the same regular thing, getting up in the morning and doing the religious services, chanting and meditating, and then going to bed at a certain hour. Since they feel their whole life is based on that pattern, they might feel trapped. At the same time, they might feel inspired. Of course, for monks and nuns they clearly feel that they are doing something spiritual, something supermundane. In reality, that may not mean very much. The actual physical work is often repetitive in the monastery. For the Carthusians and the Benedictines, for instance, the schedule and routine are quite fixed.* You are not supposed to miss mass in the morning. Your life may largely consist of taking communion, making daily confession, eating food, saying your prayers, and then going to bed, except for celebrations like Easter and Christmas. Life is very routine; you do exactly the same thing, over and over, on and on all the time. Perhaps some people would find that satisfying or even exciting, because life is so simple. The whole flow of daily life is designed to be smooth and repetitive. People appreciate it. However, suppose such a lifestyle were not a spiritual situation but something designed as a daily routine in a therapeutic community established for the treatment of addiction or mental illness. Then it's quite likely that the clients or inmates would react against such an approach. They would regard the whole institution as unworkable, an enormous imposition. So it seems our attitude is very important to how we experience a work environment.

I'm not suggesting that we seek a work situation that is more meditative in nature. Rather, what way of working in any situation will have more human potential, so to speak? What

---

* Chögyam Trungpa visited Pluscarden Abbey during his honeymoon in 1970. The abbey is home to a community of Roman Catholic Benedictine monks. On the abbey's Web site, it is described as "the only medieval monastery in Britain still inhabited and being used for its original purpose." Elsewhere on the site, the atmosphere is defined as one of "quiet reflection and of work dedicated to the glory of God." In *Dragon Thunder: My Life with Chögyam Trungpa*, his widow, Diana Mukpo, speaks of Trungpa Rinpoche's great appreciation for the genuine contemplative atmosphere at Pluscarden Abbey. For more on this, see *Dragon Thunder*, pp. 81–82.—Eds.

approach to work will provide more potential for you to put your effort and your style into the situation and become creative? The work doesn't have to be meditative in the sense of being repetitive or simple. There could be a great deal of room in the work environment for inspiration and communication, which is outer meditation or meditation in action.

Creativity in your work comes from your mind. The idea of work being creative is that the mind can connect with the sharpness or the inspiration within any situation. There is always something acute and precise happening in a situation, which can lead you to other possibilities. That quality of mind connecting with the potential could be called imagination, I suppose, but it's not dreamy imagination; it's practical imagination. It is seeing that every step contains possibilities of furthering whatever your process is. That includes your contribution and the whole environment around that particular job. There is room to learn, room to develop.

When you don't feel the creativity or workability in a situation and you have a lot of negativity happening, it begins to seem as though the whole situation is negative. This is true not only in work situations but in any situation. You get into a situation that seems ideal to begin with, and you get used to that. At a certain stage, however, you detect a faint hint of chaos. That hint does not remain faint; it intensifies, and soon you find that you want to step out of the whole scene. That happens in all kinds of situations in life, but it can be particularly heightened when you are engaged in spiritual practice. This is because you expect spiritual practice to provide something profitable and convenient to your ego, something secure. Often, when you realize that it does not provide security as expected, the situation becomes excruciating. You feel a sudden sense of doubt, a loss of independence and security. Such situations are unique ones that cannot be strategized. They are in fact very opportune and precious.

To work with those situations, you need intelligent patience, not naiveté. You need some understanding that the situation is saying something. It's saying something that you have been ignoring for a long time, and finally it's beginning to speak up. If you try to strategize in that situation, by telling yourself that the negativity is valuable, you turn it into a stage prop in which you view the negative things coming to you as positive, and it loses its direct quality.

In fact, no matter what you tell yourself, you don't really believe that the negativity is helpful. You are not really convinced, because things are so painful. You would like to use strategy to control the chaos, but in reality, you can't control the chaos in any way. If you try to control it, then you're asking for more chaos by trying to control it. That's a well-known effect.

Self-confidence does not come from control. If you have a certain conceptual notion of self-confidence, that view has to be constantly maintained. That kind of self-confidence is going in the wrong direction. If it is built on the wrong foundation, then automatically, it is weakened.

Chaos is actually a sign that there is tremendous energy or force available in a situation. If you try to blindly alter the energy, then you are interfering with the energy pattern. For one thing, you become much more self-conscious. Then you are not able to see where the energy is actually occurring in the situation. The alternative is to go along with the energy. This means, in a sense, doing nothing with the energy, as though it were some independent force. When you go along with what is happening, you uncover the real energy in the situation and then you are able to relate with situations fully, in a true way, a complete way.

In order to accept or reject something in your experience, you have to see the complete picture to begin with; otherwise you have no idea what the right thing to do is. Acceptance might be the skillful choice, or rejecting might be skillful. Before you make a choice, you should find the choiceless quality, which exists as an element of the situation. It's like buying merchandise. Before you buy something, it is best to know the qualities of the merchandise, its value, and everything about it completely. If you fail to investigate it, then you won't make a good buyer or seller.

If you blindly accept something, you might be inflicting pain on yourself or you might be overindulging in pleasure, which brings future pain. Blindly rejecting things, on the other hand, is usually based on aggression or fear. Before you make *any* choice, you should try to see the choiceless aspect, which is always there in any situation. You have to feel it. You have to relate with things as they are, and then you can reject or accept. Within the overall experience of seeking to understand things as they are, you actually include all the possibilities of rejecting and accepting the situation altogether.

To clarify, you have to learn to see situations first, completely, before you make any decisions. First you feel the situation and open yourself to it without anticipating rejecting or accepting. Without any idea of rejecting and accepting, you deal directly with the whole situation. If you can work that way completely, then rejecting, if necessary, becomes a natural process, and accepting, if necessary, becomes a natural process. You communicate with the situation completely, without any judgment. Communicating thoroughly inspires sound judgment, by itself. You might think that people are unpredictable, but a person actually can't react to you in an unpredictable way. If you are actually one with the situation, you will see why and how that reaction happened.

The main idea I would like to get across here, in terms of how to relate with work, is that no matter what job you have, no matter what work situation you are involved in, it is necessary to see the whole thing with an open mind, without preconceptions. Earlier, we were talking about transcending concepts. That applies very much to this view of relating to work. You have all kinds of choices, and you might well have a blueprint in mind for the life you want. That is one source of preconceptions. There may also be a certain snobbishness that says, "I'm not designed for certain kinds of jobs." This is not particularly a matter of money; rather, in this case you become indignant because you feel a job is beneath you.

This kind of snobbishness often came up in the monastic life in Tibet. If a monk or a great scholar or even a great teacher in the monastery got too carried away with himself, the abbot might ask him to work as a tea server or wood collector until he corrected his arrogance or transcended it. This was much more effective than an alternative such as asking the offender to do five hundred prostrations in front of the sangha. That would have been more acceptable to him than a lowly job, because it was a religious practice allowing him to redeem his mistake. Being a tea server or wood collector was harder to swallow. Of course, in Tibet there was a great deal of social consciousness within the strict hierarchical structure. The need to save face was greater than it is in North America. Tibet is similar to Japan in that respect. Both of those countries have a much thicker mask of social propriety than we have in the West. People want to belong to certain pigeonholes in society. Strangely enough, the Communists worked quite well with that. They had daily exercises in which the president and prime minister had to go out and do gardening and collect rubbish and excrement from the street. They had to carry that in a basket on their back and bring it to the rubbish heap. Of course, this remedy was off the mark in getting beyond preconceptions, because there was a game involved, the game of "the humbler you are, the more respected you are." This was a reverse version of the problem it was trying to cure.

Whenever there is a game like that connected with work, the whole approach is based on concept, and your ability to relate to the work situation openly and directly is undermined. In the case where you feel a job is beyond your intelligence, or more likely, beneath you, you feel resentful toward it or uninterested. The result is that you automatically prove the job does not suit you by not doing it well, by not being a good worker at all. The reality is that you would benefit from more of that kind of work.

Another conceptual approach to work is that of an ambitious person who is intent on doing something, on achieving his own glory, yet he lacks commitment to the discipline involved. He desperately wants to do some specific kind of work, without knowing what it is really like. He may have tremendous romantic expectations, and then he doesn't find the actual work romantic at all; he finds it disappointing. Maybe he wanted to be a professional photographer, and he loved the idea because he saw some other artist's beautiful photographs. However, he never realized how much discipline had to go into becoming such a skillful photographer, and he ended up doing badly at photography because he didn't actually want to go through that discipline at all.

There are many examples of people floating from job to job because of concepts they have in their minds about what they would like to do. When they encounter the actual work situation, they are not able to stick to it; they are not able to work through it patiently and explore the whole area. They are unable to painstakingly work through the challenges. As a result, instead of proving themselves, they disprove themselves; they humiliate themselves personally and in front of other people. They give up the work they wanted so desperately to do, and perhaps they tour around different countries, getting involved in exciting or exotic things. This lifestyle is, perhaps, a youthful or exuberant expression of life, but without depth. Quite possibly, during their travels, they get involved with meditation and visit ashrams and religious centers where they meet interesting people.

At a certain stage the money runs out, and they have to come home and do something constructive. Maybe you plan to write a book about your travels, but you never get around to it. You might write two or three chapters of a book, but then you stop. You are not able to stick with a situation and patiently go through it, explore the whole area and patiently, painfully go through the process to achieve something. There again, you are back to square one. "Shall I go back to photography, which wasn't beautiful? What other sorts of excitement can I find?" Strangely enough, many such people end up being teachers of yoga, meditation, or Buddhism, because that's the easiest work, in a certain way. In that lifestyle, you don't have to produce a sample or a product of your work. You can just go on talking, and you find that your background of tourism also helps tremendously.

Work usually involves producing an end product, whether that product is a thing that you make, a degree that you receive, or a project that you complete. You might say this orientation goes against Buddhist philosophy, but that's not true. The fact that work produces a product is different from the problems of goal orientation, where you ignore the value of the process, which we discussed earlier. I mentioned many times already the Tibetan proverb that it's better not to begin something, but once you do, you should finish it properly. In a work situation, having begun something, you should pursue it to the point of its final achievement. People come up with many excuses for not doing that, particularly people who want to "explore themselves." They might say the situation does not give them opportunities for self-exploration or that the place where they are working has bad vibes. They make all kinds of excuses that don't mean very much. The problem is that those people have become too cunning. Their laziness has become very active and resourceful; in fact, it has become very intelligent and awake. Their sort of laziness is not at all sleepy or dull. It's very sharp and precise in its ability to find excuses. It becomes a spokesman for the fundamental ego.

Particularly people on the spiritual path are in danger of not being able to persevere in the work situation. They can be particularly apt at finding excuses not to work and very clever in developing the practice of laziness. The moment they don't feel like doing something, the appropriate spiritual quotation comes to their mind.

The basic problem in all of these cases is that people have some concept about a job or project, and when it does not fit that concept, they do not want to go through with it. As I have said, they often find the work beneath them.

The great teacher Guru Rinpoche, Padmasambhava, did all kinds of different work. He was ordained a monk, but as he traveled around, he learned poetry, he learned mathematics, and he learned carpentry and other handicrafts. Also, the traditional Indian way of training a king was to give him lessons in many kinds of work, such as painting, sewing, carpentry, poetry, and physical exercises. Princes also studied warfare and the use of weapons. They learned how to ride on a horse and on an elephant. Building houses was also part of their education. All of this was part of a royal upbringing. If a prince had to be a blacksmith, he could do it and do it beautifully. He still maintained his dignity as a prince—not through pride but by his example.

These days people sometimes say they can't do certain work because they haven't taken a course in it. A lot of things in life don't have to be taught in courses. You don't need a degree to do the work. You just need to drop your hesitation and use your intelligence. You need to get into it and just do it. You can achieve the same end result as those who have received a degree in that particular thing. There are many areas where people's intelligence has been undermined by systematized study. They read books on how to make a fire, how to mend their shoes, how to hike—all sorts of things like that. However, getting into work you haven't done before can be an awakening experience when you have to use your basic intelligence to feel the ground. You use your basic common sense to get things together. Just apply it and work, and you will find that the process is opening and enlightening. Fundamentally, we are capable of anything.

You might say that a certain person would not make a good

fighter because he isn't aggressive enough or that someone else would make a bad watchman because she hasn't got the right kind of concentration. If you look at things from that angle, choices become very limited. That supposedly bad watchman could be quite a wakeful person if the situation required it of her. She might be able to do the watchman job beautifully. I remember an incident that occurred during my escape from Tibet. One night when we were getting close to crossing the border into India, we came over a ridge and suddenly saw a Chinese-built road just five hundred yards away from us with military trucks moving along it. We made a plan to creep up to the road and have everybody in our party cross simultaneously, with one person going behind with a branch to wipe out all of our footprints, because it was a dirt road. We got everybody set and made our move. We thought the people who were usually the toughest would get across first, with the slow people coming later. However, when the time came, the slow people were much faster than the tough people. It's a matter of how awake someone is at a given time.

If there is enough interest awakened in a person to communicate openly with the work situation, I'm sure he or she will be able to do the job quite beautifully. We shouldn't categorize people too much. There's always potential. Everybody has basic intelligence that is capable of surprising us. If a person is able to reach the point of breaking the conceptual barrier to open communication, his or her work becomes open and creative. That possibility is always there. There are hidden qualities in us, always.

8

. . .

COMMUNICATION

To review, basically, spiritual practice is dealing with our psychological state of being. The difference between the enlightened and the confused state of mind depends on whether you see situations as they are or you fail to see them as they are and are confused or frightened by them. The kind of spirituality we are talking about is not at all a matter of faith born from the revelation of an external entity. In this case, faith and understanding are born out of the precision and clarity of perceiving the universe as it is. Therefore, there is no point in trying to make a getaway from the world by entering into a trancelike state of absorption and trying to make the best of that as a home, a dwelling place.

The tendency of spiritual materialism is to try to find some dwelling place where you are secure and satisfied. True spirituality should not be based on that sort of aim, which seems to encourage establishing set patterns that one can identify with and disregarding spiritual development itself. For instance, you take a vow to go to a solitary place and practice meditation for ten years. You go to a quiet place, and you settle down and start going through your ten-year period of, so to speak, development—ten years of practice anyhow. Then you count every hour, every day, every month, every year that has gone by and also how many are still left to go. Those ten years go by very fast. One day, you find yourself saying, "Tomorrow is my time to come out." Then you come out. For ten years you haven't heard any news of what's happened in the world, and you have to adapt to all the changes that have occurred. In addition, you have the difficulty of adapting again to a normal living situation after having lived in solitary for all that time. It probably doesn't take too long to make those adjustments, maybe a month or so. You begin to visit your friends and relatives and get involved again in the lifestyle you used to have. You are back to square one, except that ten years of your life have been different from everybody else's—I mean physically different.

The same thing could also be said for practices like a hundred thousand prostrations, a hundred thousand mantras, and other traditional Tibetan Buddhist practices. You do them very diligently, very fast, competitively, and soon you have accomplished your hundred thousand thises or thats. In the end, after you finish them, you still have your old familiar problems. You still have the same old hang-ups and the same old clumsy style you used to have. The same situation is still there.

Quite possibly, you might get some kind of credit or credential for the practice you accomplished. People might be inclined to say, "She has achieved something. She *must* be different." But that's purely a concept, just words. I wouldn't say that such practices are not valuable, but if we approach them from an external point of view of heroism, or if we have a material or physical commitment to those practices without the attitude of working on our basic psychology, that makes them rather futile.

What's wrong here is that spirituality is regarded as something extraordinary, something completely out of touch with everyday life. You step out into another sphere, another realm, so to speak, and you feel that this other realm is the only answer. That is why it is so important for us to talk about spirituality in connection with all the aspects of relating with our familiar world. It is possible for us to see ordinary situations from the point of view of an extraordinary insight—that of discovering a jewel in a rubbish heap.

You have to start with what you are, where you are now. Concept cannot exist in the present state, but awareness is very much there. You are aware of the present state. You are *now*, you are not past, you are not future, but you are now. In that state of awareness, you don't need to cling to a concept about who you are or who you will be. Before you even go to college, you don't have to say to yourself, for example: "I will be a professor when I graduate from school. Therefore I *am* a professor, so I should behave like a professor right now." That approach is the source of a lot of problems. That's what is wrong with a lot of dictators. Hitler, for instance, hadn't conquered the world, but he behaved as though he had. That's partly why he failed. Everything came back on him because he was not realistic enough about his present strength, his own physical, mental, or spiritual health. When doctors tried to tell Mussolini that he shouldn't overwork because he was a sick man and needed rest, he just brushed them off. He ignored the present state of his health. He behaved as though he were strong and in good health and a universal conqueror. And he failed.

That doesn't mean to say that you can't do or plan anything. You can plan everything, but you plan in accordance with your present state. You don't plan something in terms of what you would like to be. No one can do that. You can only plan based on what you are now. Now you need a job; therefore you are working on finding one. The real way of being without aim or object is dealing with the present situation, the completely present situation. The more you are realistic about the present situation—how much money you need, what kind of job you are capable of doing, what state of health you are in—the better your chances when you look for a job. If a person is off the track of relating with the present moment, consumed with what might be, then quite likely her job search would be disastrous.

I'm a very ambitious person myself, extremely, dangerously so! However, I relate with *now*. On that basis, you see how far you can go, how far you can't go. Your ambition isn't focused on the future. You may think, once you get a job, you'll get a house, you can have all of these nice things and this and that, and *then* you could get *this*. Instead of actually going through the whole process, you just mentally jump to your conclusion— what you would like to be rather than what you are. Then you are in trouble. There's nothing wrong with ambition, as long as you stay with *this* situation, this very realistic thing.

In terms of work, sex, and money—which is our broad topic—if work becomes a practice in the present moment, it becomes an extremely powerful one, because the regular daily problems are there anyway. But now these problems cease to be problems—they become a source of inspiration. In the case of money, with this approach, nothing is rejected as too ordinary and nothing is overvalued as sacred. Instead, all the substance and material that are available in the life situation are simply used. We know basically what money represents, what money is for. If we know that and are able to work along with that understanding, if we can approach the ordinary situation in this extraordinary way of not rejecting anything or overvaluing anything either, that will provide quite a surprise for the habitual pattern of ego.

Usually our whole approach is based on conceptualization. Once we begin to operate with the concept that something connected with our life is good for us, with the notion that we are supposed to gain something from it, that approach turns into a process of trying to find a suitable, comfortable nest to dwell in. We begin seeking an enriched environment created for our ego, for the maintenance of *me*, myself. When, on the other hand, there are no concepts, we just throw ourselves overboard, off the cliff, so to speak. We just let go into the situation and into the learning process as it is; then openness can begin to develop. Other people might say that this is ludicrous, impractical. They might tell us that we should have more self-respect, that we should be a proud person, and we should have an aim and object, a goal in mind. However, they have never approached the situation from the other, nonconceptual, angle. The people saying those things about a goal orientation, in fact, have no authority, because they've never seen the other side of the coin. They don't see it because being without concept is too dangerous, too frightening. In fact, although they haven't seen it, there is another way of approaching life beyond defensive self-respect, beyond pride. The only way to discover this may be to make friends with ourselves. Then we don't have to put ourselves through the torture of the competitive process at all.

Sex, like work and money, is usually based on preconceptions. The notion of being faithful in sexual relations is based on preconceptions about husbands and wives and lovers. The main notion that governs sex seems to be a sense of *debt*. That seems to determine what behavior is expected. However, the basic point of sex, its fundamental meaning, its essential philosophy, is already lost once we begin to approach it from this obligatory angle. Sex or sexual experience should be considered the essence of human communication. Communication here, of course, is dependent on a physical body. Sexual communication can only be carried out by the obvious means of physical gestures or words. However, implied behind those gestures is mind, which is very difficult to perceive.

In Buddhism, there is a mythological description of the god realms that are connected with the four *dhyana* states, the four states of meditative absorption.* Supposedly, as you progress higher from the first dhyana state toward the fourth, each of these realms has less solid bodily substance than the one below. There is less and less solid body until eventually everything is based on the meditative body, the body connected with the highest, trancelike, state of absorption. This is said to be because the higher you go the less ego-clinging there is. In the realm corresponding to the first or lowest of the four states, the way the gods communicate sexually is by means of sexual intercourse. In the second realm, sexual communication consists purely of holding hands. Beyond that, in the third realm, sexual relationship consists of smiling at each other. And finally, in the highest realm, sexual communication is purely gazing at each other.

This description of communication in the dhyana states relates to the human dependence on body as the basis for relationship, the need to communicate in accordance with the solidness of the physical body. The human way of paying respect to a spiritual teacher or teaching, for example, can be by prostrating; or in the Catholic tradition, by kissing the bishop's ring; or in stories of Buddhist renunciation, through sacrificing one's physical, bodily energy to the teaching, as in the case of Milarepa carrying stones on his back to build a house for his teacher. I don't mean sacrifice in the ordinary sense. It's an act of offering. It is as though you are acknowledging that there is solid substance there, which is the body, and you are using that as a vehicle or method. Physically surrendering is an expression of commitment.

As human beings, it seems that our approach to body is a rather clumsy one, at least from the point of view of god realms, or more ethereal realms of being. In some sense, however, the

* *Dhyana* (Sanskrit) simply means meditation. The term is often used to refer to forms of meditation based on absorption, which are still ego-centric experiences, no matter how refined they may be. In particular, *dhyana* refers to the four states of absorption, sometimes called the "four dhyanas." See the glossary for further information.—Eds.

description of sexual communication in the four god realms or dhyana states is a description of human experience. Viewing it as anything else is just speculation or imagination. As a human being, how you communicate depends on how heavy you are. I don't mean heavy in terms of being physically fat or anything like that. It's a matter of how heavy your mind-body is. In fact, tantric visualizations of yourself with your consort reflect a similar approach to communication as is described in the dhyana states. As you go higher and higher into more formless levels of tantra, you have higher means of communication with your visualized consort, the *dakini*, or female consort; or the *heruka*, or male consort. In more everyday, ordinary terms, this is just saying that there are many levels of subtlety in human communication. There are many means of expressing affection, not all of them based on a gross or heavy sense of physicality.

The physical act of sex has often been described in scriptures and other teachings of Eastern spirituality as *abrahmacharya*, an act of noncompletion.* Sex is seen as a clumsy way of releasing your *bindu*. Bindu in this case is the essence of the body; often it is equated with semen, but that is not necessarily a good definition. Both men and women possess bindu. Bindu is the essence of the mind and essence of the body. This is like describing the money system as the essence of society. Bindu is another type of currency in the context of human communication.

The Indian teachings in both the Hindu and Buddhist traditions agree that abusing bindu is an act of abrahmacharya, of noncompletion. When the body contains the bindu essence, you are a completely healthy person. When you abuse that, when you throw that away, that becomes abrahmacharya, disrupting the completeness of Brahma, who is the complete one, the wholesome one. Brahma represents or contains the wholesome, healthy, unified situation of your life and body.

---

* In Hinduism, *brahmacharya* has two main meanings. Broadly, it refers to control of the senses. More specifically it refers to celibacy or chastity. So abrahamacharya is the negation or violation of that.—Eds.

The question comes down to how not to abuse bindu, how to use that particular type of currency properly and with respect. The idea of conserving or not wasting bindu could be twisted into a kind of bindu materialism: "I have to hold on to what's mine rather than give it up, so that I can be complete." That approach, however, in itself would be losing your bindu anyway. You are bargaining your bindu; you are losing it because you are not giving psychologically, not communicating completely. That could also be described as abusing bindu. Supposedly, that kind of holding back mentally can cause a certain amount of physical pain and sickness, which your body produces in response to your holding back.

Abusive attitudes toward bindu could be compared to abusive attitudes toward money. For instance, we have stories of millionaires who use dollar bills to wipe their bottoms, or they roll bills into cigars. They abuse their money. As far as sex is concerned, there is a certain tendency to think that sex, unless you are married or in some other prescribed situation, is something naughty. If you have sex outside the usual or conventional pattern, it is something you have to do on the quiet. The whole attitude toward sex is very frivolous. A lot of people have a guilty conscience about sex: "I shouldn't have engaged in such an act, but I couldn't help it. It just happened."

Such attitudes automatically undermine the sacredness of sexual communication. Society and culture and the conventional moralistic pattern often do not acknowledge the sacredness of sex but regard it as a superficial act. We are somehow indoctrinated into this view. We fail to see the sacredness of sex, the actual communication quality. Once someone begins to regard the sexual act as a frivolous thing, the whole approach toward sex becomes very cheap. The attitude of people toward each other becomes frivolous as well, as though they were using each other purely as property, purely as a functional element.

We should have the attitude that sex is basically sacred; the spiritual implication should be there. By spiritual quality, we mean here the aspect of communication. Communication cannot always be carried out by a verbal or mental process alone; sometimes the communication has to be physical. This should not be purely a biological matter of releasing pressure sexually but should be a question of learning psychologically to open one's whole being to somebody else. Sexual expression is an act of communication and openness. That seems to be the essence of the whole process.

The same thing could be said about eating food. In the Tibetan monastic system, there are elaborate mantras and visualizations connected with eating. Through those, food is made into an offering. There is also an awareness of sacredness with regard to wearing clothes. Walking up or down stairs is even seen in a spiritual way. Any physical act has spiritual implications, from this point of view. For example, if you are a Tibetan monk, when you are putting on your belt, you say, "I am putting on the belt of discipline." Or you say, "I am putting on the shoes of energy and patience" or "I am walking up the steps to the awakened state. I'm coming down the steps so I will have compassion for all sentient beings" or "I'm closing the door of samsara. I'm opening the door of wisdom." All of these actions are regarded as sacred things. There used to be a posting above the toilet reminding you of the sacredness of that function. While you were on the toilet seat there were certain visualizations to do and mantras to say, to the effect that your urine and excrement feed *pretas,* or hungry ghosts—the elixir of your life coming from your body feeds them. That's a profound thing. At this point, however, it would be premature for us to try to do a practice like that, since the teaching is still very little known here in the West in relationship to the depths of people's psychology. A practice like that could become a special cult of its own, which wouldn't be good. However, such an approach contains tremendous truth in it—that anything to do with life contains sacredness.

Still, one doesn't have to have a prescribed ritual for each thing. Otherwise the whole thing becomes religion rather than spirituality. It is more a matter of relating to this very moment, whatever it is.

Basically, any kind of unwholesome behavior comes from frivolousness, not having enough respect. You just let things happen haphazardly, casually, with no respect toward life of any kind. Respect is one of the very important things that spiritual disciplines and rules and regulations are based on. To realize sacredness, you have to be deliberate, open, and prepared for the experience to be sacred. You have to, so to speak, prepare the right vessel to contain the sacredness so that you can understand it. You have to have preparation that is beyond frivolousness. This is a very important point, because more accidents and chaos happen in the world because of frivolousness than anything else. Frivolousness is quite simple. It is being disrespectful toward situations and unwilling to use them as part of your development.

On the other hand, if you try to use sex as a self-conscious spiritual act, you are ignoring the actual relationship that is taking place in the moment and trying to impose something on top of it. It's another double cross of ego, and of course it wouldn't work. You are no longer relating to the present situation. You try to put an extra thing on it, which just becomes a nuisance. When we talk about sacredness, we are talking about a personal experience of a state of nonselfishness, a state of pure giving, pure action beyond watcher.

In the tantric Buddhist teachings, it is said that when you have a real orgasm, you don't exist and the other person doesn't exist either. That's possible to experience. In the *Tibetan Book of the Dead,* it talks about how, with a complete orgasm, you have a glimpse of clear light. There are four situations where you can experience that vision of the clear light. One is sudden awareness. If you are frightened, panicked, or shocked, you may enter into a complete state without thoughts. The second experience is connected with death. The third one occurs when you are half-asleep, just going to sleep; there is a glimpse of clear light. Finally, this experience occurs in the state of orgasm, complete fundamental orgasm. There is complete openness that is beyond thought. In fact, it's known as "beyond joy."

The joy of communication is described altogether in tantra as the four types of joy. There is joy, supreme joy, beyond joy, and finally coemergent joy. Joy here is related with the yogic practice of dealing with the chakras, or the various centers of energy in the body. Gradually communication moves into a more and more subtle state, which is less physically oriented. Finally the whole thing becomes coemergent, almost joyless, joy, which is, I suppose, the equivalent of smiling. We could almost call it a smileless smile, or maybe a smile without a face, like the Cheshire cat.

In talking about sex, we are getting into a very big topic. We are getting into the fact that every life situation has meaning behind it, or a process of communication *in* it. Communication can't be established unless there are two parties, one of whom is the activator and the other the receiver. On that basis, any communication could be said to be sexual, although I'm not being Freudian here. The passionate quality of sex, the gross level of sex, doesn't have to be involved necessarily. In order to communicate anything, however, you do have to have the true element of union. From the tantric point of view, everything is interpreted that way—in terms of union. There is the union of samsara and nirvana, the union of phenomena and conscious-ness. We interpret it all in terms of the feminine and masculine principles.* Everything is seen that way.

* The feminine and the masculine principles are concepts in mahayana and vajrayana Buddhism that refer to qualities of one's mind and one's world. These may be joined in nondual experience. Wisdom and skillful means is one of the common pairings that refer to the feminine and the masculine joining together. Here, wisdom is the feminine and skillful means is the masculine. In the chapters on sex and relationships, the author gives us more information on

Sexual communication doesn't have to be physical communication alone. When two people are attracted to each other, they have a tendency to want to open to each other as much as they can. However, if there are no opportunities to open physically, they don't have to become frustrated. Subtle communication that has the element of ultimate friendship in it seems to be the crux of the matter. When that is present, being faithful becomes a natural situation—if one is particularly keen on that discipline. That is because the communication between the two of you is so real and so beautiful and flowing that you can't communicate the same thing to anybody else, so automatically you are drawn together.

However, doubts and negative suggestions can come up and present temptations to drop out of this communication process. They can cause us to drop our faithfulness and friendliness toward each other. At that point, you become more afraid of losing the communication than attracted to enjoying it moment by moment. You begin to feel threatened. Although your communication is going beautifully just now, still you feel threatened by something, some abstract possibility of something going wrong. The seed of paranoia has been sown, and you begin to regard the communication purely as ego entertainment. Then all sorts of chaotic things happen.

At that point, communication and naked openness toward each other could quite easily become naked aggression, hatred. That is when the dynamics of what is known as a love-hate relationship become quite obvious, quite natural. Once the seeds of doubt are sown, people become rigid and terrified, because their communication has been so good and real, and they are

these two principles, which have nothing to do with gender per se. However, in the vajrayana, the practitioner may visualize the masculine and feminine as a heruka, male deity, and dakini, female deity, joined in union. For more on this topic see the glossary and also *Glimpses of Space: The Feminine Principle and EVAM*, Vajradhatu Publications, 1999.

afraid of losing it. Then at a certain stage, they begin to find that they are bewildered as to whether this communication is loving communication or aggressive communication. This bewilderment means losing a certain amount of distance and perspective, and neurosis begins to arise from that. When you lose the right perspective or space within the communication process, then love can become tremendous hate. Then it is natural, in the hatred process as within the love process, to want to communicate with the other person physically. In this case, it means that you want to kill the other person, physically injure her or him. In other words, in any relationship that we are involved in personally—a love relationship or any relationship—there is always the danger that it will be turned the other way around. The moment there is a sense of threat or insecurity, that relationship could be turned into its opposite.

There is a story of a disciple who murdered his teacher. Because of his personal feeling of communication with his teacher, when he began to reject his master's teaching, sudden bewilderment occurred. The bewilderment automatically began to look for another, alternative way of achieving communication. That sense of sudden communication turned to hatred, and he murdered his teacher on the spot.

Sometimes frustration arises in a relationship when you give and you watch yourself giving. Then you begin to feel that you deserve to receive also. That brings tremendous resistance from the other person; the other person feels you are demanding rather than actually opening yourself. The whole relationship becomes a case of overcrowding. Then you begin to wonder whether you are really opening properly, so you try to open up much more, beyond what you've already done. The whole relationship becomes more and more difficult. Again, the principle that applies here is generosity without expectation.

In terms of working with sex and communication in everyday life, it would be too much to ask everyone to become a perfect lover. That would definitely be too much to ask. However, the profundity of the emotional level in an ordinary relationship could be seen properly and completely, and that could bring you into a meditative state.

In meditation, ultimately there's no dwelling place anywhere. In the Zen tradition, you may learn to meditate by focusing on the abdomen, or what's called the *hara*. Maybe you use a koan to burn out your intellectualizations. Then, finally, you reach the state of *shikantaza,* just sitting without doing anything, not even meditating as such. As long as you are relating with any particular focus in connection with your bodily situation in meditation, you still have an aim and object. You might think that meditating by focusing on an object such as the hara provides a better sense of balance. It stabilizes you. Supposedly then your mind is clearer. However, this approach can sometimes be a problem. When you relate your sense of balance to a particular focus, then the balance is dependent on something. So, fundamentally, it's not really balance at all. You still have a division into *that* and *this,* even more strongly than usual. When you have an expansive sense of awareness, you do not have a process of relating to "this" at all. Then meditation becomes much more spacious. Rather than focusing on what is "here," your focus is totality, everywhere. This applies to communication in general. When we say "everywhere," of course that includes *here* as well, but "here" is not particularly important. Here is just here. This is just this. But "that" permeates everywhere.

When you relate with particular centers of energy connected with the symbolic mandala of the body, whether in meditation or in sexual yoga or whatever it may be, you are dealing with specific and very powerful energies. Those energies could become accentuated and very demanding, very fussy. Unless you pay constant attention, it is likely you might psychically blow up, or explode, so to speak. It has been said that a yogi who is purely working on psychic phenomena is like a drunken elephant—unpredictable and quite likely to step on anything dangerous that might be around. To avoid that wildness or to tame it, you work on space. That way you will not be treading on any toes at all. You will just be using the space that permeates everywhere.

The point is to go beyond any faint handle on our experience, anything that keeps us from being an open person. The subtle reference points keep us from being creative, because we have something to nurse, something to hang on to. Anytime meditation depends on even the faintest quality of dwelling on something, then something is still not quite free. However, somehow freedom arises from or depends on imprisonment. First you have to recognize your fundamental imprisonment. Then, if you cease to imprison yourself, you are truly free. So whenever there is an experience of faint imprisonment, you are free to give up that imprisonment—just a little bit. In order to experience freedom, you have to give an inch.

I suppose we could describe stepping out or leaping out of conceptual reference points as some kind of blowing up in the positive sense. However, the notion of a leap may hold you back from *being* leaping. Something there is still not quite free. What we are trying to relate with here in terms of communication altogether is not only about egolessness. We are working on the basis of the absence of *anything*. You see, once you develop the egoless state, you remain aware of egolessness. The absence of ego itself becomes a dwelling place. There are all kinds of dwelling places. So it would be a good idea to let go of any dwelling place whatsoever.

There is an Indian story—I think it's a Punjabi story—about a follower of the Sikh religion who was trying to meditate on the name of God. Each time he tried to think of the name of God, the name of his lover came up in his mind. He found himself repeating the name of his lover again and again instead of the name of God. He was very frustrated, and he went to his teacher to try to solve the problem. The teacher said, "It doesn't matter; repeat the name of your lover." So he continued to do that. In the meantime, an accident occurred in which his lover drowned or died in some other way. The Sikh found now that in his meditation, although there was some sense of emptiness about her, his lover's name kept coming through. Then at last he realized that there was no longer any lover to relate to. At that point, suddenly the name of God started coming through in his mind constantly, and he developed a state of meditation then.

The important point is getting into the situation and completely feeling it without a watcher. Initially you have a watcher in your meditation. You have the sense of watching yourself meditating, up to the point that the watcher herself begins to take part in the space; then the watcher is not required anymore. The watcher loses her function. Emotionally, you can get into a state of complete absorption without the watcher. Although, in the long run, that experience may be an ego thing, temporarily it could be a useful stepping-stone. In that absorption, you might not distinguish between love and hate. There's a point where the criteria begin to wear out. The particular experience you are involved in begins to become *everything*. You lose criteria of all kinds, and the experience becomes like a state of *bardo*, like an obsession without gap, a constant obsession.* That may

---

* *Bardo* is a Tibetan word that means an "intermediate" or "in-between state." The idea of bardo is most commonly understood in connection with teachings in *The Tibetan Book of the Dead*, and generally people associate bardo with teachings on what occurs at the moment of death and in the after-death state. The traditional teachings on bardo speak of six bardo states, several of which are associated with the process of dying and experiences that occur after death. Other bardo states include birth, the dream state, and the state of meditation.

In this chapter on communication, Trungpa Rinpoche is describing bardo as a solid obsession of some kind. To understand this view, we might look at Judith Lief's introduction to Chögyam Trungpa's book *Transcending Madness: The Experience of the Six Bardos* (Boston: Shambhala Publications, 1992). Judith Lief, the book's editor, clarifies the meaning of bardo and how it relates to the six realms of existence: "This volume . . . is based on the interweaving of two core concepts: realm and bardo. The traditional Buddhist schema of the six realms—

be very confusing. Then you may find that the confusion may be something more fundamental than ordinary confusion.

Passion as the ground of communication could be extremely dangerous, like riding on electricity. However, in some situations, that's the only means. You might think that if it reached the point of being like electricity, the passion would be so intelligent that it wouldn't be dangerous at all. However, it could go either way, equally. It depends on how you deal with it. The most dangerous things have the greatest potential.

---

gods, jealous gods, human beings, animals, hungry ghosts, and hell beings—is sometimes taken to be a literal description of possible modes of existence. But in this case the schema of the six realms is used to describe the six complete worlds we create as the logical conclusions of such powerful emotional highlights as anger, greed, ignorance, lust, envy, and pride. Having disowned the power of our emotions and projected that power into the world outside, we find ourselves trapped in a variety of ways and see no hope for escape."

She continues: "The six realms provide a context for the bardo experience, which is described as the experience of no-man's land. The bardos arise as the heightened experience of each realm, providing at the same time the possibility of awakening or of complete confusion, sanity or insanity. They are the ultimate expression of the entrapment of the realms. Yet it is such heightened experience that opens the possibility of the sudden transformation of that solidity into complete freedom or open space" (p. xi).—Eds.

9

■ ■ ■

THE FLAME
OF LOVE

Our subject in this chapter is sex, which is a part of the larger question of love. We can only discuss this topic if we understand how it relates to ego. Like everything else in our everyday life, sex and love can be based either on the central reference point of ego or on a more centerless approach that is beyond ego. It is very important to understand the role that ego plays—or doesn't play—in all of our activities.

Ego contains ignorance, which refuses to look back at its own origin. From that fundamental ignorance or confusion, fear or panic arises. Ego expands from fear or panic into the further processes of perception, impulse, concept, and consciousness.*

---

* Chögyam Trungpa is referring here to what are known in Sanskrit as the *skandhas*, the five building blocks of ego. These are form (where ignorance first arises), feeling, perception, concept, and consciousness. Impulse is an aspect of

Why, after ignorance, should perception and impulse and all the rest follow? It is because there is a vast store of energy that is being processed here. That vast energy is not ego's energy at all; it is the energy of the primeval background, which continuously permeates whatever is going on.

The primeval background of the universe (or the unconscious—whatever you would like to call it) is not at all just a blank, vacant state of nothingness. Rather it contains tremendous energy; it is completely filled with energy. If we examine this energy, we find it has two characteristics. One is the firelike quality of consuming heat, and the second is the quality of direction. The primeval firelike energy has a direction, a particular pattern of the flow, such as you might see in a spark. A spark contains heat, and it also responds to the air that directs it toward a particular location—the spark takes on a pattern of movement within the atmosphere. The whole process of the primeval background energy follows a pattern, which is the same whether it passes through the confused filter of ego or not. Its pattern goes on and on, continuously. It cannot be destroyed; it cannot be interrupted.

This spark, this energy that contains heat, is mentioned in connection with the yogic practice known as *tummo*. This is one of the six yogas of Naropa.* Tummo practice has been described as the development of inner heat. The energy involved here has a consuming quality, an ever-burning quality, like that of the

---

the third skandha, perception. For a complete description of the evolution of the skandhas, see the chapter "The Development of Ego," in Chögyam Trungpa, *Cutting Through Spiritual Materialism* (Boston: Shambhala Publications, 1973, 1987), pp. 121ff.—Eds.

* The six yogas are meditation practices transmitted by the great Indian Mahasiddha Naropa to his disciple Marpa. They are practiced widely within the Kagyü school of Buddhism. They are the practice of tummo, or inner heat; the illusory body; dream yoga; the yoga of clear light; the transference of consciousness at death; and the practice of bardo, or the intermediate state. Many other Tibetan schools of vajrayana Buddhism also incorporate similar yogic disciplines.—Eds.

sun. It continuously burns and consumes until it reaches that point where, psychologically speaking, it no longer allows any room at all for doubts or manipulations. This vast power goes on and on and on, leaving no room to manipulate, leaving no room for confusion or ignorance or panic or doubt. However, when this heat is filtered through the ego process of ignorance, a very interesting development occurs. Rather than remaining a pure consuming process, it becomes slightly stagnated as a result of ignoring the basic ground, as a result of ego's refusal to look at its own origin.

This, one might say, is where the basic twist of love occurs. Ordinary love, love as we usually encounter it in our lives, seems to contain a basic twist, just as the other aspects of our ordinary lives do. This is the basic twist of refusing to see the vast, all-consuming energy we have been talking about. As a result of refusing to acknowledge this energy, ego is forced to accommodate this vibrant energy in some sort of container. Ego accommodates that energy in the form of confusion.

Confusion is a kind of network, like a wire net that forms a container. Once that network of confusion has been created, we try to contain the vast primeval energy within it. Once the energy is caught up in the net of confusion, the basic twist of ego starts to occur. However, the intelligence of ego is not the equal of the power of this burning heat of love. It is only capable of distorting that burning heat. Ego can distort it, but it is unsuccessful in getting hold of it completely. The result of ego's unsuccessful capturing of the basic energy is that the energy churns out a partial burning heat, a partial flame of love.

When the heat of love is captured in the net of confusion, it still churns out an outward-directed flame. However, this outward-directed process is only an expression of fascination, because the flame has not been completely let loose into the open. Only a partial aspect of the flame has managed to escape the net and extend its tongue. That fascination with the other, or the object of love, is the basic burning energy that has been unsuccessfully filtered through the confusion of ego.

The reason I say ego is unsuccessful is because the ultimate wish of ego is to completely control all the energy, to capture it entirely so that no aspect of the basic flame escapes through the gaps in its network of confusion. Something does escape here, however, but this flame is only a partial manifestation of the energy. So the flame must retreat, or come back into the net, in order to replenish itself. That is how our ordinary confused passion works.

To repeat, ordinary passion extends outward, but because of the network of confusion that entraps it, it has no capability of extending in a limitless way, so it automatically falls back. When it comes back, it has already been somewhat programmed, or readjusted, because of the confusion that runs through it. But strangely enough, this love, desire, or passion hasn't been completely captivated by the ego. It is the one emotion that partially escapes, that is able to operate outside the realm of ego—unlike anger, pride, envy, and the other *kleshas,* or emotions, which have been successfully captivated. Passion is a very powerful thing. It is the powerful expression of the basic origin. We haven't actually managed to captivate or spoil it 100 percent.

Ordinarily, when we project ourselves onto external situations, we extend our passion or desire, and then we try to possess that object of desire. So we extend our desire, our passion, and we would like to draw something in. If our attempt is unsuccessful, we feel very frustrated; if we could only possess the object of our desire, we feel we would have conquered something. It is rather like someone who sets out to do some window-shopping on a busy street filled with expensive stores. She admires the displays, but she also wants the items for herself. She would like to buy a lot of the merchandise, but she realizes she hasn't got enough money, so each time she sees something that she admires, she feels terribly pained. Still, she looks, because she enjoys the first glimpse. Another person would slowly walk along, simply admiring the displays in the store windows. So we have these contrasting approaches: the possessive way of seeing and the admiring way of seeing.

The possessive approach applies to relationships as well, much more than to objects, because relationships between people are extremely sophisticated. In a relationship, not only does one person have the means to extend his flame out toward the other, in an effort to consume the other, but at the same time, the other person has the same possibility. As soon as one person wants to possess another, the whole process of relationship becomes an intense game. It becomes a question of who has the more powerful and overwhelming personality, which one of the two people is able to subdue the other. Once we take the possessive approach, that is generally the way we look at it.

Trying to possess another person has a primitive, almost apelike, quality. You might want to possess someone purely because of the person's physical beauty. Because he or she is handsome or pretty, you would like to possess the person. Or maybe the person has particular interesting and subtle qualities in his or her psychological makeup, and you would like to possess those aspects of the person. Both cases are extensions of an apelike approach. Possessive sexual relationships are very apelike, that is, purely driven by the basic structure of ego. You see the other person as a kind of juicy steak, and you would like to gobble the person up and be done with it—nothing more than that. It's the animal instinct continuing on our human level.

I'm not suggesting that people should be more sophisticated and develop a particular art of possessing the other. Once our approach has that possessive setup, the more we try to be sophisticated about it, the more we make fools of ourselves—because everybody knows everybody else's tricks. In this field, everybody is a professional, and we know that very well. Trying to be subtle here is rather like the Chinese story of the man who wanted to steal a bell. The story goes that a fool sets out to steal a beautiful bell, a very expensive one with a beautiful sound.

He sneaks quietly into the house where the bell is, and he finds it and picks it up. The bell rings and he panics. It keeps ringing because he is panicked and keeps moving it around. He tries to cover both his ears, while still hanging on to the bell with one hand. He keeps on saying, "I don't hear it; I don't hear it."

Not only in sexual situations but in all kinds of situations, we play this bell game. We are quite sure the other person realizes what game we are playing, but we still don't want to let on. We just continue playing the game pretending nobody knows.

Karma plays a role in this game. Karma is a natural law of cause and effect. Whatever you do now, you are planting seeds for the future. This particular chain reaction started from confusion or ignorance, the creation of ego at the beginning. You decide to act in order to get a result. When you decide to do something to benefit your existence, to ensure your security, then the duality starts right at the beginning of that action, and that is called relational action or dualistic action. Because there's duality involved at the beginning, there is also dualistic action involved throughout that process as well. So whatever you've done in the past has a bearing on your present moment—up to now. Whatever you do in the present moment will also have a bearing on the future. The process of karma cannot be eliminated in the past. But what you do in the future is connected with the present moment. Karma is like growing a flower. If you plant a certain kind of seed, a certain type of flower is going to grow from those seeds. It's a natural force that happens everywhere, all the time. If you hit something hard enough, you will break it—that's karma. It's a natural chain reaction that always happens.

Within the Buddhist monastic tradition, there is a traditional, orthodox, and very disciplined way to work with passion in order to go beyond possessiveness and grasping. You find this approach in many spiritual schools of thought that acknowledge the existence of passion but also seek to control it. It is interesting that at the beginning stages of this orthodox approach, controlling the passion does not decrease its intensity at all. In fact, in trying to control it, one learns to live with it on a more intense level. The experience of passion increases until you reach the point of passionlessness, where you realize that putting passion into action and not putting passion into action are the same. You have to achieve this kind of passionlessness before you get to the point of learning to live with passion.

This approach acknowledges the existence of this passion mentally. In your mind, you develop your relationship to passion to the point of controlling it. Through tremendous discipline of this kind, you can develop passionlessness. You do this, not by expressing the passion, but by learning to live with desire. Where you can go wrong here is by suppressing the passion. If you try to suppress it, you are not acknowledging the existence of such passion anymore at all. Whatever comes up, you suddenly shut down, because you feel guilty that you are committing a sin or whatever. Then, because you refuse to look into it, it tends to bottle up. It collects like air in a balloon and one day, sooner or later, it will tend to burst out.

Repression is a very unskillful way of dealing with passion. It is not that there is something wrong with the traditional teachings, but you take them the wrong way. If you panic, if you feel terribly shy about your passion, this doesn't let you see it. It doesn't let you examine it. If you do see it, you realize that physically carrying out your passion is not the point. Acting on it seems to be a secondary matter. What is important is seeing the passion clearly.

So in the Buddhist monastic tradition, celibacy is a powerful way of dealing with desire, not by suppressing passion, but by examining the mental aspect of it. In the Buddhist tradition altogether, rather than suppressing any desire that comes into your mind, you look at it. You have to become familiar with the desires; then the need to express them physically automatically wears out. You see that the physical expression is no more than an extension of the desire itself—you see the childish as well as the chaotic quality of the expression. However, the basic communicative quality of the desire has to continue. You channel your energy into the process of communication. In this way, the basic monastic tradition simplifies life.

Again, monasticism here is not based on suppression or pure asceticism. It is based on simplicity, the simplicity of noninvolvement and the simplicity of being alone. You become familiar with desire and then relate to it with the simplicity of aloneness, or even loneliness. Eventually, loneliness itself becomes a kind of consort, a companion. That is why, in the Buddhist tradition, tantric practitioners who are leading the celibate monastic life continue practicing the inner discipline of yoga, which involves relating with the principle of sexual union, on the mental level. In any monastic situation, both monks and nuns could have an experience of loneliness as their consort or companion. There has to be a way of working with passion, even in monastic life.

Sometimes laypeople believe that it is best to save their sexual energy for spiritual purposes. They think that if they expend their sexual energy, they won't have it available as spiritual energy. As it is explained in yogic texts, that all depends on how individuals relate to sexual relationships altogether. It depends on whether they put all their possessiveness—their greedy quality—into the process or not. If they do, then that transforms their energy into a sort of heavy passion, and that affects their spiritual lives adversely. However, if someone can relate to the physical, sexual expression of passion as part of a process of communication, I don't think sex will adversely affect the spiritual life at all. In fact, it will be an inspiration, because the physical expression of desire then becomes a symbolic gesture, the same as doing prostrations and various other yogic exercises, or circumambulating a stupa or the like. All sorts of physical exercises have been recommended in the traditional teachings to learn to use your energy properly and bring your body into contact with the earth in a way that inspires further spiritual energy.

In the Tibetan monastic tradition, first you receive the

samanera ordination, which is becoming a novice monk or nun. Then you receive *bhikshu* ordination, which is becoming a fully ordained monk or nun. Then beyond that you receive bodhisattva ordination, which is connected with the practice of compassion. Then you also receive the initiations of the Buddhist yoga tradition connected with the vajrayana. These can also be taken outside of the monastic ordination. A lay practitioner can take vows in the Buddhist yoga tradition as well as bodhisattva vows. You are then committed to practicing compassion, while you remain a householder who continues to live an ordinary secular life. In the case of taking the monastic vows, you uphold the monastic discipline of celibacy as long as you remain a monk or nun, which may be for the rest of your life. However, in the Tibetan tradition, there is no punishment for giving up your robes. If a lama wanted to give up his or her robes and cease to be a monastic, then the next choice would be whether to continue his or her spiritual work or whether to become a businessman or a householder or even a hunter, for that matter. That choice depends on individuals. Still, after giving up the robes, the practitioner's bodhisattva practice as well as his or her yogic practice continues. The monastic tradition is very much based on a physical relationship to simplicity, such as we have been talking about. The other disciplines are more connected with the state of mind. So even if a monk or a nun decides to disrobe, his or her mind shouldn't be affected. Spiritual health will continue.

10

...

PURE
PASSION

C elibacy, as an orthodox discipline, is only
applicable to certain types of people. Not
many people can achieve passionlessness by totally denying the
expression of passion. Most people are still left with the desire
to express their passion physically. If we don't embrace this
orthodox discipline, how do we manage our passion? There is
another view of passion and relationship, which takes another
approach to the subtlety of the basic primeval energy we were
talking about in the previous chapter. We could call this second
approach working with pure passion. In many ways pure passion is just passion in the ordinary sense, but at the same time,
it is what is called vajra passion. It is vajra, which means indestructible in nature.* It is called vajra passion because it is wild

---

* *Vajra* is a Sanskrit word meaning "diamond," "adamantine," or "indestructible." The thunderbolt scepter held by Indra, the king of the gods in Indian
mythology, is known as a vajra. In the adjectival sense in which the term is
employed here, it refers to absolute indestructibility that is beyond all conditioned existence.—Eds.

passion, in that it has no egoistic networks or wire mesh around it. It is free passion, wild passion, *unleashed* passion. It is passion that hasn't been directed by any sort of switchboard, passion that is more powerful than the apelike quality we discussed in the previous chapter. It contains qualities of sparkling light—a wisdom quality—as well. It has tremendous consuming energy, which does not pass through any filters or networks. That kind of passion, whether it is connected with sex or anything else desirable that arises in life, is genuinely wild passion.

Ego and its intelligence are living in a world that does not acknowledge any other dimensions. From ego's point of view, it's all ego's world. That complicates our efforts to liberate this pure passion. The more we try to step out of ego's game, the more logical answers ego supplies, attempting to block our efforts. These solutions are all very limited, based on the fundamental twist of ego.

The world of real passion is a different atmosphere, a limitless world. When you have a glimpse of this, when some unprogrammed moment of ventilation allows you to feel something outside the ego, that could inspire you to try to step out altogether. You realize that it's possible to go beyond your habitual patterns—the maze of ego.

However, just continuing to wander through the maze of ego and trying to find your way out doesn't solve the problem, because once you get out of one maze, a further maze or contraption will start up. While one is going through the maze, one is also producing more and more karmic force. The only way out is to directly see another parallel dimension, outside the egoistic setup. That could appear as a momentary perception, which provides a parallel way out, one that doesn't rely on ego's logic. In one moment, you can step out of the maze completely.

The pure or liberated dimension of passionate relationship relies on the energy of no-mind. In other words, in the experience of pure passion, mind transcends logic. It requires courage to access that dimension of life. Generally, logical answers provide security. Logical conclusions bring us some comfort. Our logic tells us that if we do this, then that is going to happen. It creates a seemingly predictable world. One tends to plan everything out, program oneself altogether. One has to learn not to indulge in that particular comfort of overlapping answers. It requires bravery to stop doing this kind of obsessive logical analysis and abandon the chain reaction of answers. It requires the bravery that is willing not to involve itself with that comfort. One must stop fantasizing for one's security and come to the point of no-mind, or nonlogical thinking.

The only way to turn off that process of logical thinking is just to step out of it. When there is no logic, we begin to see things very clearly, but we also begin to feel cold. That area, which is free from habitual mind, may feel very bleak and cold because it seems so unfamiliar. So when we experience it, we usually try to reestablish our familiar territory further and further. In order to liberate yourself from habitual patterns, whenever you feel any kind of cold and bleak mysterious corner, instead of trying to fill that mysterious area with anything else, you should just step into that cold and bleak area—because it is not participating in the logical process of ego. That's all you can do. In a way, what you do is to just not do anything.

Whenever there's a mysterious dark and bleak corner where there could be mental spiders or mosquitoes or bats, we tend to manufacture some logic, some kind of alternative to explain away those scary things in the dark. There could be anything in that space. Instead of investigating these terrible things, we would like to make everything homey and cozy. We try to reassure ourselves that everything will be okay. We're always trying to avoid those dark areas.

When you feel this fear of the void, that's exactly when you need to leap. Just go into that space. I don't think you'll be afraid while you're leaping. You're afraid beforehand. The leap itself transcends fear. It is rather like a parachute, isn't it? You are terrified by the thought of parachuting, but once you are in the air, you are ready. The fear dissolves, and the open space of no-mind opens up.

When we talk about wild and free passion, we may tend to think something neurotic and erratic is meant. With vajra passion, however, this is not the case. If we let primeval passion loose, it isn't neurotic anymore because of the very fact that it has been let loose. There's no boundary that resists anything, and passion that operates beyond the question of any boundary automatically acts with wisdom and intelligence. In such an approach, intelligence automatically finds its way. At that point, you are able to have proper communication, real communication, because your basic nature is allowed to come out.

When we talk about wildness and freedom, we tend to think in terms of an almost animal or apelike quality, as we have discussed. We think of something like a gorilla escaping from the zoo. That, however, is a description of ego's passion. If you really let loose properly, however, this basic nature is comparable to the gorilla in the wild, at the stage before it has ever been captured, before it has ever been put in a cage, as though it were still in the primeval state of roaming in the jungle. If you really let that primeval aspect of passion loose, it isn't going to destroy anyone, because that passion has a balanced state of being as part of its natural instinct.

If our approach to sex, or anything else in our life, is connected with that primeval quality, we find there is a possibility of wonderful skillful communication. At the beginning of such communication, we wouldn't feel self-conscious as we do with the neurotic, ego-oriented approach. If at first, at the very starting point, you are completely natural and open, then in the process that follows, you won't feel any self-conscious inhibition. In that case, you will find that your process of communicating, of meeting and seeing the qualities of your partner, is quite extraordinary. This is because you are not judging him or her in terms of the rugged and juicy aspect alone. You are seeing in terms of the whole, the whole quality of the other person, which is like pure gold. Like pure gold, it is beautiful, solid, majestic on the outside, and it is also solid, beautiful, and majestic on the inside. This is because you are not seeing just surfaces, but you are seeing the whole way through. This is the open and skillful way of relating to passion.

Say you're married and you are attracted to somebody else. You might think that is very free passion. However, I don't think that is really free passion at all. It is a reaction against something in your marriage that is making you feel attracted to someone else outside the marriage. Because you are married, you feel that you are stuck together, and therefore you psychologically begin to feel an anarchist attitude. That is not real freedom at all. It is a kind of dissatisfaction, feeling that the relationship is not right—and the sooner the relationship could be abandoned the better.

Free is a very interesting word. It could be "free-free" or it could be "free-wild." "Free-free" is that you are free not because you have been freed by somebody else but because you discover that you can do what you like—you discover that you have the space to move about. "Free-wild" is that you begin to feel you have managed to snatch freedom from somewhere else; it is reacting against imprisonment. Then, instead of creating space, you tend to fill up the space with all sorts of other things. It becomes wild because it is like an echo—once you shout more, the sound will come back to you more as well. That is a continual creation of your own spider's web. It becomes wild at the end. It has to be wild because it is frantic. It is wild in the sense of neurotic. Immediately when you realize you've got freedom in the "free-wild" sense, you begin to shout, you begin to fill the whole of space, and the sound comes back to you. You shout more and more until finally the whole thing becomes complete chaos. You are creating your own imprisonment under the pretense of freedom. So freedom is a question of whether you have real space or not.

When you apply passion with wisdom, you see the whole process and are not fascinated and overwhelmed by the exterior alone. Instead, when you see the exterior, that simultaneously puts you through to the interior as well. You go the whole way, completely and thoroughly, so you reach right to the heart of the situation. Then, if there is a meeting of two people, that relationship will be very enlightening. You don't only see that person as pure physical attraction or pure habitual pattern, but you see both—the outside along with the inside. This applies to any form of communication, not only sex. Such communication is whole-way-through communication.

Now we have another problem, quite a grave problem. Suppose you see all the way through somebody, and that person doesn't want you to see all the way through—he or she might be horrified by you and run away. What do you do then? Well, since you have made your communication completely and thoroughly, you now have to see that this is the other person's communication. Running away from you is that person's way of communicating with you. So you don't pursue matters further. If you do, if you chase that person, sooner or later you are going to turn out to be a demon from that person's point of view—a vampire, in fact. As that person sees it, you have seen all the way through his or her body to that fat, juicy meat inside that you would like to eat up. The more you try to pursue the person now, the more you are going to fail. You have to realize that there must be something else wrong with you if that person reacted that way. You can't always be completely right. Perhaps you looked through the person too sharply with your desire. Perhaps you have been too penetrating. Since you possess beautiful keen eyes of penetrating passion and wisdom, you don't want to abuse that.

I'm not necessarily talking about how to win that person over. If the person runs away from you, there must be something wrong with *you* in your application of that unleashed passion. If people possess some particular power or exceptional energy, many of them might be inclined to abuse that power, to misuse it by trying to penetrate to every corner, every remote part of the other person. Something is lacking there, which is quite obvious—a sense of humor.

Humor in this case also means panoramic awareness, a feeling of space, of openness. A lot of stories from the Buddhist scriptures tell us that the work of bodhisattvas failed because they were lacking in a sense of humor. They have been too honest, too deadly serious in their application of the teachings. Even if they had a good understanding of how to apply the teachings, they didn't provide the necessary accompaniment to that, which is a sense of humor. They became blunt bodhisattvas.

In a situation where you want to open completely to someone but the person resists you, it is similar to the bodhisattvas. You may have wisdom, compassion, and everything you think you need to communicate with others, but you lack a sense of humor, which is an expression of dhyana, meditative awareness. If you are insensitive and try to push things too far with another person, that means that you don't feel the area properly. You only feel the space as far as your relationship to it takes you—you see what's wrong there, but you don't see what's on the other side. You don't see the other person's point of view, and you don't see the silhouette of the whole situation. Such an overall vision should accompany your relationship to any situation. That is what provides a sense of humor, which is very much needed.

Sometimes people run away from you because they want to play a game with you. They don't want a straight and honest, serious involvement. They only want to play a game. If they are lacking in a sense of humor and you are too, then you both may become demonic in each other's eyes.

This is the point where lalita comes in. *Lalita,* which is a Sanskrit term mentioned earlier, means dancing with the situation. It is the dance with reality, with phenomena. *Dance* here means exchange. When you want something very badly, you don't just reach out your hand to take it. In the case of vajra passion, you don't extend either your eye or your hand automatically. You just admire what you desire. You wait for a move from the other side. That is learning to dance with the situation.

Often we are very blunt. If we don't like something that is going on in our life, we feel tremendously self-conscious. We don't know how to end the scene that is troubling us, because we are creating that scene, putting it together. It is our unskillful action. You don't actually have to create that whole scene at all. You can just watch it, you can work with it. In that way, it doesn't become *your* scene; instead it becomes a mutual dancing together, of you and your world, your phenomena. If you take this approach, in fact, you end up with an ideal situation. No one ends up being self-conscious because it is a mutual scene. Self-consciousness means stagnation. You are stuck because you don't know how to go beyond that scene, but if you go beyond self-consciousness, the situation becomes very creative. Relationship becomes tremendously creative and dynamic.

In vajra passion, which is passion combined with wisdom, a relationship between two people can be very beautiful, because both partners are completely relaxed. Both are participating together completely, so no one has to take the lead. Sexual relationship can be one of the most important examples of this kind of communication, though the same approach also applies to other forms of communication. All types of communication always include both the feminine and the masculine principles, the chaotic or seductive aspect and the skillful aspect. These are present in any communication, whether it is conversation or correspondence or even just communing with nature. In any communication, these qualities of prajna and upaya, wisdom and skillful means, are always present.* In the sexual relationship, this is particularly vivid, particularly obvious.

---

* *Prajna* is a Sanskrit term meaning "transcendental knowledge," which is knowledge that sees through duality and recognizes emptiness. *Upaya* is also

The symbolism of the yogic tradition of deities in sexual union is applicable here. This symbolism is not purely a metaphor for something; in sex it becomes a real, living application. Sexual relationship is a living, basic example, a living symbol, or mudra as we call it.* In all communication, whether in a relationship between two partners, or friends, or any other communicative situation, the feminine and masculine principles are there. There is all-pervading openness—open space is created or the communication could not take place at all, and in order to communicate, a leap into that space is also necessary. The leap is skillful means, the masculine principle, and the open space that you leap into is the feminine principle of wisdom. The open space that is present must be met with skillful action, action that deals with that wisdom, knows how to swim in that ocean of wisdom.

The interplay of masculine and feminine principles is the basis of inspiration in all aspects of life. If a proper foundation is in place, allowing harmonious interaction of the principles, then the masculine and feminine principles act together very creatively and beautifully in situations. Relating harmoniously, they develop a mode of activity that is known in the vajrayana tradition as the four karmas, the four enlightened actions. Through these actions you can bring about peace and gather richness; you can magnetize situations, and you are also able to subdue

a Sanskrit term. It refers to compassionate action that is actually effective in situations. Prajna and upaya are associated with the feminine and masculine principles, respectively. Enlightenment is sometimes defined as the unity of the two.—Eds.

* *Mudra* is a Sanskrit word that literally means "sign, symbol, or gesture." A mudra can be any sort of symbol. Specifically, mudras are hand gestures that accompany various Buddhist practices, which express different moments of realization or aspects of the practice. Here the author is referring to the more general sense of mudra, in which the symbol and the symbolized are inseparable.—Eds.

or conquer or destroy whatever you need to.* In other words, the relationship between the masculine and feminine principles is the basic formula for a mandala.** The ground where you build the mandala is the feminine principle of openness, and the skillful way you use that ground in constructing the mandala is the masculine principle. In this case, the two principles are also called prajna and upaya. If you examine the vajrayana tradition, I'm sure you will always find the two basic principles in action. Understanding this could be tremendously inspiring.

You might ask why we say that wisdom represents the feminine principle. Wisdom contains an inquisitive quality: wanting to learn, wanting to know everything, wanting to survey every corner. The feminine realizes she's the ground of everything, and she would like to explore that ground. That is what you call the dakini principle in the Buddhist tradition.

Wisdom is learning, knowledge, isn't it? Knowledge can be creative, producing further knowledge, so it is the mother principle. Knowledge can also be destructive, because you know how to create chaos as well. Therefore, there is a destructive quality to the feminine as well as a creative quality. It's the mother principle, basically.

---

* *Karma* refers to the law of cause and effect in general. The four karmas referenced here refer to the four enlightened and advanced actions that are practiced by a realized yogi or teacher, which arise from the understanding and ability gained through prolonged practice. The four karmas are pacifying, enriching, magnetizing, and destroying, which the author describes here. He has sometimes characterized the four karmas as the expression of crazy wisdom.—Eds.

** *Mandala* is a Sanskrit word. The Tibetan term *kyil-khor* means center and periphery, or center and fringe. While we often associate mandalas with two-dimensional Tibetan diagrams used as an aid in visualization practice, in general, a mandala is the unification of many vast elements into one view through the experience of meditation. Seeming complexity and chaos are simplified into a pattern and natural hierarchy. *Mandala* can sometimes be almost synonymous with *world* or *worldview*. Here, the author describes how the relationship between the masculine and feminine principles gives rise to a complete pattern of energy, or a world.—Eds.

The masculine principle shows the feminine principle the skillful move to put its pattern in the right order, so to speak. Wisdom is knowing, pure knowing. It is not connected with action. The contrast between masculine and feminine here is rather like the contrast between practice and philosophy, or theory.

We might wonder how passion is related to compassion. Compassion is also communication, the ultimate communication. It doesn't necessarily mean feeling sorry for something; rather, it is basic communication that is not hesitant to become involved. In compassion we are willing to put ourselves into the situation of helping others, no matter what is required. Compassion sees the nature of the samsaric game that is being played, and whenever action is required to cut through that game, the action of compassion comes into play very accurately, right on the point. If necessary, it can be ruthless. The four karmas mentioned above are actually a description of the different aspects and qualities of compassion. When the feminine and masculine principles act together in harmony, that is also the essence of compassionate action.

Mahasukha, or the great bliss, represents the union of the feminine and the masculine principles. It is the ultimate communication connected with vajra passion. When you are able to establish complete communication, there will be tremendous joy, because there is no chaos within the dance anymore. It is like the meeting of teacher and disciple, which is the ultimate meeting point that expresses great joy. Such joy exists as the sudden realization or experience of vajra passion.

Vajra passion doesn't inspire you to fill the space at all. When you constantly have the neurotic desire to express your passion in this and that way, then whenever any space is created, you try to fill those gaps by doing things, which is a result of panic. If you try to approach limitless passion from the point of view of filling space, you can't do it at all. With that limited approach you are completely powerless. But vajra passion, open passion—or we could even say transcendental passion—does not inspire you to fill the space. It just inspires you to create more space. You don't necessarily have to do anything. You just enjoy the space more.

11

■ ■ ■

FAMILY
KARMA

I thought I might say something about relationships in the family, starting with the relationship between parents and children, both in the West and in a traditional society like Tibet's. This could be a bridge to our discussion of money, actually, because it starts to look at the bigger situation of how relationships function within society.

In Tibet, when the parents got old, the adult children usually remained with them in the house. Children would eventually take over the running of the family business, and the parents would become like their children's advisors. They expected to be given very good hospitality in the home, being well cared for and having their occasional advice acknowledged. Children were dedicated to their parents and very obedient. In traditional Tibetan society, the elders wouldn't be put into old-age homes or any situation like that.

There might be feelings of resentment, hostility, and guilt between generations, but still, the whole family situation was contained and prescribed by the society. The practice of that society was to give as much hospitality as you could to your parents and to look after them until they died. Young people may sometimes have found the situation painful, and sort of ghostly. Your parents might be watching you, behind your shoulder all the time, which could be extremely discomfiting, but still the children put up with it. Socially, to remove your parents from the home would be regarded as a disgraceful thing to do. So the children tried to be patient with their parents.

However, it wasn't always easy. There is a story that exemplifies this. A man and his wife had his blind father living with them. The father was very nosy, and he listened to everything. Because he was blind, his hearing was very sensitive, and he could catch every subtlety of what was being said. He always tried to mind his daughter-in-law's business. She finally decided that the solution to this problem was to kill him, but she didn't want to kill her father-in-law by obvious means. She wanted to find a subtle way of doing it. Then she heard about a snake whose venom was very poisonous, and she thought: "Well, now there's an opportunity!" She caught one of these snakes, and she cooked it. She made a broth out of it and served it to her father-in-law. Surprisingly, a certain chemical in the snake broth cured the old man's blindness. When the grandfather ate the snake broth, he began to regain his sight. After that, he was even nosier. So her plan backfired completely.

Our situation in the West is quite different from the approach in traditional societies like Tibet's. However, the relationship between parents and children is still an important one. The only way to relate with your parents in the current situation is to acknowledge them and to try to communicate with them. The relationship between parents and children is absolutely beyond money. It's a relationship that can't be calculated in terms of dollars. I don't know whether anybody has attempted to quantify such a thing or not, but it's impossible. The karmic debt is impossible to pay back, from either side. A huge sum or amount of energy has been put into the relationship. That energy would be worth an incalculable sum of money. Children and parents need to relate to one another in terms of that energy, which means relating to one another as persons.

In many cases, when the relationship with the parents breaks down, children begin to give up hope about the relationship, or they resent it. They might even resent the fact that their parents gave birth to such a child. "It was a terrible thing to do, creating me." That's quite tragic. It's necessary to go beyond that attitude and relate with your parents in terms of a human situation. A lot of young people haven't been able to do that successfully. However, it could really help. When parents realize that their children are not just frivolous and reactionary toward society and toward what their own parents have done, then the parents begin to appreciate their children. They can see that their children have some gratitude for their upbringing. Then children may be able to share with their parents what they have learned in the process of their life.

Interestingly, the problems with your parents are also connected with your money problems or your money karma. One could say that 25 percent or even 50 percent of money karma is bound up in that relationship to your parents, their way of bringing you up, and their way of relating with you in life situations. Your neurosis in the money situation is partly based on your neurosis in dealing with your parental situation. Because of that, the money situation becomes much harder and more difficult to deal with.

Altogether, our family relationship to money is a very, very powerful thing. The fundamental attitude that people have toward money seems to pass down through the generations, century after century. Whereas other aspects of parents' relationship with their children can be shuffled around, somehow money remains an inflexible point. Other things may change, but the attitude toward money is usually left intact from generation to generation and passed down as it was; a very old-fashioned approach still goes on. Karmically, money becomes a binding factor between the generations.

Parents as well as children need to work on their relationship with one another. If parents don't regard their children as guests from the moment when they are born, then they will begin to regard their children as property. With that approach, you lose valuable opportunities of relating with the person who is your child. When the child grows up, you feel that *your* property, your territory, is enlarging, expanding, rather than feeling that your guest is doing well.

Regarding a child as a guest means that you appreciate him or her as a friend, a human guest, not a pet, not just "my son" or "my daughter" but a friend who also has his or her own independent intelligence. Ideally, you should be honored that this particular person, your child, has decided to accept you as her parents. Often, parents lay heavy trips on their child rather than regarding the child as a guest who could make up his or her own mind. If the guest decides to leave tomorrow, you thank this guest for having visited. "We hope you enjoyed your stay here. What else can we do for you? Could I call a taxi for you, help you book your air tickets?" If you can go ahead and do that, it's beautiful. The guest might come back and accept your hospitality again and again.

On the other hand, children may come home purely out of obligation, although they don't feel welcome. Or sometimes when children come back, their parents regard it as a chance to talk to them and remold them. "I would like to have a word with you. Mommy and Daddy would like to have a word with you. You have to think about what you are going to do next." In that situation, we expect children to do what we think is good for them, so that they won't be social outcasts. We threaten to withhold their inheritance. That is a problem. There's no sense of generosity at all. Viewing a child as a guest is a mark of generosity. Then the whole thing is open. You let the child know that he or she can take off any time the child likes, and you are willing to help with the journey, whatever you can do. Then the whole relationship becomes more direct. Fundamentally, if you regard one another as friends, the concept of family—father and mother and children—opens up tremendously.

As a parent, you can't ignore the child's independent quality. When you see a child purely as an extension of yourself, then whatever the child does has some bearing on you, and you're not appreciating the child as an individual person who is growing up. Acknowledging others' independence is part of developing generosity toward them altogether.

Beyond that, children can actually help their parents in many ways. So the birth of a child should be regarded as a teaching or learning process for the parents. It works both ways: parents learn from their children, and the children learn from the parents. It should be normal for children to relate to their parents. This indicates that their destination, or their karmic situation in life, is all right. If after they have grown up, children fail to relate with their parents, there is something not quite right about the karmic situation for the child. He is trying to escape or ignore the reality of the karmic situation.

When your children are young, if you take the approach of seeing them as guests, then discipline is quite straightforward. You can tell your children exactly what's wrong in a situation or what's required, but there's no further implication behind it. Discipline arises in that moment. You may say, "That's a dangerous thing to do" or "That's a chaotic, confused thing to do." That's it. There's no further antagonism behind it. Of course, you can't quite take this approach at the beginning, when a child is only a year or so old. At that age children are just starting to walk, and they pick up everything in sight methodically, and throw things around. You can't expect them to respond logically at that point. As time goes along, however, this approach to discipline becomes quite workable.

As a parent, you may find it irritating and painful to see that your child is dirty or has made a mess. With that thought, you rush in and give him or her a bath and good clothes, and make things tidy. Then you can say, "Isn't he cute; such a nice clean person!" Helping someone in that way is for your own entertainment. It's part of your pride. You are relating to that person exactly the same as owning an object. On the other hand, situations could be related with directly. That person needs a bath and new clothes, so you provide those things, but it doesn't matter to you what the outcome is. You just do it, without any demand.

Later, after the children have grown up somewhat, if problems haven't become too extreme or gone on too long, then both parents and children can connect to one another and work on the relationship. If the situation is only halfway stuck, then either the parents or the children are intelligent enough to approach the relationship from a different angle. Or sometimes another element could be introduced by someone who has been closely related to the family. This person could present another version of how the parents and the children could relate. But once problems have gone unresolved for too long, solving them is like trying to stop an arrow that's been shot. It's on its way already. You can't change the course; it's done already. So it's better to work on the relationship earlier.

When children don't listen to you, it's usually because something fundamental in their view of you has been set in their mind. It's difficult to change the situation unless parents and children are willing to work with the situation, willing to give up their view, willing to say, to a certain extent, that they were wrong in the past. You might have to go as far as that, and then you can relate to one another as grown-up persons. There is no other way.

As a parent, the only way to work with the relationship is to approach it *outside* of already existing expectations. In other words, your son or daughter has a certain fixed idea of you, and he or she will approach you from that view, and you probably do the same thing. However, you can approach your child from beyond that usual style, outside that style, as though you had just met him or her. It would be as though you were meeting her for the first time, as somebody else, or as though she met you as somebody else. The two of you meet and become friends. One can approach one's relationship with an adult child from that angle. Otherwise, as much as you may have words of wisdom to say to her, you will run into the worst pigeonholes of her expectations of you, and your advice is not going to help her at all. You *could* approach her from a different angle, from a different direction, with a different style and see the situation differently. That is possible.

We can't deny that there is biological continuity between generations. That continuity can be worked with on the basis of pride and obligation or in terms of direct contact between people. Pride is saying, "Look what a good son I produced." Obligation is saying: "I must relate with my father because he is my father." However, both sides can approach the relationship more directly. The continuity between generations is there, and you don't have to fear losing that continuity at all. It's impossible to lose it. It will be there in any case. It could be the basis for becoming good friends, the basis of an absolutely beautiful friendship.

The karmic situation is the source of the whole subject matter we are discussing. As children, we have a certain karmic link with our parents and a certain karmic relationship with them, just as we have a karmic link with money and a certain neurotic relationship with money. The karmic situation is the reason we find ourselves in inescapable situations. If you are skillful and selfless, relatively selfless—or at least a candidate to be selfless— some thought should be given to the relationship with your parents and trying to work with them, trying to work with their situations and understand them. In some cases, parents have preconceptions of you as a child and won't listen to anything you say. But in other cases, the parents are trying to understand and trying to learn, trying to take an interest in your livelihood. Then there are tremendous possibilities of approaching them and trying to work with them as selflessly as possible—relating with them rather than trying to push yourself into their territory.

Some of the major difficulties between people, especially different generations, come from a feeling of guilt. This doesn't serve any good purpose, but nevertheless it always seems to be there. Guilt serves to perpetuate the difficult situations that brought the guilt on in the first place. Parents feel guilty toward their offspring, and children feel guilty toward their parents. Some individuals are aware of the cause and effect of their actions, and this type of person seems to feel the most guilt. Then there are those who purely want to grasp their own opportunity, just run away and do their own thing. With such people, there's little or no guilt at all. They just go ahead and do what they like without consideration for how it affects others. Although they might have to go through a long period of struggling to get what they want, and they might have to inflict a lot of pain on others to accomplish what they want, still they are delighted once they've attained their goal.

Still, I'm not recommending guilt. Guilt is not fundamentally healthy, because it has the quality of condemning whatever happens and not seeing the inspiration or positive aspect in things. Often a guilty conscience comes from self-hatred, constantly condemning oneself. The only way to overcome guilt is by seeing that there is nobody to blame for the chaos or the difficulties in life. Chaotic situations are not punishment, but they are stepping-stones. Then you can see the positive within the negative.

I also have some advice for practitioners of meditation or

those who join a spiritual community. The Buddha required his students to have their parents' permission to become monks. These days, I don't think it's absolutely black and white that a young adult needs his or her parents' permission to practice or be involved with a spiritual community, but you should have some attitude that sooner or later you are going to communicate with your parents about your spiritual path. We have to recognize that the karma of those people, your parents, has to be taken into account by you as a practitioner. If you try to tell your parents why you are involved with meditation, you may run into their lack of knowledge about what meditation is really about. (This could apply to anyone you try to talk to about your practice.) There are lots of misunderstandings resulting from a lack of knowledge, a lack of education about what meditation really is. It could be difficult to communicate. The misunderstanding could come from you or from your parents. One misunderstanding is that spirituality automatically means giving up anything to do with the world, thinking that we should run away from the world and get absorbed in a state of bliss and happiness. If we talk like that to our parents, we are not providing them with accurate information. It's an educational problem on our part.

Another wrong approach is knowing better but letting your parents be ignorant and just providing some basic logic they can relate to, because you think they would be happier if they had some simplistic logic to go on, something to believe about meditation. So you provide a stepping-stone of ignorance for them. In fact, you allow your own ignorance to become that stepping-stone for them. Whenever anything is mysterious or beyond your comprehension, you immediately go back to the original confused state of mind, and this is what you share with them.

For the time being, when you first start to practice meditation, you might not tell your family what you are doing if the environment is totally unsympathetic. But that shouldn't be regarded as a permanent situation. If children cannot talk to their own parents, then friends of theirs may be able to talk to their parents and explain things, because your parents will be less defensive with your friends. In any case, you should have some hope of communicating with your family at a certain stage, relating with them rather than abandoning them altogether. You can't give up all hope for the relationship. By the way, this applies not only to children telling their parents about meditation but to any of us who decides to do something that is not "sanctioned" by our family and friends.

The Buddha himself found that there was no way of explaining to his parents why he wanted to leave his situation as the crown prince, so he escaped from the palace. He ran away in the middle of the night. Later, after he practiced and attained what he wanted to attain, he returned to his parents, and he began to teach them. As a result, his father became devoted to him, and his own son, Rahula, also became his follower, his disciple. So the Buddha went back to his family and talked to them.

What we are discussing here is not black-and-white prescriptions. You can't really follow any kind of party line. You have to work things out very flexibly.

I would also like to say something about the situation of marriage. To begin with, let's look at the problems that sometimes develop. We can't just talk about the ideal. Relationship problems arise when people feel they are in an obligatory situation rather than relating to each other as friends. Two people find they get along extremely well before they get married, but after they get married the relationship often begins to deteriorate. They may begin to lose their friendship. They are not friends anymore; they are husband and wife. Friendship doesn't seem to apply anymore, because their relationship has become obligatory. Partners stop referring to each other as friends. Instead they say "my husband," or "my wife" to refer to each other. They lose the playmate quality they used to have. Quite possibly during the honeymoon period, they may have the sense of being two kids playing together. But as soon as they get home to the kitchen-sink level, they lose that sense. They are serious citizens now. They begin to exert their willpower and conviction to maintain their marriage by working at the whole thing very seriously and faithfully. They tend to lose their sense of humor about everything. Legality has turned their relationship into a solemn situation rather than just being a statement of the continuity of what is already so.

If the friendship continues to develop in a marriage, the husband and wife may eventually develop a level of common understanding where they no longer even have to finish their sentences when talking to each other. Just a word or two, and the other person already knows what her partner is going to say. In marriage, ideally communication takes place very freely between the husband and wife. They are able to communicate with each other more fluently and openly than they can with other friends. They know one another very well because they spend so much time with each other, so they are able to let loose completely and be open about anything. Perhaps they can also do that with other people, but it is much more challenging and tiring. Other friends tend to have their own interpretations of what is being said, much more strongly than the two partners do with each other. Their relationship can sometimes reach almost to the level of telepathy because they have gone beyond any kind of inhibitions.

In a relationship, if you feel a sense of generosity, that is the ground for good communication. We could say that generosity is the real ground of monogamy, or commitment. The committed situation makes you feel that you can accommodate whatever there is. You have a sense of safe ground, and you can afford to expand. You don't have to be frugal with your feelings anymore. If you begin to feel poverty in a relationship, however, things become very tight. You begin to question how much attention to pay to this or that situation in the relationship.

Commitment can provide generosity and openness. You share your experiences without making a big deal out of them. You are not particularly defeated or threatened by the other person. There is a sense of security, but the security mentality in this case comes from a sense of having nothing to lose. Therefore, you have nothing to gain, but things are so, as they are. This is the highest sense of generosity.

Marriage is about two individuals sharing common ground. When one of the partners is in trouble, the other one is there to help. When the partners help each other, that maintains the common ground of the relationship. There's an almost computerized sensitivity in a good marriage. When one person is in trouble, the other one comes along with solid help and works the problem out. Or as the vows in some marriage ceremonies say, "For better or for worse, in sickness and in health." You vow that you are going to take care of and accept the other person as your husband or wife. You swear you are going to take care of the other person's whole being, be responsible for his or her welfare. If you are in a better position than the other person, if your partner is in a low-energy state and your energy is normal, you will influence or help that other person to bring her or him up to your level. The idea is to influence each other in a healthy way.

However, as we know, marriage can become completely different from that. Marriage can develop a pattern in which, when the other person is low, you take advantage of that to lay your trips on your spouse. At that point, I'm not sure that a marriage is really a marriage. Who knows who's laying heavy trips on whom?—that's where the trouble begins. One person feels that he is on a higher level than the other, that he is more mentally balanced, and he pushes his game. That game can go on and on, and finally there is apt to be a split.

As I have already said, in a healthy marriage two people don't particularly relate as husband and wife. In a genuine marriage, you accept the other person as a friend, a beautiful, communicative friend, and your partner views you as a good friend as well. Then, when you have a child, you actually do regard that child as your first guest. You have to feed and clothe this guest, bring her up, and educate her. You are the host and hostess. That would be the ideal.

12

...

THE QUESTION
OF MONEY

Money plays a very important part in our lives. These days it seems to control the whole process of our lives. We have to earn a living. Earning a living, earning money, is what allows us to make choices. The question of whether we will be able to study or whether we will be able to meditate coincides with the question of money. If we have money, then we can study more or meditate more. If we run out of money, we can't meditate as much, because we can't afford to pay a meditation center to accommodate us. It seems to be a very simple thing: if we have enough money, then we can live luxuriously, and if we don't have enough money, we have to work and we might have to submit to hard conditions.

That's the way money seems to us—very, very simple. Do we have money in our pockets? We do? That's great. We have enough money to get back home. Isn't it nice that at least we are quite sure that we will be able to sleep peacefully in our bed tonight. We're also going to have enough money to buy new socks. Isn't that great?

Actually money isn't as simple as we think. You see, money is more a matter of thoughts than anything else, those thoughts that are constantly cropping up as we go through life. Do we have enough money to go to a restaurant to eat? If we don't, we don't go to the restaurant—it's back home for us. Do we want to see a particular movie? Yes; but no, we don't have enough money—back home for us. We want to go to a meditation center. Do we have enough money? No? Then we have to go back home. Or we have to start working to make enough money to go to the meditation center, because the people at the meditation center want money as well—they're hard up.

It is interesting that money seems to have so much controlling power. I have experienced this power of money myself. Whole organizations, whole institutions, are based on money. The entire authority in certain organizations is based on money. Let's take an example. Say you saw an ad in the newspaper for a meditation center, advertising an ideal place to meditate. Very factually, that newspaper advertisement happens to be there because the meditation center had the money to pay the newspaper for the ad. Because of that, you happened to see the ad, and this also happened because you bought that newspaper. You paid the money, so you got the paper. Everything seems to operate through money. Because they paid money to put the ad in the paper and you paid money to buy it, it all comes to the point where you're filling out a form applying to go to that meditation center. You write them and say: "I can pay to stay at your meditation center." Or you say: "I am a poor student, and I can't afford your rates—will you accept me on a work-study basis?" And you get the answer: "You are welcome at a discounted rate, but you will have to work. We need you to work, because we need to keep our center alive, and your work means a lot to us. If you work in the vegetable garden or doing construction on our new facilities, you will be saving us money. On that basis, you are welcome. Please come, you are welcome."

Then, the moment we set foot in this meditation center or ashram, or whatever kind of place it is, the first thing we realize is that we have fallen under institutionalized control. We realize that the organization is in control of the money; they control the financial matters. We are somewhat upset and irritated to find that we are actually in the hands of an institution rather than those of a spiritual leader. Immediately, we begin to think: "I haven't got any money. How long are they going to let me stay here?" Then we go ahead into the program, and we study and practice and work. We find that the whole process is worked out exactly by the organization on a financial basis. Everything you do depends on how much you've worked and how much you have failed to work. It's all based on whether you generate a profit for them or not. All of these things are worked out in a very matter-of-fact way, because the comptroller or the administrator of that particular organization is very conscious of money.

Of course, the spiritual leader of this organization is also very aware of money, but he is also conscious of human relations, because he has had to recruit people and build the organization. He tries to be polite and make conversation, and he tries to inspire people as much as possible—because he feels guilty about the money thing. As you go along, he tries to put you at ease. He says: "Please make yourself comfortable. Our place is unlike any other place. It's different—we don't think about money at all. Our focus is very much on the individuals who are here. Get to know the rest of the people in the community. Relax and meditate. Do whatever you want to do. In fact, you don't even have to meditate if you don't want to. It's voluntary." He says all this because, underneath, he is conscious about the money.

Or another approach might be: "I would like you to take part in my organization. However, anybody who stays on my property must participate in the yogic exercises and take part in the meditation. If you don't do that, you are not worthy. We cannot accept you here. Whether you have money or not, I don't regard you as worthy if you have come here for frivolous reasons. You are too frivolous because, number one, you don't have any money, and the second thing is that you don't want to take part in the meditation." Now you feel obligated to take part in the meditation and yoga sessions because you don't want to be rejected, and by now you care less about your spiritual development than you do about your acceptance in the center and successful financial arrangements. You say to yourself: "I would like to stay in this center. I like it. It's a nice setup, the people are nice. So I have to follow the rules, otherwise I'll be chucked out." So you take part in the yoga, the meditations, and everything that they do there.

In one center I know of in California, you not only have to do the practices, but you must take part in discussion groups as well. In such places, the leader of the place, who conducts the discussions, develops very keen eyes. He checks out the new arrivals to see if they have a link with him or whether or not they are likely to have faith in him. He checks this with his sharp keen eyes, like a vulture looking at a fresh corpse. Then his approach in discussions is based very much on whether the newcomer has long hair or short hair, whether he is smartly dressed or dressed in the colorful hippie style. What he says is mostly based on impressing the newcomer, because he wants to convert him. If the newcomer has come in the hippie costume, then he will accommodate that. If the newcomer is more of a business type, he will present the religiosity of his community in a matter-of-fact way and try to show in a businesslike fashion that his philosophy is valid.

If you have newly arrived, by the time the discussion finishes, you are terribly tired. You have encountered and talked to so many people. You are completely tired out and want to relax in bed. But before going to bed, you would like to make yourself a cup of herbal tea or have some hot milk. However, the moment you try to do that, the light in the kitchen switches off. "It is eleven o'clock. Our institution does not allow people to stay up any later than that. Go to bed or you'll be out, no longer a part of this community."

The moment people have their hand on the switch, they feel a great deal of control or power. They can do that because they are in control of the money. They have the authority, which is based on their dignity of controlling the money, which now amounts to the status that goes with controlling basic factors like light. It could well be that this place has fancy chandeliers with lots of lightbulbs. In any case, the authorities control the setup in this particular little society. They are in control of that room where you want to make your tea. They are going to switch the light off, so you have to go back to your room and sleep. The next day you wake up feeling somewhat awe-inspired by this place, and on some level, you are in awe of the authority connected with controlling the money here. You are interested in all of this, and you want to be on the good side of this authoritative and impressive organization.

However, when you come out of your room, someone tells you that you didn't get up early enough. They had a morning service this morning, and you slept late. So you feel guilty about that; you even feel guilty about having breakfast now. However, somebody working in the cafeteria might feel sympathetic to you, and that person provides you with eggs and toast. Maybe he gives you breakfast because he feels that he has to keep up a certain standard of behavior in the organization. He gives you breakfast quite nicely. So the morning goes quite smoothly, with no confrontational problems, and lunch goes in a similar way.

These are the kinds of institutions and situations, particularly within religious or so-called spiritual institutions, we encounter in this country or any other country. They express the weight of the power of money.

If you start an organization, you will experience this tendency for the power of money to take over. It's true that you do have to take money into account; you have to be practical. Soon your practicality begins to be associated with a sense of authority. That authority becomes associated with your qualities of a dignitary, your status—where your house is located, its impressiveness, and the colorfulness of its display. The whole situation begins to reflect the power of money. That's complete nonsense. It's completely mad in a sense. You may think that as the person who started the organization, you are special. You may think that this is connected with where you came from, your exotic place of origin. However, whether you come from Tibet or whether you come from Afghanistan, Timbuktu, Ceylon, Polynesia, or wherever you come from, it doesn't mean anything. The mysteriousness of a place doesn't make it important at all. What is important is what we are in this country. In this particular place, we are interested in human relationship, human basic contact. The place you came from doesn't make you important at all. Whether you come from Moscow or the North Pole or anywhere else is irrelevant. Where you came from is just a place on this earth. We all know about this earth. We have everything marked on geographical maps. Everybody knows the names of places; whether they pronounce them right or not doesn't matter.

The whole problem here arises from trying to make money out of confusing people, out of creating awe-inspiring environments for them. I am particularly talking about religious organizations and institutions, because I myself come from one of those, and that's what I have the most experience of. Indeed, in my life I also made the mistake of creating a religious institution. I didn't mean to do it, but it happened like that.

When we create institutions to confuse people, the results are very sad, terribly destructive and evil—but funny. Creating such an institution is very similar to a child building a sand castle and then selling tickets to it. We could say that it's all child's play, but there is a difference between when children do this and when adults do it. That single factor is—money! A child doesn't talk about money, but those of us who have achieved adulthood think of this game as a very serious, solemn game. We would like to charge other people money to get into our game.

It is degrading to think in terms of selling the dharma, selling the teaching for money, selling the Buddha. Dharma means truth. If religious centers have the mask of truth and the image of the Buddha, they can exhibit the combination of the two and sell it. They can exhibit it externally and sell it, and it becomes a cheap commercial practice, very much based on ego. Ego is striving to attain its reward. The thinking is: "If I start this organization, can I use it to build myself up further?" This sort of competitive attitude is based on ego, and it also becomes involved with money. Whenever we invest our ego in a particular formula, the question we are trying to answer is, "How much are we going to gain from that?" That easily ends up connected with money. Here it ends up in the spiritually completely disillusioning process of selling the truth for money. In this kind of environment, complications in the relationships among the people involved in the organization automatically develop because no one is fundamentally being cared for. All we care about is money. The whole focus is on developing the community, the institution, into something prosperous that has a dignified exterior that can inspire awe in people. The whole thing is falsely dignified, and the leaders talk about how much money has been collected, how much wealth has been gained, and so on.

In the ordinary case of just earning a living, money is not a problem to begin with. We may be inspired to do certain work. We would like to get an interesting job. That's fine. The result of the job is that we get some money, and at the same time we continue to enjoy the work. Once we accumulate a certain amount of money, our concentration may begin to drift away from the work and begin to move toward what we can do with the money. We think of travel destinations, and we begin to calculate whether we will be able to go first class or will have to settle for business or coach class. Those kinds of preoccupation develop.

While we are working, before we actually accumulate a sum of money, our work process may seem very creative. When the money actually is handed to us, it seems very flat. Just getting money in exchange for our work feels very flat; it's just a piece of paper in our hand. We don't know what to do with it. We immediately want to exchange it for something else that is more creative, but doing that is difficult for the very fact that we have to consider our money situation.

Ego's reaction to the physical presence of money is interesting. Suppose I hold up a hundred-dollar bill. Whether it is one hundred pounds, one hundred Euros, or one hundred dollars doesn't make any difference. You have an attitude when you see this bill, an immediate psychological attitude. It doesn't matter whether you are a millionaire or penniless. You get a certain feeling on seeing this, this bill with the design on it; a certain attitude immediately comes into your head, which is psychological materialism. I'm talking about your psychological reaction to this hundred-dollar bill, the psychological implications for you of seeing it. This kind of attitude is very silly, isn't it? In fact, my showing the money, handling the money, seems very silly, absolutely silly. I'm sure you would be thinking: "What is he going to do with this money? Is he going to put it back in his pocket or is he going to tear it up?" It's not necessary to do anything exhibitionistic. Just by my holding up a hundred-dollar bill, you see the psychological implications of perceiving this banknote.

Before, when you were working, the work might have been very creative, but when you are handed a bill like this at the end of your work, when you see that you've been presented with so many dollars in your hand, the whole thing is flat like a flat tire.

The whole result is very flat—because you have worked, you got *this*. People's creativity is very much alive, but then when they get paid for their creativity, they often experience that as rather meaningless. Money is the reward for their creative process, but it is very one-dimensional, a tremendous comedown. That's why it is sad to reduce every creative force to monetary terms. It's terribly sad, sacrilegious in a sense. It's quite shocking but quite fascinating. The psychological attitudes that can be observed here are extremely interesting.

For people who have it, money represents a potential for ruling the world. It is potentially so in their minds, but it is not actually so. For example, a person who has a great deal of money might think: "Because I have a lot of money, I can make a donation to such and such a place, and by making that donation, I will be able to manipulate the people there into giving the place thus and such a form." That is a kind of game that a rich person might play. Suppose, however, that the place you are planning to contribute to refuses your money. This goes against your automatic expectations; you presume they would love to have your contribution instead of refusing it. If they refused you, you would be completely suspended in midair. Such attitudes are so interesting.

What I have been saying doesn't at all mean that I think money should be regarded as unimportant. It is a very important force in our lives. Money shouldn't be regarded as something that just comes and goes. That's very naive. No divine administration prints banknotes for you and disburses them. Money doesn't just come and go like that. Money comes and goes along with your greed and attachment. You sometimes avoid spending money because, strangely enough, you have such a strong sense of worship toward it.

You may have a feeling of the divinity of money. However, the moment you see something you really want to buy, you forget about the divinity of the money and you spend it. Before you know it, you have just a few pennies left in your pocket. It is interesting that if you are not careful all the time about the process of giving and receiving money, you don't spend your money properly at all. If you handle your money without awareness and mindfulness of how much you are giving out and receiving, then the money just flies away, even if you have millions of dollars in your pocket. If instead you are aware of how many people worked hard for this particular banknote, how much energy they spent for it, then you begin to think more carefully about buying and selling. You begin to develop a relationship to money. It is another relationship in which we can see how much we waste our energy. We see—not necessarily in money terms alone—how much we abuse our energy in situations. We would like to get some kind of response in a situation; therefore we spend more energy than necessary. Often we do get some kind of response but not a complete one.

In this case, money represents the energy principle; you can connect with that when you're aware of how much you're spending. It's no good thinking, "If I spend more, I'll get more" and thoughts like that. You won't. You have to understand the cause of spending as well as of taking in money. The cause of your expenditure is very important. Do you have a feeling of balance and love, or are you exerting your energy in order to get power over another person or to make a demand on another person? This kind of expenditure of energy is in a sense a spiritual currency of its own, which is represented in a mundane sense by money.

From this point of view, every dollar you make or spend represents your energy of the moment. If you misuse the dollars, if you just dish them out, spend inattentively, then you are disregarding your energy. You lose track of how much energy you have to spend in order to get one package of some product.

If we look at it this way, the way we deal with money connects with a basic characteristic of our state of mind. We should see it in terms of the expenditure of energy and how we are going to transmute that energy into a proper use. Obviously communication and exchange are taking place all the time. How are we going to use that?

It seems that money makes a huge difference in the process of our communication and relationships—because of our pre-conceived attitudes toward it. Money becomes a key point. If your friend refuses to pay his part of your restaurant bill, auto-matically you get a feeling of resentment or separation from your friend. Immediately you experience a break in communi-cation. So money is not just a physical thing, but it has much to do with the energy principle—which is connected with our attitude toward it. The energy flow of our preconceived ideas becomes the currency of exchange. Our preconceived ideas actually take the place of money. So the question of money becomes the question of how you relate to the energy of your preconceived ideas. In that situation, money is related with the pride of ego as well as the energy expenditure of ego. But what happens when you transcend these egoistic fixations through the generosity of helping other people?

In that case, when you take the point of view of openness and space, you don't think in terms of money at all. Instead, you produce money in order to free other people who are thinking in terms of money. You can do this by offering another person a cup of tea and a piece of cake or giving the person a box of chocolates. If you pay for a cup of tea, money doesn't come into it at all—it's just a cup with tea and hot water in it. It very much depends on individuals, whether they think in terms of money, which is preconceived ideas, or in terms of actual things. If you think of ordinary things as they are, rather than relating them to a monetary value, you can destroy the conceptualized idea of money. You can bring about real communication, which brings with it a loss of ego.

You can just see things simply and directly rather than think-ing in terms of how much money things cost. When it comes to things as they are, it doesn't matter what you pay for them. The value of something isn't a question of a price tag. You value it because you feel that you have a basic link with that thing. Then it's also meaningful or powerful to just give it away. That particular object may not be valuable at all, from a monetary point of view, but because of the emotional context, it has much more value.

To develop detachment from money, you don't particularly have to cut down on your expenditures. The whole thing is about your attitude toward money. You can see that attitude when people buy things. If you see people buying dia monds in a jewelry store and you watch their faces as they negotiate and choose a particular diamond, you can see that they have a very definite preconceived attitude. It's a very fixed mentality. They go through their motions very "meaningfully"; the whole transaction is weighted with significance. However, if you happen to have a lot of money and would like to buy diamonds, you don't have to negotiate with this heavy meaningfulness. If you see a diamond you want, just spend the money and buy it! It may cost a lot of money, but that doesn't mean that you have to make a big deal out of the whole thing by doing it very meaningfully. You don't have to spend your preconceived ideas.

In this case, preconceived ideas are expressed in terms of the monetary system. The weight of your preconceptions is the value. The number of layers of preconception you are laying on the situation is what you're spending. When you spend, you feel the loss of your preconception, but you gain another preconception, because of how much what you have just bought cost you. There is often that kind of attitude behind buying and selling. That attitude tends to make everything into a family heirloom. It all comes from how serious you are, how lacking in a sense of humor. That is the basis of the evolution of this kind of monetary system—no sense of humor. When you see a big banknote, you have no sense of humor about that. It becomes a solemn thing—very embarrassing in a way. Handling money becomes a solemn, meaningful, very serious game. If you have a sense of humor, handling this hundred-dollar bill doesn't seem like a heavy thing anymore at all. It could be anything—just a piece of paper. It is interesting to see it as just a piece of paper with this meaningfulness added to it. The mere contrast of seeing just a piece of paper and at the same time the added-on meaningfulness provokes tremendous humor. We see the lightness and the heaviness at the same time. We could have a completely different attitude.

In the example of people buying diamonds, it seems that they are buying things in a very meaningful way. They are very invested in that exchange of richness. One person is selling the diamond, and one person is paying thousands of dollars for it. This exchange shows on their faces. They look like babies who are about to receive rich ice cream in their mouths. There is a very centralized intense feeling about it. The same intense face can be seen in gambling casinos.

I'm not approving or disapproving; I'm just remarking on the funny side of this. Altogether, I'm not recommending that you do something or not or that you do something else. I'm just illustrating the contrast of this and that. In this case, one sees the greedy quality of the situation, the greedy quality of the face, the intense quality of it, as opposed to an attitude toward money in which one could give casually, with a casual sense of exchange. You could quite easily go to the jewelry shop and spend thousands of dollars buying one diamond. Just like that—you could do it, with a less solid attitude toward the whole thing. I suppose I'm not millionaire-minded myself, particularly. I spend money very easily, but I get what I want and I enjoy those things thoroughly, very beautifully.

However, the whole process is not mindless. You choose particular qualities. You can compare the quality of one thing with another. When I'm buying a suit, for example, I go to a lot of shops and compare one suit with another suit. I go through that process myself. That's quite all right, as long as you aren't thinking very greedily and heavily. There's nothing heavy about this approach. Each time you see another suit, you smile; you laugh. You comment on that suit.

To work with your attitudes toward money, I wouldn't recommend extreme measures, such as tearing up a dollar bill as a spiritual exercise, or using it as a cigar wrapping. Whether you do it privately or publicly, tearing it up doesn't help very much, because you tear it up meaningfully. You wouldn't tear up a plain piece of paper meaningfully, would you? But this banknote paper you would tear up meaningfully, which amounts to the same thing as avoiding tearing it up. I think the point here is illustrated by Mahatma Gandhi's attitude toward the lower-caste people in India. The lower caste was called untouchables. After Mahatma Gandhi's movement, they were called *harijan*, which means the "sons of gods." However, somehow it amounts to the same thing. If you give these people this special name of "sons of gods," then you still have the same attitude toward them—you are just changing the name. I'm not disparaging Gandhi here; I'm simply pointing out that you may be turning black into white on the surface, but underneath, nothing may have changed. It's the same thing with tearing up a dollar bill as opposed to a plain piece of paper. When you tear up the dollar, you still have a special attitude toward it. So I don't believe in this little bit of exhibitionism.

In the case of tearing up the bill, it's just a matter of trying to change your ego clingings to a different fashion, a different approach. They still start from the same place, however. You are purely changing the locality of your grip. When you let go in one place, you begin to grip the next area.

Generally when we spend money, we are paying for a certain psychological result. As long as we don't have the attitude that we are buying a particular energy by paying money, then that's all right. We try to buy preconceived ideas with our money. It's like exchanging a lump of earth for air. Because money is very flat and stale and ordinary, we pay out the money in order to get hold of some kind of creativity. That's the wrong attitude. If you think of spending in terms of expanding your energy, that's fine. However, very few people actually think that way. Spending money to get into something creative soon becomes reduced to numbers and quantities. The minute you start to measure the quantity of your wisdom, that's the wrong approach. Measuring the quantity of your wisdom is the last thing you want to do.

We could say that money is just money or that money is a symbol—but both of those are saying the same thing. Money is money, but because of that, it's a symbol. Therefore, the discussion of money is very flat. Nothing happens. It's very depressing. On the other hand, it's nice to have money, isn't it? Having money shouldn't be a burden; it should be a delight. It's nice to have money, because you can spend it on worthwhile things. You can channel your energies in worthwhile ways. You don't have to feel guilty because you handle money. That's the whole point. Feeling guilty about handling money is like feeling guilty because you breathe air. Some people might feel they're being extravagant because they're breathing other people's air. That doesn't make sense. Handling money is nothing negative, nothing bad.

Nevertheless, a lot of us tend to think money is connected with solely materialism and therefore is bad. I was having dinner in New York with a prominent businessman and some of his colleagues. All through the meal he was apologetic about being a materialistic person. Actually, being a materialistic person often just means being a practical person. You don't have to feel guilty about money and dealing with material objects at all. There's nothing wrong with that. You can do your business completely and properly. The problem comes from something behind that. It comes when you think of building up your business as building up your empire. Money has a very interesting temptation to it, the temptation of imperialism. You begin building up all sorts of other things with the money—your personal realm. Then you tend to relax when you have enough money to play with. At a certain point, when you're relaxing into the pride of having enough money, corruption takes place. It is dangerous when you begin to feel you can afford to play in the field of ego; you can just play around with things.

Ambition is not a problem in relationship to money unless you are trying to build your empire. If you are working factually, with the facts and figures of a situation, I don't think there is anything wrong with trying to succeed. The problem arises when you would like to look down on other things, celebrating your own achievement. When you begin thinking that your achievement is greater than somebody else's, when the competitive quality comes in, then your ambition becomes part of ego, because ego's process views things as a battle.

You might have intense emotions about succeeding at the things you're doing. There could be intense longing to accomplish something that uses your intelligence properly and fully. That has a certain uplifted feeling to it, a feeling of putting things into practice. That could be said to be emotion, or enthusiasm in a sense. But in another case, your emotionality could be egotistical. You get emotional because you would like to win the game. Whether ambition involves ego or not depends on whether you are involved in a competitive game. If you're involved with competition, then you are connected with ego. If you don't involve yourself with the competitive game, if you are purely keen to put your practice into effect, that isn't ego. Bodhisattvas might have a tremendous desire to help others to find their path, which could be said to be an expression of emotion. Compassion could be said to be emotion, an intense longing to put things into practice. That wouldn't be ordinary emotion in the sense of ego.

If you have money, you don't have to use it every minute, every step you take. You can learn to use the things you already have, as well as paying for things with money. The psychology should be that you could have lots of money, but you could still hitchhike occasionally. You could ask someone for a ride. You don't hitchhike because you're desperately poor. In this case, hitchhiking—which is not necessarily literal here—would be enjoying every moment of your relationship with people, enjoying walking and being independent. If you have money, you may feel completely prohibited from doing anything naturally, simply. That's a very sad thing. If you have lots of money, you might buy expensive silk flowers rather than just having ordinary flowers in your house. You could buy ordinary flowers or you could grow them. They needn't be expensive, particularly. The point is to work with what is, whether you have lots of money or very little.

In Asia there is the tradition of the monks wandering through the countryside and begging for their food, which is a little like hitchhiking might be in this country. I don't think we can practice this approach in America, particularly. For one thing, it is not socially acceptable. Also, if you started doing this without the proper background, you might begin to feel you are a special person. You might make a spectacle of yourself, which would just create a self-conscious egotistical problem. Generally, in Buddhist countries in Asia, mendicant monks are part of the community. They are accepted in society. In Tibet there were lots of monks doing the practice of begging, and they had no problem of survival at all. They didn't have to go to more than ten doors begging for food. They would get chunks of meat and butter and bags of barley flour and all the other things they might need. If they went to more than ten families, they would get more than they could carry. The relationship to giving food was very different in Tibet. People weren't hesitant to give. They were concerned about taking care of the person who needed food, and they cared about the relationship. They gave large quantities automatically. It was just the habitual way of doing things. Somehow I don't think we can really practice that here, sadly.*

* This talk was given before the advent of most food banks in America. Contributing to food banks, food drives, church suppers for the homeless and working poor, and other practices like this might be a contemporary way of practicing the kind of community generosity described by the author here.—Eds.

For the monks, this way of life expressed simplicity. It wasn't an expression of poverty mentality. With this monastic approach, you don't worry about survival. You live day-to-day. You think just of today; you don't think of tomorrow. Tomorrow comes, it doesn't come—either way, you don't worry. You continue to live in a very simple way. It is an everyday life of simplicity.

When you have very little money, it can in a sense simplify the whole process of life. You have to be quite efficient in calculating how much you have and how much you can spend on food or anything else. But, similar to the practice of begging, one doesn't particularly have to fight for anything. I faced this situation myself when I was living in Oxford. We had something like nine pounds a week to feed three people in our household. Life can be quite simple if you know exactly how much money you have in the bank and that's all you have to spend for the basic things you need. It might feel harsh or bitter if you are fighting to gain more, trying to squeeze other things out of that small amount of money.

The problem is not always how little money you have to spare but, rather, whether you are allowing enough space for yourself. The sense of poverty often seems connected with a lack of space. It may seem pretentious or insensitive to suggest to a destitute person that they need to create more mental space, if they are living in financially troubled conditions. However, if you can appreciate the aspect of simplicity in your life, then you don't have to involve yourself with money more than is really necessary.

You should try to create a space of loneliness as much as possible in your lifestyle, whether you are rich or poor. When everything is crammed into you, when all the undesirable things in life seem crowded within you, you are putting yourself through all sorts of unnecessary pain simply because you are not able to see the space and the open situations that exist.

13
■ ■ ■

THE KARMA
OF MONEY

Money acts as a lubricant for all kinds of material interchanges in our lives. It's like karma. You can't say that karma is an entity of its own, but at the same time it has its own energy characteristics. Other situations are a part of its force. From the Buddhist point of view, karma is just mechanical and reacts to the natural chemistry in situations. Money works along with that.

Karma has many different aspects, and one of those manifests in our karmic relationship with money. Almost everyone has an unresolved problem with money, just as they have an unresolved problem with life. That seems to be their money karma. In some cases people have a lot of money, but still they are always short of it; or else they have very little money, but it lasts for a long time. There are all these different and intricate relationships with money. Some people can manage money very well; they have less neurosis about it. Some people find dealing with money very difficult. For them, every penny has to be fought over.

One's money situation is part of one's karmic relationship with life, definitely. For instance, you might want to be free of obligations, but one thing is holding you back—money. You find you have to resolve your money problems before you can move forward. Then, being held back to resolve the money problem brings you to involvement with another situation. So you are hurled back into your life in that way. Or you might be pushed ahead. You might have an inclination to do certain things or to go certain places and suddenly out of the blue somebody sends you a check. It's as though the check were saying, "Go and do it; here you are." That kind of event is always quite mysterious.

For some people, it seems very difficult to get free from a sense of hoarding money, like always wanting a bigger house, cars, and material things like that. One wishes that one could drop that mentality. In a lot of cases, people get an impulsive sense of renunciation, a sudden impulse to give everything away. You want to give away your car, your wristwatch, your camera, your house—everything. When you do that, you feel much better, temporarily. You feel heroic. However, even after you have given everything away and you think you are free, somehow your money karma still follows you. Just giving things away, getting rid of them, doesn't help. You still have a problem.

Usually people are not aware that money is karmically related to them. Some people may be more aware than others, but the usual tendency is to think that giving your possessions or your wealth away will be like having an operation to remove a malignant tumor, and then you will be free of it. Money doesn't work that way. That whole karmic situation comes back to you, always. So again the same old saying is true, "Better not to begin, but once you do begin, do it properly." We have to be able to have money and work with it but not be attached to it. It is similar to any transmutation process. You have to make a relationship with money and a relationship with possessions and not get into an extreme, impulsive renunciation kick.

In the Buddhist monastic tradition, monks and nuns renounce having personal belongings beyond the bare minimum: your robes, your begging bowl, your practice materials. However, the basic point is renunciation and simplicity. Certain contemplative traditions of Christianity might say that monastic life should be the equivalent of living in the same way as the poorest person in the country. In the case of Buddhism, however, poverty is not the criterion, nor is the idea to live like this or that kind of person. Rather, the idea is to be fundamentally simple. You do only the necessary things in life, without introducing extra complications. Eating, sleeping, and defecating are the necessary things, and apart from those, you do not have to engage with anything else. Doing only those three necessary things is what is called in Sanskrit the *kusulu* tradition.* So in Buddhism that ideal has to do with leading a simplified life rather than with any notion of being rich or poor. It's about being content with simplicity and not introducing further entertainment.

In the previous chapter, we talked about the mendicant practice in India and Tibet of monks begging for food as an expression of simplicity. Today one would feel self-conscious adopting this lifestyle in the West, saying that one has renounced worldly things and is asking for food. Some young people have suggested to me that receiving welfare here in America is the equivalent of monastic begging in Asia. However, deciding not

---

* The term *kusulu* is sometimes used pejoratively to refer to someone who is ignorant, but there is also a use of the term that refers, as the author does here, to a practitioner who profoundly simplifies his or her life. According to another great Tibetan Buddhist teacher, Khenchen Thrangu Rinpoche, as well as others, there are two approaches to the spiritual path: one is to study the Buddhist texts extensively and is called the path of the scholar (*pandita*), and the other is to meditate directly with less emphasis on study and is called the path of the kusulu or the simple meditator.—Eds.

to work and receiving welfare is quite different. In the case of monks begging in Tibet, they had to spend much of their day walking outside, and they had to endure a lot of cold weather and other hardships. You had to lead the life of a beggar in a complete sense. Doing that thoroughly and properly could be a karma-free practice. However, if you are taking money from the nation, then you are collecting heavy karma. There is a Tibetan term kor (dkor), which means a gift through trust. Such a gift has powerful karmic debts connected with it, because somebody gave you that gift because they trusted you. Such a gift should be spent properly, used properly.

There are many stories about the karma connected with this kind of gift. There is a well-known Tibetan story of the lama with a black horse who was quite successful at collecting gifts. His monastery became extremely rich and had gold roofs, and he had a golden saddle, and so on. When he died, he was reborn in the ocean as a giant fish with hundreds of little fishes nesting on his body and eating it. Those who had given him gifts became those little fishes that were feeding on him. They ate him up down to his bones, but they never managed to get at his brain and his heart. He kept regenerating and getting eaten up again and again.

There's a sort of Robin Hood idea in the youth culture today, the idea that it's all right to rip off a big corporation or a supermarket or some institution that's impersonal. People feel that sort of thing could be done without heavy karmic repercussions, just because of the impersonality of the situation, but it could also involve a sort of vandalism or basic hatred toward society. A basic, subtle, psychological aggression is coming out. You feel it is a safe way of expressing aggression, a convenient way. Generally, destroying public or government property— even though it may be cloaked as a statement that these big institutions are corrupt—is going in the wrong direction and is not beneficial to people. That kind of relationship with national karma could be extremely heavy. You are sharing in everybody's karma, but at the same time you are being destructive and creating more karmic debt.*

Another reason for resenting money, as we have already discussed, is a general tendency to view spirituality as being away from the world, apart from worldly concerns. People with that view find it irritating that they still have to deal with money in relation to spirituality, which means to them that spirituality is also a worldly concern. However, spirituality *is* a worldly concern, in fact a much more subtle one. Without samsara, there couldn't be nirvana at all. By getting into spirituality, people are not getting out of anywhere; they are not escaping from anywhere. The ubiquitous Mara or Yama still follows them everywhere.**

Often people's attitude toward spirituality is based on searching for escape or at least relief—seeing spirituality as the ultimate pleasure, as we talked about earlier. And when money is brought into the search for ultimate pleasure, it's a tremendous shock. Even in a spiritual context, money still catches up with you—it's a terrible thing. We make too big a separation between spirituality and living in the world. We make such a separation that we are making spirituality the goal itself rather than relating to it as a way of living.

---

* The talk on which this chapter is based was given in the early 1970s. Today the culture of corporate greed might be identified as the prevailing source of equally heavy karmic repercussions in North American culture and could also be said to be based on aggression and lack of respect for others. In either case, there is a feeling that one can take advantage of others, or profit from others' resources, without karmic consequences.—Eds.

** Mara, in the Buddhist tradition, is a personification of the seductions and deceptions of the dualistic view of reality. Yama is the mythical Lord of Death, but also the ruler of the six realms of existence, under whose dominion the ravages of time—including birth, old age, sickness, and death—are pervasive. Rinpoche's point here seems to be that no matter how one may try to twist and dodge, no matter how spiritual a context one may try to cook up, the factors that haunt samsara remain to be dealt with.—Eds.

In the Tibetan monastic tradition, entering the monastery was not a way to get away from dealing with money. In the monastery, the monks often didn't all live in one building. Many times, you had your own house on or near the grounds of the monastery. You were supposed to find three sponsors: one for your education, one for your spiritual development, and one who was responsible for your financial welfare after you joined the monastery. One of these people might put you up in his house. So you lived with that family and took part in the householder's life. There might be six or seven people living in the same house. At the beginning, you might be asked to cook for the family or to fetch water or collect firewood. Your parents also might provide you with your share of food and other supplies to contribute to the household or to the monastery.

As well, there was a certain time of year that you went out collecting food. You might do that twice a year. In the early winter, you would go out into the lowlands and collect grain. You would visit family after family. You might give them spiritual instructions and help them that way. In the summer, you would go up to the highlands and collect butter and cheese and things like that. Or else you might become the family's teacher in a particular household, in order to pay for your monastic training. You would spend three or four months participating in that family's household, and you were their meditation teacher. Each member of the household would come to you separately to receive instructions. In return, you were given bulk food that you could bring back to your monastery. In general, people would give you a gift of food or money in exchange for teaching. The rest of the year, you would live on those gifts of food, and you would also share it with other monks, who had all been doing the same thing. If you were a novice monk, you might go back to your own home for a period each year, particularly in the autumn, and help your family with the harvest or do other work like that. You were supposed to maintain contact with your family.

SHAMBHALA PUBLICATIONS

If you'd like to receive a copy of our latest catalogue of books and audios, please fill out and return this card. It's easy—the postage is already paid!

Or, if you'd prefer, you can e-mail us at CustomerCare@shambhala.com, sign up online at www.shambhala.com/newsletter, or call toll-free (888) 424-2329.

NAME

ADDRESS

CITY / STATE / ZIP / COUNTRY

E-MAIL

And by also giving us your e-mail address, you'll automatically be signed up to receive news about new releases, author events, and special offers!

The monasteries also held winter festivals, New Year's festivals, and other ceremonies and celebrations, all of which required a monetary base. When a monastery decided to have a festival, the people in charge would meet and decide either to buy property or to request some land from a landlord. The property for the festival would often consist of three or four fields of barley. The monastery would also be given twenty or thirty head of stock, as well as a certain amount of money to help finance the festival. Then the property would be turned into a household, and often the poorest people in the vicinity would be asked to take charge of it and run it as a business. They would sell the grain and the butter and whatever else was produced on the land. In return, they were given a certain amount of the profit for themselves. The remainder—a fixed amount of grain, butter, and tea—was then offered to the monastery for their use during the festival. During the ceremonies, tea would be offered to the whole assembly of monks, which might be anywhere from a hundred to three thousand monks. Some meals were provided to the monastic community, as well as various materials that were needed for the festival, including such things as objects for the shrine. Guests from the neighboring monasteries were also fed and entertained out of the profits from the festival property. So each festival relied on its own property, and this was one of the ways that the central finances of the monastery were maintained.

Working with money is always part of the psychology or the philosophy of a situation. So we need basic criteria for working with money. Working with money requires discipline to know how much money you need for a week, how much money is required to live for a day or a month. Living in any society requires this process of discipline. We have to work along with the pattern of society. In that context, it seems that a relationship with money is necessary. We have to actually face the whole problem of money as it is.

In this country, I have met many young people who have a

general hesitation to work. When you are short of money, you have to put in effort and go through the whole pain of getting a job and committing yourself to situations that are not appealing to you and are often a source of more pain. That pain is seen as worldly pain without any redeeming quality. You see it purely as suffering. If you have the attitude that you fundamentally don't want to work with pain, then when you become interested in spirituality, you don't want to deal with any pain whatsoever. You are seeking transcendental pleasure, and work and money seem unromantic. They're too close to home. They're contradictory to your whole idea of spirituality, which is to receive the highest pleasure, bliss.

However, you find that you have to go back to the original pain that you wanted to escape. You begin to see that spirituality is not pleasure seeking and that your work situation is also spirituality, but not spirituality with pleasure or any reward. You are not trying to gain anything, but you are trying to go deeper and unlearn, to undo yourself. It has nothing to do with pleasure at all, actually. The point of spirituality is to face the facts of life, and you might learn the facts of life through working. Then maybe your relationship to money may change. Because your fundamental attitude toward work is different, money becomes a naturally easier matter. There's nothing evil about it.

Work is also something *real,* just as much as spiritual practice. So work doesn't have to have any extra meaning behind it, but it is spirituality in itself. Work doesn't need another philosophical reinforcement. You may want to work for a good reason, something that proves that what you are doing is valid. Maybe you think that you can't relate to work unless you have a good philosophical reason, and without that, your work remains mechanical. Then quite possibly you are missing the point of spirituality altogether. Spirituality is not other than work, just to make the point clear. Work is spirituality, work is real—as much as anything else.

Pain and pleasure in relationship to work seems to be a relative question. If you think about somebody on a yachting vacation in Europe, you will resent being stuck with your little job, doing repetitive work. Our outlook is definitely connected with ingrained criteria. In fact, that's exactly what we are working on: to see how you fundamentally relate to pain and pleasure, good and bad, how they come about. Never mind about what you've been told, but how do you actually relate with pain and pleasure?

Fundamentally, we need to relate with the earth, with our actual work situation. Then, situations are going to tell us quite bluntly: "I reject you" or "I accept you." In both cases it's quite painful.

The pain is that we have to deal with many different things that we really don't want to relate to. Fundamentally, we'd prefer that *they* would relate with *us* rather than our having to open ourselves up to them. That is because we prefer to stay within our shelter; we want to keep our basic ego shell intact. Once anything demands that we step out of the shell and communicate, then the situation becomes too complicated for us.

The basic pain is losing security, losing the sense of maintaining your ego intact. You can't have pain unless you have associations with things in life. The association itself, the duality itself, is the pain. It's the basic notion that you can't maintain yourself by yourself; you need something else. In the case of a hungry baby, being hungry makes her insecure, and not being hungry makes her secure. In the case of this young child, ego is not that big a thing. It is an experience of simple duality.

When a baby is hungry, he or she will cry. There's nothing wrong with that. We are not trying to get rid of *that* level of fundamental duality, necessarily. However, that simple situation also contains other possibilities. It wouldn't continue to be as simple as that. In other words, we are not trying to get rid of ego, but we are trying to get rid of the chain reaction of ego.

On the one hand, a simple ego could transform into wisdom. It *is* wisdom. Ego has basic instinctive awareness of this and that. However, the simple ego also has the tendency to get into "I" more, and that goes with aggression. It seems a baby doesn't even have the "this and that." The baby doesn't even know that it's hungry. However, it feels insecure. Instinctively, it feels that way. Hunger is connected with loss and death, and being fed is connected with gaining and surviving. That's quite simple, but we tend to complicate things way beyond that. We come to have a fixed notion of pain as being pain, and pleasure as being pleasure. We acquire limited and particular conceptualized ideas of pain and pleasure. We are not able to retain that childlike quality.

So we need to look at the karmic complications that develop in our relationship to money. Sometimes, when people feel that something's wrong in their relationship to money, they become very shy about dealing with money. These days, some people are so embarrassed by money that they refer to it as "bread." Someone might say, "How much bread do I owe you?" They don't want to use the word *dollar*.

Referring to money as bread is very sneaky. People would like to have synonyms for money. There's something funny about that. Working with money is ultimately a proud path. Referring to money as bread implies that it is something dirty, something obscene. Straight talk about money is too embarrassing. In French the word for bread is spelled p-a-i-n. So you might say to someone, "How much pain do I owe you?"

Even our actual physical currencies reflect our larger relationship to money. On American money it says, "In God We Trust." That communicates quite a lot about American society. On Tibetan money, we used to have the eight auspicious symbols and the six symbols of longevity. The writing on the bills said something like: "The currency of the heavenly appointed government, the ruler of the temporal and spiritual domain." That communicates another worldview entirely. The last Tibetan coins circulated before the Chinese takeover had three symbols of friendship on them. That money was very short-lived! It lasted only two or three years.

Money in Tibetan society was thought of in terms of what is called *yün* in Tibetan. *Yün* means prosperity or fundamental wealth. It is actually the *force* of wealth rather than actual concrete wealth. There is a belief in abstract energy that can pass from one person to another. It is an abstract magnetizing quality that gathers and radiates wealth. That quality could pass through you to other people. There is an old custom in Tibet that if people have to give somebody money, they take the bills or the coins out of their pocket and rub them on their collar before giving them to the other person. The idea is to transfer the yün to your collar so you don't end up giving the fundamental wealth away to the other person—you just give them the money.

Even the great Tibetan lineage holders had to deal with the karma of money, in a sense. If you have read the story of Marpa, one of the great forefathers of the Kagyü lineage, you will remember that when he met his teacher, Naropa, Naropa asked him, "Before I transmit the teachings to you, how much gold do you have?" Marpa gave him eight solid gold pieces, each in the shape of the knot of eternity. Naropa said, "I know you have more than that. Give me some more!" Finally Marpa had to empty his whole bag of gold coins and give them all to his teacher. Then Naropa threw the gold into the air and stamped on the ground. The whole ground turned into gold; every pebble turned to gold. Then Naropa said, "I have much more gold than you, actually, but I'll give you teaching anyhow."* There

---

* The first four teachers in the Kagyü lineage (one of the main schools of Tibetan Buddhism) were Tilopa (988–1069), Naropa (1016–1100), Marpa (1012–1097), and Milarepa (1040–1123). Their life stories, which illustrate how the awakened state of mind is transmitted from guru to disciple, are well known to practitioners of Tibetan Buddhism and are regarded as exemplary.—Eds.

are many stories like that about receiving the teachings. When Tibetans went to India, they always had to bargain for the teachings. (Actually, India hasn't changed that much.) Of course, the student always had to give in; otherwise he or she didn't get the full teachings.

The teaching becomes more expensive, or perhaps we should say more valuable, as the lineage goes on and on. The longer it continues, the more people have had to work hard for it and sacrifice their lives. So the teachings become more valuable.

It has been said that the best gift from a student to a teacher is practice, full commitment. Then second comes physical service. The third best gift is giving money or gold for the teachings you receive. Even in the case where the student is providing the gift of practice or service, the student still has to support himself—the teacher is not going to support him. That's what we see in the story of Marpa's disciple, Milarepa: he provided service to Marpa, and he also had to support himself.

Any gift is a symbol of commitment. In the old days in Tibet, if you were going to give gold to the teacher, you had to work for it; you had to gather it. Its value came from the fact that it cost you a lot of effort and energy to acquire it. Giving a gift was a sign of committing your energy in the right direction, in the direction of the teaching. This was true in those old days when Tibetans went to India to receive teachings, just as it is true here nowadays.

14

. . .

BUSINESS
ETHICS

As an extension of how we work with money altogether, being in business can be an activity that develops our sanity and thus helps to propagate the dharma. Beyond that, the world of business expresses richness, in the sense of expanding the vision of the buddhadharma into our lifestyle and activities. I have been presenting a series of what I call the Shambhala teachings, which are precisely about how to extend the vision of Buddhism into the understanding and practice of everyday life.* The Buddhist view is based on overcoming ego and dedicating ourselves to helping others. The Shambhala view is extending that understanding and those values into a complete way of life and into the creation of a whole

* For an overview of these teachings, the reader may wish to consult *Shambhala: The Sacred Path of the Warrior* by Chögyam Trungpa, which is also published by Shambhala Publications.—Eds.

world, starting with a society based on dignity and wakefulness, which I call the Great Eastern Sun. With that view, developing a business can provide people not just with a job but with a social structure and a way of life, so that everybody involved can benefit.

We have to look at what kind of human power or economic power in our approach to business will produce genuine accomplishment. First we need to consider the question of value, in terms of richness, poverty, and politics. In your mind, the value of your business might have to do with achieving your dream of striking it rich. You want to come up with something that will make you a millionaire. Or you might want to set up your individual economic kingdom, so that you can have people running around working for you. A third notion of value is based on establishing a business that will be an expression of personal accomplishment and an expression of your individual freedom. You don't want to commit yourself to any higher ideas of the truth, such as the dharma. Your business will speak for itself, and hopefully, it will rescue you from poverty. The fourth approach to value is that you value your business because you're excited about the project you're working on, which makes you feel good and creative. For a long time, you have wanted to express yourself, and this is your·chance to express your talent, your genius.

There might be problems with all of these approaches. There is, however, one value system that is workable and helpful, without question. The basis of the approach to business, in this case, is to relate with your everyday life situation and with the economy as neither a burden nor a promise. Rather, you feel a sense of duty, from the point of view of the bodhisattva ideal of putting others before yourself. You think in terms of providing resources for yourself and for others. You accommodate all sorts of people, and you employ them in your company. The basis of this approach is bravery, which is also connected with the basic Buddhist vision of helping others.

Along with that bravery comes skillful means: being resourceful in working with the situation around you in terms of economics, human power, and whatever other issues you might have in your business.

You can also trust that, if your approach is true to yourself, it will be true for others. With that introduction on the value of the economy, or the value of wealth altogether, we can look at the question of ethics in business.

OBSTACLES TO DISCIPLINE

1. *Habitual patterns.* Let us begin with the obstacles to discipline, or to what is called *shila* in Sanskrit. The first obstacle in your business is your habitual patterns. We cannot separate our business from our general practice of sanity or our relationship to the principles of truth, or dharma. You might be extremely well mannered and civilized, soft-spoken and gentle. When you walk into the office, however, you are a problematic person who expresses neuroses right and left. There your personality is entirely different. In that situation you are trying to mimic or express the notion of "job" and "duty" in the wrong way. The schizophrenia in relating with sanity and insanity becomes evident. This is due to your previous habitual patterns. You have a kind of nervousness, which needn't be there, but which comes out when you relate with your employees, your partners, or your clients.

When you see this pattern of behavior, you feel that you don't want to go on behaving this way. To overcome this problem, you need to develop a totally unified behavior pattern or psychological state of being that includes every activity. You should relate to your sitting practice of meditation and your business deals in exactly the same way. That is absolutely necessary.

If you're the boss and you don't have this unified approach of discipline, the employees see what's happening and are subject to the transformations that you are going through. You have a psychological problem, and your insanity shows through. Falling back into habitual patterns of this kind creates a problem for everyone in the office. Even if there is a lot of prosperity and working capital, if the staff members don't feel enough trust, they will also express the boss's insanity. You begin to find that the entire business establishment goes berserk during working hours.

In the evening, when you go home, you might take a shower, change your clothes, and go out to eat in some civilized place. You might go to a party, or you might give a talk to some group, or you might have to meet with one of your clients—or even a meditation student. In any case, you try to change your mask.

That whole setup becomes ludicrous. If somebody could see your daily performance from morning until you go to bed, it would be very embarrassing. And in some sense, people do see what you are up to. Often you think you can hide, that you can lead a double life, but in fact, everybody knows what you are doing. People are not all that stupid. They can pick up on your behavior patterns. That pattern of leading a double life and indulging your habitual patterns is one of the biggest obstacles to discipline.

2. *Slander.* When there is a lack of discipline in the workplace and you are indulging your habitual patterns, this leads to employees bad-mouthing others in the establishment. Again, if you are the boss and you are indulging your habitual patterns at work, then you influence the other employees. Eventually they feel that they can't contain themselves. They can no longer just watch what's going on. They begin to speak out; then those in charge speak slandering words to their employees. It can become a messy situation. Before long, the employees begin to lose their feeling of basic loyalty to the business, which is quite natural in that situation. If no real sanity is expressed and preserved in the working situation, then the notion of genuine hierarchy, or any respect for authority, falls apart altogether.

If you work with someone who is indulging his or her habitual patterns and neuroses in this way, you should try to find a supportive way to speak with this person. A business endeavor only works when everyone has good intentions, which means making a commitment to manifest sanity beyond your habitual patterns. If the situation is not founded on that kind of good intention, then slandering or bad-mouthing arises naturally, because people have to release their negative energy.

3. *Lying.* In that kind of schizophrenic work environment, we find ourselves not telling the truth. We might end up adding more zeroes to our profit figures, inflating the value of the company so that we can get another bank loan or arrange more financing for the company. There is only one saving grace, which is to return to our own sanity. The practice of meditation is very important in this kind of situation. Sitting practice might add 50 percent to our sanity. It can prevent us from doing something totally crazy.

4. *Laziness.* When you wake up in the morning and you have to go back to the establishment that you have created or where you work, you feel tremendous hesitation. You try to delay stepping into your office as long as you can. You try to have as good a time as you can outside your work. That attitude creates an unhealthy situation, because you have no real enthusiasm for work.

If the owners and the employees don't show up on time and don't work together, a lot of underlying depression is created. Everything becomes a hassle. You wind up not working hard enough to see projects through. The only time you really work hard is when you have to push something through because your whole business is in danger of falling apart. Then you must do something. But other than that, you have no incentive to work, no motivation to celebrate doing business at all.

The opposite of these obstacles is to be free from habitual patterns, free from slandering, free from telling lies, and free from laziness. These are the basic disciplines that we need to apply in business. Maybe the examples I gave are not applicable to you, but if you look at your own business situation from this point of view, you can see how these principles apply quite vividly. If you look at what is going on in your state of being, in relationship to your work environment, then you can overcome what needs to be overcome.

MEDITATION

Next I'd like to discuss the application of meditative discipline in the workplace. We're not speaking here of literally meditating at work but rather of how to bring this state of mind into your business. Meditative discipline is working with our state of being altogether. In this case, we can talk about positive attributes.

1. *Gentleness.* We should understand the need for gentleness. Gentleness means being free from aggression, and it also means extending ourselves further, in our business and in our life altogether. Again, we are talking about having no separation between business and domestic life but seeing that everything is related. When basic discipline has developed in you and you are free from habitual patterns, slandering, falsity, and laziness, then you can be gentle. You are free from depression. Therefore you can afford to smile. You can afford to be kind and inquisitive.

2. *Free from hypocrisy.* At this point, we can also be free from hypocrisy. We do not regard our business as a way to run away from the truth or the sanity of the buddhadharma. We also do not regard our business as a way to entertain ourselves, a way to build an economic kingdom, or a way to build up our personality.

3. *Free from competition.* Because of having developed the qualities of the previous categories, we can be naturally free from competition in dealing with colleagues or other businesses. We don't have to jump into situations immediately and twist the logic around. We don't need to think that we are the smart-

est businessman because we can pull some trick before anybody else thinks of it. Such competitiveness is problematic and it leads to conflict. The problem arises when there is not enough steadiness in the sense of *samadhi,* or the basic meditative state of awareness. Things become very jumpy, jumping back and forth. Your motivation is purely based on passion, aggression, and ignorance. It's necessary to overcome that state of mind.

DISCRIMINATING AWARENESS

The final topic is how to apply discriminating awareness or appreciation in your business. Discriminating awareness is called prajna in Sanskrit. It is connected with seeing situations clearly and distinguishing, or discriminating, all the details of what is taking place.

    1. *Loyalty.* The first category of discriminating awareness is loyalty. In this case, loyalty is based on developing appreciation for your colleagues, which comes from your discriminating awareness. You don't regard other people in the workplace as objects, and you don't regard them purely from the reference point of being in business together—in the negative sense. Rather, you appreciate their unique qualities. Developing this sense of trust and loyalty is connected with gentleness, which we discussed already.

    Gentleness brings a basic sense of loyalty, because you are free from aggression toward others. Loyalty manifests as harmony between the staff members within the working situation. When that is present, you can expand your vision. You can develop further discriminating awareness in terms of acquiring the technical knowledge that is required to run your business. If you lack adequate information or vision to conduct your business, that manifests in a lack of professionalism. However, you can gain the knowledge you need. In part, you can learn from other people who have already developed knowledge in your field.

Sometimes, however, there's a problem if you base your vision purely on someone else's knowledge or success. You want to mimic them, to get on their business bandwagon or their artistic bandwagon, or whatever it may be. If we have basic discriminating awareness, that will provide potential choices and ways to improvise that aren't purely based on adopting someone else's cultish concept of success. It will also allow us to connect with all kinds of people beyond our sphere. We could employ them or work with them quite freely.

Because we have developed our basic discipline, or shila, already, which includes not lying or slandering, we are able to tell the truth in the work situation. In our business, we can use the familiar atmosphere or environment surrounding us for support; at the same time, we have to expand constantly beyond it. It is always necessary in business to bring fresh blood into the system, as well as fresh capital, so that we don't just recirculate things all the time. If we did that, our business might dry up altogether.

We have a small planet. There is a limit to how much we can pee on it and still have fresh water to drink. If we pee too much, we might wind up with very salty water. Similarly, we need to bring fresh blood, fresh resources, into our system as much as we can, but without losing our integrity.

I have noticed that when people encounter economic problems in their businesses, they often freeze. They act as if they were completely cornered. Frequently you feel you have no other choice but to shout something out. In such situations, you need to extend your vision, based on discriminating awareness, and then you will see how to improvise with whatever resources are available to you.

On the other hand, sometimes when people have a small success in a business venture, they think they can run around and go wild. Often successful businesspeople think that they do not need the protection and friendship of their long-standing colleagues. They feel that they can make friends with new people who might appreciate them more than their old friends.

Those are two extreme positions, both of which require the application of discriminating awareness. They are the problems of eternalism and nihilism that arise in our business ventures. Eternalism is thinking that you have conquered the situation completely and you no longer need any support. You can't imagine that anything will go wrong. Nihilism is feeling fatalistic when you have a problem in your business, thinking that the immediate obstacle will destroy you.*

2. *Tell the truth.* In relating to your employees in a business, it's very important to tell the truth. If you try to act like a guru with your employees, by trying to find various devious ways of dealing with the situation, it won't work. You have to be quite straightforward, particularly in business. This is based on the further application of discriminating awareness. Here it is sharing what you know quite straightforwardly and without pretense.

In any business situation there are facts and figures, the mechanics of how things are put together. Out of sharing that, you can relate with people quite straightforwardly. The facts and figures are plain and ordinary. You should make your communication very plain and straightforward to begin with.

If you are having a problem with an employee who doesn't contribute much to your business, even if you share the dollars-and-cents perspective with him, it may not help. At some point, you may have to tell your employee that he doesn't have the capability of dealing with those facts and figures, and then you may have to tell him to find another work situation. However, you don't have to reprimand him beyond that. The less innuendo, the better. A straightforward message is best, because business is very direct. It is full of facts and figures, and the logic

---

* In the study of Buddhist philosophy, nihilism and eternalism are often discussed as fundamental obstacles on the Buddhist path. They refer to problems in one's view of reality altogether. It is interesting here to see the author apply this to a problem in the relative, everyday world.—Eds.

of that provides evidence of someone's workmanship on the spot. If you don't relate to the facts and figures, you won't be a good businessperson. If you begin to philosophize the whole situation, it will create difficulties.

BASIC INTEGRITY

When you run a business, your task may seem gigantic, monolithic. When you begin to look at everything you need to do, you might have a list of five hundred problems that need to be overcome. But you can do it, as long as you have basic integrity. You can do it and you've got to do it. It's choiceless.

There is no other way than to have basic integrity. Without that, you will have lots of problems. Basic integrity is the outcome of applying all the categories discussed above. Through the aspects of discipline, meditation, and discriminating awareness we have discussed, you arrive at a situation of basic integrity in your business.

There are many different situations in which we need to apply basic integrity. For example, a businessman or -woman may feel that there are chapters and chapters of things he or she has to straighten out at work. You don't know where to begin, so you pick one thing at random, something that seems easy to accomplish. You try that approach for a few weeks. Then that initiative falls apart, and finally, the whole business or your whole life falls apart. At that point, to compensate, you might buy a new hat or a new car or a new suit, to try to make yourself feel better. On the whole, however, if everything is charged on your credit card, then somebody else owns you, rather than your owning yourself. So there is a need for basic integrity rather than spending money randomly to make yourself feel better.

You can help other people through your business to relate to money and ownership with a sense of integrity. For example, if someone needs help getting a loan, you could help or sponsor him or her by cosigning a loan, which is much better than encouraging someone to lie about their credit. In the Buddhist tradition, at a certain point, people may take a vow to devote their lives to helping others. When a teacher lets the student take such a vow, the teacher is cosigning for him or her. The person is not a bodhisattva yet. The teacher is saying, "You are becoming a bodhisattva now. You can develop all the transcendent qualities you need to help others. I am your spiritual friend, and I'll help you to do so." So the teacher is the cosigner. Step-by-step, the person learns to be independent. He or she doesn't come back to you for advice all the time, because as a spiritual friend you are harsh as well as friendly at the same time. We can take a similar approach in our business relationships.

There is a danger in business, and I have found this in Buddhist businesses in our community as well, of falling back on old habitual patterns and trying to find out how much you can cheat monolithic organizations such as your bank. You hope they will make mistakes in your favor. That is twisting the logic, and businesses suffer a lot when they have that kind of limited vision. It is very important not to twist the logic of business ethics at all. You will feel better afterward.

The question of how to approach carrying debt in your business is very interesting from this point of view. If you own your own tie 100 percent and you own your own suit 100 percent, you feel good that you have them. They are yours, all the time. When I first got credit cards, I was hesitant to use them. Although I had a credit card, I preferred to use cash. Taking on debt should be viewed as your choice, rather than feeling that you have to get into debt more. It's also good to feel that something is yours, that you've paid it off. That gives you good credit.

One of the problems that we face in business is the notion of a quick turnover and a constant turnover. You juggle things around all the time until you are a million dollars in debt. Even then, you think you are rich and you acquire more debt. We have seen that logic applied in many disastrous business situations in this country. The business appears rich, but it's a gigantic paper tiger. In that situation, you are frightened of how much you owe, yet you don't really own anything.

People should work for and own what they have. You can acquire genuine value or credit that way. You collect some things of value, like buying antiques for your home. From owning a Ming vase and putting it in your house, the economic value in the situation grows altogether. What you own provides an economic base. So, for example, I would recommend that you own your own home and not turn it over or sell it right away. If you move somewhere else, rent out the original house.

When you have a quick turnover, you are riding on a roller coaster. You have no ground. You don't have the principles of heaven, earth, and humanity operating properly. You just have heaven, but it's a funny heaven, not even a good heaven. You have no earth at all. Humanity is floating around up there in heaven, with no earth, no working basis. So bring something of real value into your business and into your home, as much as possible. If somebody offers you a good deal, if they offer to give you a million dollars for something you own, I wouldn't take it.

Whether it's a house, or jewelry, or even your shoes, you should have something of substance in your business. Personally, you should have something you can bring home, something that is actually yours, not something that belongs to somebody else, which you are going to sell for them. The expression "You lost your shirt" is quite appropriate from this point of view.

If you keep busy making quick financial transactions all the time, you might feel rich. But the dollars and pounds and Euros purely pass through your hands. It's as though you had a form of financial diarrhea. It's like flushing your food down the toilet without eating it, which is a terrible thing to do. It is ultimate poverty. Quick transactions cause lots of problems, as we have seen in many businesses in the past.

Of course, borrowing money is appropriate in many situations. It's based on your vision and your resourcefulness. The point is not to cheat people and not to tell tall stories but just do what is necessary, on the spot. You respond to the whole situation, but everything has to be based on the truth. You have to learn to tell the truth. That is very important.

What I would like to avoid is encouraging any lower-level mafioso concept of doing business. That would be making a really bad job out of your business, and it's not at all connected with bodhisattva vision. As long as you don't exaggerate the figures and don't add extra zeroes to your profit figures, it seems all right. But business deals have to pay for themselves. That's how you should evaluate a business offer.

To begin with, you should ask yourself, is this a clean job? Does it work? If it doesn't work, it would be better to give it up. That's Buddhist ethics. Of course, in order to ensure that a business transaction goes forward to begin with, you may have to inspire somebody else. You might have to tell your client or your business partner that this will work before it's proven to work. As long as you are confident about it, that's fine. In fact, you could be opening up a new world for somebody else. However, that person should be filled in completely, so that you are doing a completely honest job of working with the person. You shouldn't feel that you might have to improvise another explanation six months later.

Ideally, all businesses should be without blame. Once you are 100 percent without blame, then you become tremendously prosperous. Perhaps the idea of juggling things around rather than being straightforward is a leftover, something borrowed from counterculture. It's like taking pride in getting into a theater without paying, trying to avoid the ticket taker and using the back door. Things like that might be profitable for a few weeks, but as time goes on, you find that you have problems. Honesty is the best wealth.

We should try to expand on the basis of being friendly

with others. We should try to employ as many people as possible, because it's helpful. There are certain people who get into business because they would like to be admired. They want to become important people on the spot. They would like to rule a little bit and give orders. When people use their business to create a personal economic kingdom, they are usually hungry to be somebody to their friends. They would like to perk themselves up by making themselves the center of the organization. They think that because they are an economic force and employ people, they can push them and pull them around and fire them at will. When people want to set up their own economic kingdoms, they have the worst notion of hierarchy. They would like to hold on to the nerve center in a crude way. The basis of working with people should be comradeship rather than false charisma. Comradeship and wisdom together should form the base, along with the fundamental notion that everybody is respected. It would be good to understand those principles as they apply to business. Please don't try to play funny games.

15

. . .

REGARDING MONEY AS MOTHER'S MILK

B ased on how far our understanding has come, it is my intention to make this discussion of money and wealth into a good celebration. It is like the springtime: trees are beginning to bud, the green grass is shooting up, and flowers are about to blossom. It is like Midsummer's, the summer solstice, which represents the center of the year, the time when things can grow and evolve further. So this is the appropriate time for this discussion.

Through the application of the Buddhist teachings, we learn to practice, to be disciplined, to be well groomed, and we learn to beautify ourselves. As a result of practice, people recognize their dignity, and everybody is brilliant and glowing.

However, aside from helping us to discover our dignity and improving our physical appearance, practice works with other factors related to our individual survival. In connection with entering the Buddhist path, we have to learn to support our community altogether. We have to support our husbands, wives, and children, our house, our motorcars, even our bicycles. We have to send our clothes to the dry cleaners. We have to maintain our meditation practice. All of that requires a lot of money.

Occasionally we would like to go to a restaurant and have a drink in the bar. Or sometimes we can't prevent ourselves from buying a nice dress, nice tie, or nice shirt that is displayed in the store window. We also have to go to the hairdresser. Driving up to the mountains, going to the movies—little things like that seem to be necessary for us. We do those things, in any case. Particularly when we feel uplifted, when we feel basically good, we tend to treat ourselves better, which automatically costs a certain amount of money.

Money is a burden, in some sense, and at the same time, it's a delight to us. That's why we are having this discussion. *Ratna* is a Sanskrit word that means "richness," especially from a vajrayana perspective. This kind of richness is free from poverty mentality. However, that doesn't necessarily mean that we have to be frivolous. The issue of money or ratna in our individual lives is complex, confusing, and many times burdensome. But at the same time, beyond our individual hassles and financial difficulties, we are trying to expand ourselves, our lives, further.

Your livelihood might involve organizing a business, or you might work for someone else. Early in your life or career, you may start by working for someone else. You might be a waitress or work in a gas station. As your vision becomes greater, you want to train yourself so that you can help yourself and others further in life. You learn to survive, and eventually to do more than survive.

The basic training in Buddhism and the Shambhala vision of enriching our own lives and of society as a whole can help us to accumulate fundamental richness in ourselves. Apart from receiving the teachings of the Buddha, the dharma, and learning how to sit with a good posture in our meditation practice, we also learn how to project goodness, brilliance, and richness, which is what we call Shambhala vision. That training might cause other people to think that you have a lot of money. Someone might look at you and think, "That guy must be very rich because he's so happy, well groomed, and not shabby anymore." You might not really have that much money. But on the other hand, you are truly wealthy. Through our practice, we actually become ratna, wealthy.

When the Buddha attained enlightenment, he went around the cities and collected small pieces of cloth that were thrown away by other people. Apparently he was a good tailor, so he sewed all those little squares of cloth together and made a beautiful monastic garment out of them. When people saw him wearing this robe, they remarked, "Look! Who is that well-dressed, well-clad person?" A tradition of sewing monastic robes out of small pieces of cloth came from the example of the Buddha. He projected some kind of richness, power, and strength. It was not a question of having expensive cloth sewn into robes; the sense of richness came from the way the robe was worn, the way it looked on him.

Richness is not purely a result of dollars and cents. When a person is worthy of wealth, he has it. The logic is as simple as that. My attendant often tells me, "You can't wear that shirt for the fourth time." I say, "Of course I can." I've worn a single shirt without laundering it many times, and it has looked fine. That's what we call merit. Merit means that somebody is deserving and able to reflect that in the situation. A person doesn't have to be extravagant in order to become ratna, wealthy, but he or she does have to have a karmic sense of basic sanity, basic worthiness. That is the general principle of how one deserves and actually acquires and reflects wealth.

When we come to business enterprises, there is a little bit of a problem, even for someone who has individually attained this kind of basic wealth. We might have educated ourselves in a Shambhala understanding of economy and our role in the economy. However, when we get into business, we tend to borrow the concepts of how other people have made money in the past. We have understood natural richness, but going into business, we may forget the merit involved. We forget that we are glowing as we are, wearing our shirt for the umpteenth time.

The land in America was invaded, which is particularly heartbreaking. It is absolutely heartbreaking to study the history of Mexico and how the Spanish gained their wealth by devastating the wealth, culture, and beauty of Montezuma's kingdom. I changed my mind about that a little bit after I learned how the Aztecs sacrificed a person to their gods every day and threw the body down in the temple. What happened to their culture could be partially a result of that bad karma. At the same time, the way the Spaniards related with the native peoples was heartbreaking. They were purely greedy for gold and willing to kill for it. We have a similar problem in the United States. Although we have a nice Thanksgiving celebration to remember how we exchanged food with the Native Americans and thanked one another, at the same time, most of this place was snatched. That has brought all kinds of karmic consequences to us, as Americans, that is.

To put it in a nutshell, in America, when we run a business, we have habitual tendencies, based on how others made money purely by cheating. It is not necessarily cheating directly, but cheating in the sense of figuring out how you can get around things.

As Buddhists, however, we are immigrants who have arrived here out of nowhere. (Maybe some of us were in Tibet together in our past lives. Who knows?) So we can change the possibilities and the ways of doing business here into something different from the American heritage. The situation has changed at this point. Vajrayana has been established in this country. The karmic situation in the United States has changed altogether. Maybe some of the karmic debts connected with the Native Americans have been paid off. In any case, it is a very good time to set up a business.

When we go into business, we should take the attitude that the reason to establish a business is to provide us and others with the financial resources to practice. We should think about how we can help our fellow brothers and sisters, our friends. Finally, we can have a positive influence on this continent. Cutting down aggression and greed is itself a tremendous contribution. We might tend to think that our contribution is insignificant, but we are extremely powerful, and we can actually do this.

In our business ethics, we should think in terms of friendship. When we deal with somebody, we should not think in terms of cutting his throat, but we should have good faith in the person. Whether we are buying land from that person or just a T-shirt, there should be tenderness toward him or her. That goes a long way.

On the whole, we should regard money as mother's milk. It nourishes us and it nourishes others. That should be our attitude toward money. It's not just a check or a dollar bill that we have in our wallet. Each dollar contains a great deal of the past. Many people worked for that particular one dollar. They worked so hard, with their sweat and tears, as Churchill said. So that money is like mother's milk, very precious. At the same time, mother's milk can be given away, and we can produce more mother's milk. So we shouldn't hang on to it too tightly. When there is more gentleness, more kindness, and more willingness to share with others, that brings tremendous gratitude, nonaggression, and the wealth of mother's milk.

The main point is not to borrow the habitual tendencies of passion, aggression, and ignorance, and not to cheat anybody. We are trying to establish a financial mandala, a financial world altogether. That world is not only a local world but a vast world that we can share with others.

When we deal with people in business from that perspective, they will be surprised by our nonaggression and by the fact that we're not relying on habitual tendencies. When we speak of developing a financial mandala, we are not just talking about creating a tight world for ourselves. Instead we are talking about a general sense of how we work with the world altogether, how we work with aggression, how we work with our behavior patterns. We should learn from our mistakes and use those conclusions to develop ways of doing business that are pure, open, and fresh.

Such vision can be expanded beyond dealing with the financial situation of the United States. This vision can be expanded to Europe, Japan, China, and other parts of the world. Money brings people together. On the other hand, money is also the place where passion, aggression, and ignorance are brought together. By working with money, we have wonderful possibilities of exploring the depth of the confused world, samsara. Money is actually the equivalent—and not even the equivalent—money *is* the workings of the twelve nidanas, the twelve steps in the chain of conditioned existence that I discussed in chapter 1. It is how things work, how things evolve, how things come to fruition in samsara.

In working with money, we should break that chain, and we should set up a new chain. It's possible. The paramitas, the transcendent actions of a bodhisattva, are a different chain. When you break the chain of the twelve nidanas—which come from greed, ignorance, and all the other expressions of our confusion—then you have a new situation, based on generosity, discipline, patience, and the other bodhisattva activities.

First of all, we have to utilize the knowledge, wisdom, and customs that exist in this country. From there, we can work step-by-step with people. You begin to make friends with them, and things evolve beyond that.

In working with money as mother's milk, we are definitely talking about maintaining our integrity and our morality. It is not going to be a quick moneymaking adventure right away. However, we can achieve some success in business with this approach. On the whole it is very helpful to communicate and share with others who are also taking this approach.

Please come along and join us. *Us* means you. If anybody is going to turn off the wheel of life, the wheel of conditioned suffering, it has to be us. That is our job. It is also our job to enrich ourselves tremendously for the sake of those who practice meditation and meditative awareness. That tradition of practice will survive for at least another five hundred years, if we support it. We are the first immigrants, the pioneers. We have just come off the boat, so to speak. It is wonderful to be that way.

16

...

KARMA

Now that we have discussed the details of work, sex, and money, we can address the fundamental question of karma. In order to do so, we need to review a little bit. As we discussed already, some meditators ask themselves, "If we are meditators, why should we work? Why should we include sex on the spiritual path? Why should money come into it?" When people take spirituality from a very idealistic point of view, they may think that work doesn't need to be included in the discussion of the path, except perhaps in terms of some bare minimum of work that might be necessary to survive. Sex shouldn't be included because it is a source of pain because of all the complicated relationships it involves. Certainly money shouldn't be included because that's the thing that grabs people and brings them down, rather than letting them get high on spirituality. Money involves relationships where one person owes money to another; it represents worldliness itself.

When people talk like this, I think they are talking about a different kind of spiritual path than the one we are discussing here. On that ideal path, the idea is to create good karma to try to escape from anything ugly, bad, or painful. That kind of spirituality is oriented toward pleasure. You enter into a state of meditation; you reach a state of absorption and go into all kinds of ecstasies. You get drunk, high, on meditative absorption, which as we discussed earlier is called a dhyana state. Then once you are high and into the ultimate bliss of dhyana, of course you don't have to work, you don't need money, and you don't need sex. When your bliss runs down, you just recharge it again.

Of course, on this path you are not a nuisance to other people. You don't have to talk about anything but your state of bliss, which you can do with a pious smile while being nice and kind. There's no fear of treading on anybody's toes, because you are not involved with sex, not involved with money, and not involved with work. You don't have to protect yourself from anything. You're a free man or woman. It's a beautiful world. That is the classic view of people engaged in pleasure-oriented spirituality.

Beyond that, in society in general, it seems that everybody wants to work for good karma. Of course! Everybody is searching for something in life. We try to gain something. We try to attain something. What we try to attain is happiness.

When we apply this search for good karma to spiritual practice, we try to reach happiness through the back door, by a shortcut, which is dealing with the mind. We think that if we can get into a meditative state, we will have attained happiness. We will have fulfilled all the desires that exist in the world—in a transcendental way of course.

Many religious approaches have that element of searching for bliss in them—Buddhism, Hinduism, Islam, Christianity. For example, people could misunderstand the writings of the great Christian mystic Meister Eckhart where he talks about the beauty of the all-pervading presence of being. There is the danger in Christian mysticism—any kind of mysticism—that it might turn purely into a search for pleasure, bliss, or eternal kindness. You begin to think that you are on the side of God, defeating Satan.

Buddhism begins quite differently from other religions, in that it begins from an atheistic standpoint. The whole revelation and inspiration for the Buddhist path comes from pain, suffering. Then you look for the origin of suffering, you discover the possibility of the cessation of suffering, and then you discover the path.* The whole Buddhist path could be geared toward antisuffering, which is exactly the same as what is being taught in other religious traditions: that the ultimate aim and object is pleasure. Insight consists in how to make pleasure last longer. In order to do that, we avoid sowing bad karma. Our perpetual good karma will grant us good results so that we can live in that good-karma territory perpetually. But of course, the trick is that we have to *maintain* that.

You have to have criteria for pleasure based on some contrast, in order to enjoy it. The pleasure of meditative absorption always contains a faint trace of paranoia. Without that, you wouldn't enjoy the pleasure. There is the sense that something unenjoyable is just about to approach; therefore we are happy because it isn't here yet. It's sort of like banging your head against the wall, so that it feels better when you stop, though it's not quite as crude as that. However, there is always a slight hint of having to maintain, always a sense of maintenance.

It's like enjoying having a huge house—centrally heated, beautifully decorated, with everything in order. You enjoy your house, your domain. Only an efficient, paranoid person can create a place so beautifully in order. You can't achieve that

---

* Here Chögyam Trungpa succinctly summarizes the Four Noble Truths, the first teaching and one of the most fundamental teachings of Shakyamuni Buddha. For Trungpa Rinpoche's in-depth discussion of this topic, see *The Truth of Suffering and the Path of Liberation* (Shambhala Publications, 2009).

immaculate order unless you look in every corner to make sure that everything is pleasurably and perfectly set up. You have to make sure that the insurance is paid up in case of fire and that everybody involved in the maintenance of the house has been paid. The house has to be kept clean, and the central heating and air-conditioning have to be looked after. Everything has to be taken care of, constantly. You can't have the pleasure unless there is the possibility of pain, at least some subtle pain. Without that, the person wouldn't appreciate the pleasure at all. In order to have perfect pleasure, there must be absolute and perfect paranoia to go along with that.

Maintaining spiritual pleasure relies on the same logic, including the insurance policy. That desire for insurance or assurance is always there, because you want to be sure you can remain in your blissful state in the face of any nasty alternatives. You try to seal yourself off completely so that you can remain in that state of absolute equilibrium.

The question comes down to this: Do we want to adopt this approach of perpetually creating good karma purely for the sake of not getting involved with work, sex, and money? If so, then quite likely we will have to maintain some safe haven so that we can stay in this meditative state, which is very pleasurable, all the time.

On the other hand, is there any possibility of ending the rat race of continually maintaining that? Can we take an approach that is not directed toward higher pleasure or higher pain but is just seeking to become more realistic? There are actually possibilities of transcending both good and bad karma. Both, as we have already explained, come from a repetitive pattern. No psychic powers we might be able to develop, no higher spiritual powers, can transcend both good and bad karma. That has to be worked out on the earth level, on the basic ground of earth.

You possess the intelligence to work with this. That intelligence sees the foolishness of searching for good karma or bad karma. Somehow the karma that exists has to be worked out in its basic nitty-gritty, which is where relating with work, sex, and money comes in. However, we do not get into work, sex, and money purely for the sake of relieving our karma; rather, we get into them to see how they can present actual contact with reality. It is very scientific. That reality depends on our body, speech, and mind, our behavior, our emotions, and everything that is part of us.

You might wonder: As long as there are emotions, as long as there is body, as long as there is mind, doesn't that mean that there's also some karma that we have to work through? Not necessarily. Body is just body, free of karma. It's a mechanical thing—it's just a certain chemistry that exists on this planet. Mind perpetually goes on developing itself—it needn't be connected with karma. It perpetually develops flashes of all sorts of ideas instantaneously. Speech is the interplay between mind and body. As long as body and mind are active, speech happens.

Body and mind are not necessarily connected with karma, because volitional action, which creates karma, begins with attitude, with concept. When we have an attitude, we have conceptualized body and conceptualized mind, which brings conceptualized speech. The necessary condition for karma is concepts. Once concepts begin to operate—including such concepts as "high" and "pleasurable" or "low" and "suffering"—those concepts continually sow a seed in the basic mind, a seed for the growth, or the start-up, of energy. With that condition of concepts in operation, karma then functions and assumes its place. It produces physical or mental results. Physically, you might be injured or in a pleasurable state, and mentally, you get either painful or pleasurable karmic results.

The key point here is concepts. Concepts come from bewilderment, from not knowing where we are, who we are, what we are doing—from absolutely knowing nothing. This complete bewilderment is called ignorance. That bewilderment of not knowing what we are or who we are makes us seek the nearest situation to get a foothold in. We describe that foothold as,

"This is me, and this is the situation. These are my projections, my house, my family, my enemies, my friends." We immediately create this pattern. When there are any interchanges going on, it is very convenient to have this set pattern to work through them with. However, adopting those patterns doesn't solve the basic bewilderment at all. The whole inspiration for karma keeps arising from this unresolved bewilderment. That is why it is so pleasurable to find spiritual pleasure and so painful to find samsaric pain. Of course, the notions of spirituality and samsara are also concepts that we happen to have very conveniently found.

There we are. That is the situation that we have been talking about throughout this book. What can we do about it? In some sense, you can't do anything about it. We might try to find some happy medium, but that doesn't seem to work here. A happy medium is where you make a compromise; you cool down the pleasure and cool down the pain. Then you get a mixture of the two in a very toned-down way. That doesn't really solve anything.

Perhaps we need to ask *who* it is that is staying in the bewilderment. That may be the key: Who is bewildered? You might say, "I'm bewildered." But then we might ask, "What do you mean 'I'?" We can't seem to catch the "I." You can't catch it! That's it, in fact! So nobody is in bewilderment. Is that true? We can't catch anybody in bewilderment, and when we do, we're back into the game of paranoia and pleasure.

Interestingly, bewilderment is an expression of wisdom as well as an expression of ignorance. The situation of bewilderment implies that you can't label anything. That's why you're bewildered. If you can't put a label on anything, however, there are also possibilities of space. There are possibilities of a gap, open space. On the other hand, there are possibilities of not discovering space, which also creates its own bewilderment and paranoia. It goes on and on. That is the source of bewilderment: not having any ground, absolutely not having any ground.

Bewilderment is not knowing whether you are or you are not. You may know that you don't know, but that just makes it more bewildering. Basically, bewilderment is uncertainty about who's who—fundamentally, really. Do you exist? Nobody knows actually. You can read books, but that doesn't give you any answers. You can ask people, but they don't give you any clear answers. You're always back to square one.

There is a difference between bewilderment and confusion. Bewilderment is the first stage. It is the ground of not knowing what's happening. There are many elements coming through you, passing through you, and there's a tendency for this utter bewilderment to become solidified as confusion. Confusion is the second stage. Confusion arises when you try to relate with your projections, or how the bewilderment is expressed in your projections. There is a conflict between the simple expression of bewilderment versus identifying with the bewilderment. There's a very subtle difference between these two. Confusion only arises from a realization that you are in a state of bewilderment and then creating an identity out of that.

The first stage is the bewilderment or not knowing whether I exist or not. And the second stage is being confused about how to relate with that or this. Bewilderment doesn't contain self-consciousness at all. It's a completely egoless state. Then after that, you begin to establish some identity. When bewilderment becomes confusion, it's a very cunning trick in which you give up searching for anything: "I don't care whether I exist or not, but there is something here, so let's call that 'me.' And then my relationship to that is confusion." You still don't know exactly what's going on, but you stumble along.

You accept that there is an ambivalent self, in a sense, by innuendo. You know that you are actually a selfless person, but at the same time, by innuendo, you want to establish that you have a self, to provide you with some identity. To undo this confusion, one must go back to the original bewilderment.

There is an alternative to confusion. Although there's no

ground in the bewilderment, there are still flashes; there are still gaps. Basic bewilderment is not as efficient as we think. There is the peak experience of bewilderment, and then there is also a gap—absolute space beyond that bewilderment. Bewilderment also has its ups and downs.

When we experience basic bewilderment without confusion, we are touching in just barely before the start of the volitional process that creates karma. That's where meditation can play a part. Meditation acknowledges basic bewilderment and the space in which basic bewilderment forgets to create its tantrum. So there's some gap, some room somewhere. However, it seems it's a long, long way from there to the everyday simplicity of dealing with work, sex, and money. When we discover this space in meditation, it's as though we have gone to the peak, to Mount Everest. Then what? It seems to be a long way down to the ground.

There are actually many opportunities for relating with bewilderment. There's the opportunity to finally stop everything. We decide not to rush, not to run anymore. And we stop for a moment, just to be quietly with the meditation technique, whatever it may be. Then there are just teeny-weeny stars shining through the darkness—an occasional glimpse.

Usually, when bewilderment happens, we manufacture a lot of other things. We build a whole world or identity around it. However, there's another possibility. Something's missing in our discussions here. There's something else that hasn't come into the picture clearly yet, which seems to be the root of work, sex, and money, something else that's vital.

Let me explain again. Basic bewilderment is, in a sense, intelligent, but it is passive. In a way, it is carefree because it doesn't have to be involved with karmic chains. It's an open thing. But we need something else. Once we are in an open state, how do we leap? Try to see what it is. It is the governing force of work, sex, and money.

Energy. That's it. Some schools of Buddhism refer to this

energy as chandali or tummo, a term we mentioned in our discussion of sex. What I want to emphasize here, however, is not the connection to esoteric aspects of Buddhist yoga but that it's possible to have energy that is free from karma.* That's what I'm trying to point out. There's original bewilderment. From that original bewilderment, in which you experience space of some kind, energy arises. Through that energy, you can work with all the troubles with work, sex, and money. It is fresh energy without a debt.

You might think that fresh energy is going to collide with a karmic seed and create karma, good or bad. It could, but it doesn't necessarily have to, because you get this energy directly from the basic bewilderment, without going through the conceptualized idea of volitional action. It is energy run wild in its own sanity. We have discussed the relative problems connected with work, sex, and money. Now we know that within those situations there is a basic tool—the basic energy of wakefulness or bewilderment, which is saying the same thing. That energy is a force that is constantly operating in the situations of daily life.

Of course, there is intelligence in the bewilderment. This intelligence is going to search for bliss or express pain. But that is just mechanical, part of bewilderment's mechanical-reaction system. It's sort of a guided missile, a missile guided by the bewilderment. But the handle on basic bewilderment, its exit, is energy.** Bewilderment's way of relating with situations is energy.

That energy has direction, which we might call the absence of panic. Energy functions on its own in situations. Wherever the energy is needed, it happens. So energy doesn't have to be

---

* For more on tummo see the discussion on page 114 and the accompanying footnote, as well as the glossary entry.

** The word *handle* here is used in the sense of getting a handle on something. Specifically here it relates to coming to an understanding of bewilderment or finding a starting point for action.—Eds.

guided consciously. Once you begin to guide it consciously, then the whole situation becomes karmic force. However, if you are in contact with that basic bewilderment in its positive quality and if you are in contact with the energy, panic doesn't arise anymore. Panic is not relevant there. The panic comes from ego, from trying to hold on to something, which is ego's game. The whole reason one can transcend both good and bad karma is that panic is not relevant in that situation of fundamental energy. If panic arises, you feel that you have to suppress it, and by then you are already working with dualistic concepts of this and that. From that point of view, karma is a conscious thing. Karma comes from concept. Concept is a very conscious thing. So if there is a state of absence of concepts, you are free of karma.

The basic nonconceptual energy of bewilderment can be the inspiration for spending or making money, engaging in sex, and being able to work. This might be difficult to grasp fully, so I'll go over it again: Bewilderment is energy, or has energy; and the most basic thing about bewilderment is that there's nobody there. Therefore, the volitional action of karma doesn't apply to it.

Fortuitously, people have flashes of this basic bewilderment occasionally. We may catch a glimpse of that basic bewilderment of being nobody—and that should be the key to dealing with work, sex, and money. In that way, the whole way we work with our life is approached in a very sane way, with nobody trying to save anything or anybody, and nobody labeling anything as good or bad. Work, sex, and money are not regarded as good or bad, but are seen in a very awake way, because fundamentally there is nobody there.

To put it more bluntly, egolessness is a kind of momentary flash. There are occasional breaks in our experience of ego. It's from there, those breaks in ego's game, that we can approach work, sex, and money. In that case, work, sex, and money become part of a very natural process.

17

∎ ∎ ∎

PANORAMIC
AWARENESS

There are two kinds of positive thinking. One kind is thinking that the future is going to be all right, which is based on panic and concerned with security. The other one is not living in the future but living in the present. The present situation is open—you could almost say solid—and real, definite, and healthy. There is an appreciation of the richness in the present.

Believing in the present is antipoverty, because it doesn't involve wishful thinking of any kind at all. It is there already and you don't have to wish for anything. It's solid and real, in a sense much more real than "me" and "myself." In the Buddhist tradition, we have a belief in buddha nature, *tathagatagarbha*, which has been described as the most positive thinking of all. Some schools of Buddhist thought would say that tathagatagarbha, or buddha nature, is not some kind of abstract "nature" but rather a living buddha inside you. Sometimes people visualize the buddha within, with a complete body. Certain other schools within Buddhism have said that it is too dangerous to believe in such a real thing's being there, because that approach could also be taken toward ego as being something solid and real inside you. These schools criticized that approach as being eternalism, one of the two extremes, the other being nihilism. In some sense, however, eternalism is more positive than nihilism. However, buddha nature has nothing to do with a solid, egoistic sense of self. Basically, it is the essence of being awake, which is already there. We don't have to think up something positive and make the best of it.

This kind of positive doesn't try to push away the negatives. Even perceiving the negatives is a vision of the positive. That's why we speak of panoramic awareness, which is basic positive thinking. Relating with panoramic awareness could be said to be a way of freeing ourselves from the chain reaction of karma, which is based on hope and fear. As we discussed, karma is a chain reaction that is based on panic or uncertainty, on one hand, or also a chain reaction of goodness in the smaller, one-sided sense of good versus bad. On the other hand, the positivity of panoramic awareness is restful. It opens the situation and brings spaciousness and a meditative state of being. At the very moment that is present, there is no furthering of karmic cause and effect; no karmic seed is planted or developed. When that positiveness is there as we are dealing with situations, we can speak of meditation in action. In that way, meditation in action is just as important as sitting meditation.

Panoramic awareness is the basic trust that the space is there already. The whole point is that we don't have to get it; we have it. When we say, "How do we get it?" that is the voice of poverty. Panoramic awareness *is* buddha nature. It may depend on the intensity of the awareness, how fully it is developed, but in any case it is some state of "awake."

To say that panoramic awareness is free from negativity sounds like there is still some poverty there. However, we are not imprisoned at all. This positive state of being is so fundamental that it doesn't need relative support from anywhere. It's the positive of transcending positive and negative. It is transcendental.

It's not a naive possibility, like saying, "Everything's okay," meaning that things are defensively okay. You tell yourself defensively, "Keep smiling," and you tell yourself "I am happy," and you try to believe that. Instead, panoramic awareness is realizing that everything is healthy, everything is fine, but you don't have to make a big deal out of that. Your awareness provides you with basic understanding that doesn't involve defensively proving anything to yourself. Rather it is believing, having faith in, and seeing the situation *as it is*.

Being in an egoless state sharpens your intelligence because there's nothing in the way. You don't have to manage two things at the same time anymore. There's always just one thing to deal with—that's why it's called nonduality. So your skill in dealing with any situation becomes sharper and more precise. Your sensitivity in dealing with other people is also heightened.

We hear so much about the egoless state, but then when we experience it, we might feel doubt: "There must be something more than this!" It is said that the secret of mind seems too easy to be true. Egolessness doesn't mean thoughtlessness, a state without thoughts. There will be thought patterns anyway. For instance, when you read sutras, there is prose in them that you can follow; they contain thought patterns of the Buddha—how he views things, how he thinks, how he presents a situation. Also, in many cases when questions were asked of the Buddha, he supposedly just smiled and didn't answer; he left the questioners to work out the answers. Even then, a subtle thought pattern is still there. So of course, there can be thought patterns without ego. As we read descriptions of enlightenment, it sounds very dramatic and glorious, but actually when we experience a glimpse of it, it doesn't seem to be as glorious as the descriptions. The descriptions make us expect too much.

Once panoramic awareness is there, it grows. Or rather it is gradually uncovered; the dirt is gradually removed and the awareness shines through. It shines through. You can't really nurse it. Panoramic awareness has to grow by itself. It's like the description of the *garuda* hatching. The garuda chick grows inside the egg, and when the shell breaks, the garuda can fly without further nursing. Once the space is there already, you don't have to do anything with it. Just go along with the action. It is self-fulfillment. That's why the notion of spontaneity comes in here.

If you solidify the space, then that becomes the watcher, the abstract quality of your intelligence. Then there's really no space at all. The watcher is like a chemical that solidifies things. There are various degrees of intelligence, and at a certain stage, the intelligence could become the watcher. That's a limitation we are facing. First there is duality, this and that, and then we begin to be aware of that, which could be said to be a very healthy step toward awakening. But then we begin to identify with that duality so much that there is a danger of making the space into characters with personalities. So what one has to do is sort of undo everything. First of all, depersonalize the awareness of duality, and second, the natural duality should also be dissolved. It's a going-backward process, an undoing process.

Once you begin to relate directly with the basic intelligence, once you have already acknowledged that, then as the situation develops, that basic intelligence becomes stronger and stronger, more real. It grows by itself. It's like when you first begin to awaken from sleep. You open your eyes; then you begin to hear sounds. That process of waking up continues until finally you get out of bed and walk about.

Taking a leap, which we discussed earlier, is the beginning of acknowledging basic intelligence. We struggle with that. You don't want to believe that there is something fundamentally secure that doesn't need to draw security from anything else. When you begin to realize there is such a thing, that could be frightening as well as pleasant. In many cases, we feel that if we acknowledge that, we will lose our occupation, the basic occupation that keeps ego busy. So we have to push ourselves into it.

There is a subtle journey going from the *shunyata* level of recognizing the emptiness of our habitual patterns to the *mahamudra* level, the attainment of vajrayana vision in which one is working directly with the energy of a situation. First of all, you perceive space, and you are in the space but still conscious of it. Then, at a certain stage, you lose even the notion of space. Sometimes you become heavily involved with "that," and you lose track of "this" altogether. That's just fascination taking over, rather than a realization of egolessness. The difference is that in the case of being one with the situation, there is no sense of being off balance, no sense of being on either side of the this-that equation. In that case, there is no need of a scale. In the case of fascination, there is a scale, and the weighting toward the object is heavier, but there are still two sides of the scale. In the case of being one, there's no scale at all. There is no sense of power on one side or the other.

There is also a difference between being awake and being overpowered by your experience. That sense of being overpowered means that there is still a scale with two sides. When you are overpowered by the situation, you are captivated, and there's a sense of stupidity. You may feel very calm, but there's no sense of dignity and no sense of sharpness.

With ego in the picture, it's more a case of overcrowded ground than not having any ground. There are so many things between you and the ground that you can't perceive the ground at all. There's a spiky quality to the ego-oriented experience. First there's irritation and then a larger sense of irritation, and then losing a sense of direction, and then finally, being completely flipped out.

Whenever anything irritates us, it's trying to communicate

with us. Usually we are looking for an answer rather than trying to communicate with irritation. There is sanity operating, but usually we don't try to learn from that at all. We try to do something with that irritation rather than just relate to it. There's no point in trying to ignore irritation completely. It's a matter of experiencing the basics of the irritation. The point is to acknowledge its presence rather than try to suppress it. The approach is not analytical particularly; it's more instinctive.

When we talk about relating with irritation here, we are talking about how to handle it at the beginning. When the first flash of irritation comes, just try to feel the abstract quality of it, the presence of it, and in that way you set a proper balance. Then the irritation doesn't become overpowering, and you don't become overpowering toward the irritation either. The next step is then dealing with the specific nature of the irritation. At this point, you have already set up the right relationship with the irritation, which allows you to handle it in a much easier way, as opposed to a confused way.

When the first flash of irritation occurs, it throws out a cloud of confusion, of bewilderment.* You are so shaken up by it that you do something sudden or panicky and upset the whole possibility of skillfulness and dignity. Then everything becomes very pathetic. Then each subsequent time you try to deal with the irritation, because you handled it wrong at the beginning, the whole situation becomes an ongoing emergency. When you try to deal with that emergency, another emergency pops up on top of the first one. Then the whole situation becomes very spiky or freaky, or whatever you want to call it. If you are able to relate with the irritation properly at the beginning, then it doesn't throw out bewilderment or confusion; rather, irritation presents itself as it is. Then the emergency doesn't arise at all, so

---

* In the last chapter, the author was speaking of bewilderment as a groundless state before ego or karma is solidified. Here he is speaking of it in a more conventional sense of equating bewilderment with confusion.—Eds.

you have time to deal with the situation. There is space, room to move about, slowly.

Generally when irritation pops up, we automatically think that we are obliged to do something with it, without knowing what to do. However, we could work with it in the same way that we work with everything in meditation. That's the whole point about meditation: you can be doing nothing but still remain brilliant. This takes away the fundamental speed connected with the irritation, which is not speed in any real sense anyway. It's like rush hour. We call it rush hour but actually we are not really rushing—just the opposite.

The courage to work with ourselves in this way comes as basic trust in ourselves, as a sort of fundamental optimism. In the beginning, you act like a warrior, and then you actually become brave. It's like the visualizations in tantric practices. When you visualize yourself as a deity, for example, first you have your belief, your version of you, which is called the *samayasattva*. You visualize yourself as the deity; it is your version of you. Then along comes what is called the *jnanasattva*—the body of wisdom, the buddha-nature quality—which arises as another visualization in front of you. That visualization comes to you and is united with your basic notion of yourself. So finally you become Buddha completely; you become the deity completely, and you begin to act like one. That is called vajra pride. That's an important part of visualization. The important part of that pride is to believe that you *are* that—you have three eyes, you have three tongues, and you have flames around you, or whatever it is that you are visualizing. You *are* that, you really are! Visualizations are not just fantasies. They are a part of you, so the pride is believing in that part of you. If you have the potential of growing a beard and you don't shave, then the beard grows. It's part of you.

In the process of visualization, finally you begin to visualize the whole world as a mandala, a sacred space, and every sound as mantra, or sacred utterance. The whole world and everyone in it is included. Such vajra pride, or indestructible pride, does not need any relative reference point. It is inborn belief that doesn't need relative support. In fact, once you begin to check back to your relative reference world, once you begin to doubt, you lose the vajra pride. You might be afraid that you can't survive without relative support, but you survive better if you don't have to question your talent, if you don't have to compare and look for relative support. You just work with what you can do. It's a fundamentally positive thing. Relative support actually diminishes your talent, because you begin to question yourself, you begin to compare yourself, you begin to have doubts. Comparing yourself doesn't help. It diminishes your confidence.

Vajra pride might seem to be a dangerous path that could easily stray into a kind of false enlightenment. The danger of vajra pride's turning into ego pride comes when you start using it to suppress the negative things you feel about yourself, your irritation with yourself. You try to use the logic of vajra pride for that. Then it ceases to be vajra pride anyway. It's impossible to turn 100 percent vajra pride into ordinary pride. But once you try to use it for mundane purposes, it is no longer vajra pride.

At the beginning of the path, ego may seem to be in control of the situation. In fact, the whole spiritual journey may start out as a gigantic ego trip. The ego brings us to the dharma by saying, "Gee, I'd like to get enlightened and do all this stuff I've read about." We have to use that. You just begin where you are. It's quite a simple process. You start with ego's version of enlightenment, and at a certain stage, ego finds that it is threatened by your commitment to the path, and it begins to wear away, to drop out. At that point, we are approaching the cliff we need to leap from, which is suicidal for ego.

There is actually a succession of sudden shocks until you fall off the last cliff. Whenever there is a cliff, ego tries to avoid it, tries to come back to a safer place by using the same logic constantly and by not being willing to take any chances. At a certain point, ego begins to find that its version of enlightenment doesn't match the teachings, the genuine dharma. But it ignores that. It creates it own teaching. Whenever there's a cliff, it says, "No, I'm not going over that cliff. I'm going to survive; so I'll make my own teaching." When a situation feels very uncomfortable, I would say there is *more* reason to approach the cliff then, because there is some gap, some crack that has appeared. When neurosis is coming up more vividly, there is often a gap. So that's a great opportunity.

When you actually make the leap, there is no landmark at all, not even limitlessness. It's completely all or nothing. Or you could say it's either one or everything. You can afford to leap; therefore you don't have to hold on to anything.

At the same time, when we talk about *all,* or unity, that doesn't mean to say that the situation becomes completely depersonalized. There is still *all* of that particular person's point of view, even when we are speaking of the buddhas, the awakened ones. That's why there could be different enlightened realms, which we often refer to as the three *kayas: nirmanakaya, sambhogakaya,* and *dharmakaya.* Even within the ultimate realm of dharmakaya, Samantabhadra, Vajradhara, and many different types of dharmakaya buddhas exist.* They are *all,* therefore they are *one.* They are all; therefore they are individual, personal.

I hope that you will be able to put into effect what we've discussed, in practical ways. No doubt what we've talked about

---

* The three kayas, or the *trikaya,* refer to three fundamental aspects, or bodies, of enlightenment. *Kaya* literally means "body." Dharmakaya is the ultimate realm of wisdom beyond reference points. Sambhogakaya is the realm of compassion and communication. It literally means the realm of enjoyment. Nirmanakaya is the buddha that takes human form, which refers to the historical Buddha but also to the enlightened teachers we may encounter now. In Tibetan vajrayana Buddhism, the dharmakaya is personified in visualizations. Two of the most important dharmakaya buddhas are Samantabhadra and Vajradhara. The point the author seems to be making here is that even in the realm of ultimate truth, there is still an immediate, personal quality to wakefulness or sanity, as personified by these buddhas. In fact, the universal quality gives rise to the personal quality of enlightenment.—Eds.

might clarify your problems, but at the same time, the discussion might confuse us more. That confusion is the starting point. It is what we have to work with in everyday life.

We have been talking extensively about the importance of appreciating and working with our mundane life as a source of sanity and awareness. Often there is a perceived conflict between our ordinary life and sitting meditation. Seeing a conflict between those two comes from the inability to perceive the background of panoramic awareness that is present in our daily situations. There is always an undercurrent of panoramic awareness that acts as guidance. That is the source and inspiration for being skillful in daily life. Relating to that does not mean having to be rigid and careful, or overly watchful. Nevertheless, there should be some acknowledgment that the space of awareness is there. There should be just a fraction of a second of acknowledgment. Through this acknowledgment, a sense of spaciousness spontaneously arises that provides the right perspective, or distance, between action and reaction.

For the beginner, relating to this awareness may require some level of watching oneself or deliberateness. In the long run, however, watching doesn't come into the picture. For instance, if a chaotic situation happens, there is uncertainty about how to deal with that, and that uncertainty flashes back on us. That uncertainty itself becomes space. In other words, each time there is doubt, the doubt itself brings a kind of bewilderment, but that bewilderment becomes space, spaciousness. In that way, a sort of natural, inbuilt understanding of the situation happens. In that sense, there is a shock absorber that is always present.

That kind of awareness is based on a certain amount of trust, or optimism. Basically, nothing is regarded as a failure or as dangerous. Rather, whatever arises is experienced as part of a creative and loving relationship toward oneself. That subtle confidence and optimism automatically bring skillful means, because we realize there is no need to be panicked. We have a warrior's attitude toward life, which could also be described as faith or belief in our life, or possibly as devotion to our experience and our world. Whatever happens, we always have a fundamental positive quality about our experience of life. Such faith could be said to be the source of an almost magical performance. If a person relies on that confidence, it is almost as though she is going to perform a miracle, and she is taking quite a chance that the miracle might not happen. However, because she has confidence, she almost knows it will happen, and she does what she has to do, and the miracle does happen. That kind of fundamental positive approach runs right through all situations in dealing with life. It also becomes a meditative experience, because it is a purely optimistic attitude without watcher, without ego, without centralizing in the self or being careful. This whole positive flow can only happen if there is no centralized security. Instead, there is basic faith and belief in one's wholesomeness, in one's fundamental healthy situation.

Editor's Afterword

This book is primarily based on three seminars, each of which was entitled "Work, Sex, and Money." The first seminar was conducted at the East West Center in Boston in September 1970, less than six months after Chögyam Trungpa arrived in the United States. Rinpoche gave one talk on work, one on sex, and the third on money.* The second seminar took place in the summer of 1971 at Tail of the Tiger, a rural residential meditation center in Barnet, Vermont, that today is called Karmê-Chöling. The seminar was a series of nine "events," which consisted of lively discussions between speaker and audience, punctuated by Rinpoche's remarks or short talks, some of which came at the end of several hours of questions and answers. The first few talks of this seminar were an introduction to the view of the importance of meditation in action in general, how karma operates and can be ultimately transcended, and the problems of materialism—physical, psychological, and spiritual—and how they affect our everyday experiences. Then Rinpoche conducted several discussions on each of the three themes of work, sex, and money. The entire seminar lasted ten days.

The third three-talk seminar, given in April 1972 in Burlington, Vermont, takes a slightly different approach to the material.

* There may also have been an introductory talk that was not recorded.

The first talk describes the mechanisms of physical, psychological, and spiritual materialism and how these affect the normal course of work, sex, and money. The second talk looks at how the practice of sitting meditation and joining that with meditation in action can help us to begin to dismantle ego's games. Finally, in the last talk, Rinpoche looks at how work, sex, and money are often an expression of klesha activity, or confused emotions, and how that approach can be overcome.

The editing of this material was quite challenging, especially in regard to the second long seminar, which was so dominated by free-flowing discussion and a question-and-answer format. Sherab Chödzin Kohn completed the first stage of the work, the monumental task of editing the original transcripts. If one has not grappled with this kind of editorial work, there may be a tendency to underestimate the editorial expertise needed to create a group of transcripts that have readability and coherence while maintaining the original voice and language of the speaker. Sherab is a master of this craft, and he produced edited transcripts that capture the "wild and woolly" character of this period of Trungpa Rinpoche's teachings.

It then fell to me to organize and, to some extent, manicure this material further, shaping it into the structure it now has. In this final form, there are no longer questions and answers, but much of the material from the discussions has been incorporated into the narrative structure of the book. In the section of the book on money, I also added material from two later talks that Chögyam Trungpa gave to Buddhist businesspeople in Boulder, Colorado, in 1979 and 1981.

The editorial perspective I adopted was to look at what Rinpoche was saying from the view of universal wisdom, separated somewhat from its original cultural milieu. Put more bluntly, there were a lot of hippies and counterculture people in the audience in the early seventies. Rinpoche spoke absolutely directly to them. There was no sense of distance between him and them, but at the same time, he always addressed the larger view, speaking from the perspective of universal dharma and its applicability to any situation.

Sometimes, I had to divorce the questions asked from my reading of Trungpa Rinpoche's answers in order to see how to edit the material. His answers were always taking the large view, although he also spoke directly, responding intimately to the most personal queries. He had a gift for addressing minutiae and the cosmos at the same time. I don't know how he did it, but you can see the results here, which to my mind are up-to-date and very helpful in dealing with current realities.

In the early seventies in America, Rinpoche taught many visionary seminars in which he laid out fundamental principles about how mind, energy, and reality work altogether and how this leads to both the normal confused pattern of our lives and the possibility of uncovering brilliant sanity in the midst of this confusion. In that light, this book gives us a comprehensive and profound approach to the view, practice, and action of meditation in action. I believe that the view Trungpa Rinpoche articulates in *Work, Sex, Money* is also, in many respects, the underpinning of the Shambhala teachings he emphasized from 1976 until his death in 1987. The approach presented in this book to work, sex, and money can be seen as the necessary foundation, within one's personal discipline, for creating an enlightened society, a theme he came back to over and over again in the eighties.

Sherab Chödzin Kohn and I were serial editors on this project, meaning that we didn't collaborate extensively, although we did consult. Sherab accomplished the beginning beautifully, and I then took the book over the finish line. It was a bit like working together in a relay race. For both of us, the more we worked with this material, the more we fell in love with it. We hope that it will speak to you, the reader, as well. May you have success on the path, and may you meet with Buddha himself, in the form of the marvelous opportunities for wakefulness afforded to you by experiences of work, sex, and money in this life.

Editor's Acknowledgments

Extensive transcription of the original talks and correction of unedited transcripts were necessary in order to undertake this book. In addition to the considerable work that Sherab Chödzin Kohn did himself, several other transcribers were involved. Thanks especially to Barbara Blouin, who has a long association with the transcription and editing of Chögyam Trungpa's work.

The Shambhala Archives has recently completed the remastering and digitization of more than three thousand lectures and other recordings of Chögyam Trungpa's teaching in the West. Its continued work to preserve and make available this large corpus of material is greatly appreciated. Special thanks to the staff of the archives, Gordon Kidd, Chris Levy, and Sandra Kipis, for their work altogether and for providing us with excellent MP3 recordings to refer to throughout the editorial process.

Sara Bercholz was the editor for this project at Shambhala Publications. I appreciated her enthusiasm and her editorial input, which was to the point and forced me to grapple more than once with the complexities of the material in ways that I hope are a benefit to readers. Peter Turner held a view of this project that inspired all of us, and he negotiated the various twists and turns of the editorial process with sensitivity and aplomb. It was a pleasure working with both of them. Thanks, too, to Jonathan Green for assistance with contracts and letters of agreement. Thanks also to the copy editor, DeAnna Satre; the designer, Lora Zorian; and the assistant editor, Ben Gleason.

Without the students who gathered around Chögyam Trungpa in the seventies and inspired him to teach in wacky and wonderful ways, we would not have this precious collection of dharma teachings. So thanks to those pioneering practitioners, many of whom are now senior teachers and practitioners in Shambhala International, the association of centers created by Trungpa Rinpoche and now led by Sakyong Mipham Rinpoche, and other Buddhist communities around the world.

Thanks to Diana J. Mukpo, Sakyong Mipham Rinpoche, and all the members of the Mukpo family for their continued support of the publication of the work of Chögyam Trungpa.

And finally, deepest thanks to the author himself for sharing this profound, brilliant, and practical dharma with us, pointing out how each moment of life is infused with wisdom and panoramic awareness.

CAROLYN GIMIAN
May 2010

Glossary

The definitions given here are based on how the terms are used in the text and do not attempt to be comprehensive. Terms already clarified in footnotes are not, in general, included in the glossary, unless additional information may be especially helpful to the reader.

AMITABHA (Skt.). An important mahayana and tantric deity connected with the Pure Land schools of Buddhism. Amitabha is the buddha of compassion and is the ruler of the western paradise, Sukhavati. Many Buddhist funeral rites, especially those of the tantric Buddhist schools, include a chant asking Amitabha Buddha to guide the consciousness of the deceased to the pure land of Sukhavati, thus releasing him or her from the round of suffering.

AVALOKITESHVARA (Skt.). The great bodhisattva of compassion; he is an emanation of the buddha Amitabha. His limitless compassion is said to help all beings who turn to him in difficult times. His Holiness the Dalai Lama and His Holiness the Karmapa are each considered to be an emanation of Avalokiteshvara. The mantra of Avalokiteshvara, OM MANI PADME HUM, is among the best known of all Buddhist mantras.

BHUMI (Skt., literally "land"). One of the ten stages, or spiritual levels, that a bodhisattva must go through to attain buddha-hood. The ten bhumis are progressive stages in the development of the bodhisattva's wisdom and compassion. They are called: (1) very joyful, (2) stainless, (3) luminous, (4) radiant, (5) difficult to conquer, (6) face-to-face, (7) far-going, (8) immovable, (9) having good intellect, and (10) cloud of dharma.

BINDU (Skt., literally "drop," "dot," or "point"). In yogic practice, which focuses on an inner or esoteric path of unifying mind and body, bindu may often refer to semen in men and to the sexual essence or essence of life in human beings generally. In the practice of sexual yoga, the idea of not wasting bindu has to do with refraining from ejaculation during sexual intercourse. Bindu is more broadly associated with mind or consciousness. In *Journey without Goal* (Shambhala Publications, 2000), Chögyam Trungpa says: "So consciousness or bindu is journeying through the energies of the world. Consciousness is the awake quality that doesn't have to refer to immediate reference points alone, but has greater scope, like a radar system. . . . The radar system is called bindu" (*Journey without Goal,* p. 128).

BODHISATTVA (Skt., literally an "awake being"). A bodhisattva is an individual who, by taking the bodhisattva vow, is committed to helping others and who gives up personal satisfaction for the goal of relieving the suffering of others. In the Buddhist teachings, a bodhisattva is more specifically one who has committed to practicing the six paramitas, or the transcendent virtues, of generosity, discipline, patience, exertion, meditation, and knowledge. The bodhisattva's development of wisdom and compassion is an ongoing journey, and it is an example of how to work with daily life with awareness and compassion, or concern for others' welfare.

BUDDHADHARMA (Skt.). The teaching of the Buddha, or the truth taught by the Buddha. See also *dharma.*

BUDDHA NATURE. The enlightened basic nature of all beings. Buddha literally means "awake" or "the awakened one," so buddha nature is related to complete wakefulness. Basic goodness, which Chögyam Trungpa discusses extensively in the Shambhala teachings, is similar to the concept of buddha nature. See also *tathagatagarbha*.

CHANDALI (Skt.). See *tummo*.

DAKINI (Skt.; Tib., khandroma). A wrathful or semiwrathful female deity signifying compassion, emptiness, and transcendental knowledge. The dakini is the embodiment of the feminine principle. The dakinis are tricky and playful, representing the basic space of fertility out of which the interplay of samsara and nirvana arises. More generally, a dakini can be a type of messenger or protector. In vajrayana practices, sometimes a dakini may be visualized alone, as the central figure of the visualization. Sometimes the dakini is visualized in union with a male deity, or heruka. See also *heruka*.

DHARMA (Skt., literally "truth," "norm," "phenomenon," or "law"). Often used to refer to the teachings of the Buddha, which are also called the buddhadharma. May also refer to the basic manifestation of reality or to the elements of phenomenal existence.

DHYANA (Skt., literally "meditation"). See *dhyana, four states of.*

DHYANA, FOUR STATES OF. Dhyana is a Sanskrit term that means meditation. In Pali the term is jhana; in Chinese it is ch'an; and in Japanese, it is zen. Dhyana Buddhism is a term that may be applied to any Buddhist school that stresses the importance of the practice of meditation. The four dhyana states refer to four stages of absorption within the realm of form, or the rupakaya. The attainment of these dhyana states is connected with attainment of special powers and with the lessening or elimination of confusion and obstacles. However, the dhyana states are still relative experiences that take place within samsara, or the confused realm of existence, although on a refined level.

FEMININE AND MASCULINE PRINCIPLES. In Buddhism, the feminine and masculine principles have nothing to do with gender differences. They are a way of looking at how reality is experienced in terms of space and what is contained in the space. The feminine principle is the container, the atmosphere, or the environment; the masculine is what arises or manifests in that vast space. The feminine is described as unborn, unceasing, with a nature like sky, and is equated with wisdom; while the masculine is connected with skillful action, including the bodhisattva activity of compassion. In the higher tantras, it may also be associated with mahasukha, or great bliss. Chögyam Trungpa gave many teachings on the feminine and masculine principles. See the footnote on page 206 in chapter 8 for further information. See also *dakini* and *heruka*.

GARUDA. A mythical bird that is half-man and half-beast, which is associated with tremendous speed and power. Like the phoenix, it is said to arise from the ashes of destruction; thus it has an indestructible quality.

GURU RINPOCHE. "Precious Teacher," the name by which Padmasambhava, a great teacher who helped to bring Buddhism to Tibet, is often referred by the Tibetan people. See also *Padmasambhava*.

HERUKA (Tib.; Skt., daka). A wrathful male deity in vajrayana Buddhism. The heruka is considered to be the embodiment of the masculine principle and in vajrayana visualization practices may be visualized alone or in union with a dakini, or female deity, representing the feminine principle. See also *dakini*.

HINAYANA (Skt., literally "small way"). The narrow way or path. The first of the three yanas of Tibetan Buddhism, the hinayana focuses on meditation practice and discipline, individual liberation and not causing harm to others. The hinayana is made up of the shravakayana (the path of those who hear the dharma) and the pratyekabuddhayana (the path of those who are individual or solitary sages).

JNANASATTVA. See *samayasattva and jnanasattva.*

KAGYÜ. Tibetan for hearing (ear-whispered), or command, lineage. *Ka* refers to the oral instructions of the teacher. The Kagyü is one of the four primary lineages of Tibetan Buddhism. The Kagyü teachings were brought from India to Tibet by Marpa the Translator in the eleventh century. He was a primary student of Naropa, a great Indian scholar and realized holder of the Kagyü teachings. The six yogas of Naropa are fruitional yogic meditation practices that are practiced in the Kagyü school. Chögyam Trungpa was a major teacher in the Kagyü school of Tibetan Buddhism.

KLESHA (Skt., literally "trouble," "defilement," "passion"). *Klesha* refers to the confused expression of emotion. There are three primary kleshas, which are often referred to as the three poisons. These are passion, aggression, and delusion or ignorance. There are many other kleshas, such as arrogance and envy. Emotions can be experienced and expressed in a clarified, direct way, which can be the expression of wisdom rather than confusion. However, this is considered to be a rather advanced approach, based on practice and letting go of ego-clinging.

KUSULU. See *pandita versus kusulu.*

MAHAMUDRA (Skt., literally "great symbol" or "seal"). The central meditative transmission of the Kagyü lineage. The inherent clarity and wakefulness of mind, which is both vivid and empty.

MAHASIDDHA (Skt.). A greatly accomplished practitioner and wise teacher in the vajrayana tradition who has accomplished siddhi, or great power. Often used in reference to teachers who are unconventional, nonmonastic masters of meditative realization.

MAHASUKHA (Skt., literally "great bliss" or "joy"). A fruitional experience in the practice of vajrayana yogic disciplines. Chögyam Trungpa explains this as "not so much that somebody is tickling you or that you are in a state of ecstasy from the effect of some chemical. . . . Here, joy and togetherness and wholesomeness has to do with something that is naturally there, completely there, a sense of arrogance and pride without neurosis, a natural state of being, which is so" (*Glimpses of Space* [Halifax: Vajradhatu Publications, 1999], p. 83).

MAHAYANA (Skt., literally "great vehicle"). The second of the three yanas of Buddhism, the mahayana is also called the "open path" or the "path of the bodhisattva." Mahayana presents vision based on shunyata (emptiness), compassion, and the acknowledgment of universal buddha nature. The mahayana path begins when one discovers this buddha nature in oneself and vows to develop or uncover it in order to benefit others. The ideal figure of the mahayana is the bodhisattva who is fully awake and who works for the benefit of all beings.

MARPA (1012–1097 CE). The chief disciple of the Indian teacher Naropa, Marpa of Lhotrak brought the Kagyü teachings from India to Tibet in the eleventh century. He is often called "Marpa the Translator." A farmer with a large family, he was known not only for his meditative realization of mahamudra but for his attainment of spiritual realization within a secular lifestyle.

MILAREPA (1040–1123 CE). A great Tibetan Buddhist practitioner in the eleventh century. He was the chief disciple of Marpa. When Milarepa first went to study with Marpa, he was subjected to many trials. Marpa asked him to build a number of houses, and then had him tear them all down—except for the last one he built. Milarepa had to support himself while he was studying with Marpa, which was difficult because he came from a very poor background. After he finally was accepted by Marpa and received the highest teachings from him, he went into retreat in various caves around Tibet for many years. He attracted many disciples and became highly renowned. He belongs to the Kagyü lineage but is greatly revered by all schools of Tibetan Buddhism. His songs of meditative realization continue to be studied, providing inspiration and practice instruction up to the present day.

NAROPA (1016–1100 CE). A great Indian siddha, or tantric master, second of the enlightened lineage of teachers of the Kagyü lineage of Tibetan Buddhism. Naropa was a greatly accomplished scholar at Nalanda University; he left Nalanda to search for his teacher when he realized that he understood the literal meaning of the teachings, but not their true sense. He underwent many trials before he attained enlightenment. Later, he was the teacher of Marpa, who traveled to India three times to study with Naropa and receive teachings from him. Chögyam Trungpa gave a number of seminars on Naropa's life and teachings, several of which are published as *Illusion's Game* (Shambhala Publications, 1994).

NIDANA (Skt.; cause or source). One of the twelve "links" that form the chain of conditioned arising or the links that make up samsara, the everyday confused world of suffering. The twelve nidanas are depicted in the wheel of life, which shows the functioning of samara. The nidanas form the outer ring of the wheel. The innermost ring is composed of the three primary kleshas: passion, aggression, and ignorance. Around that, the six realms of conditioned existence revolve: the realms of gods, jealous gods, humans, animals, hungry ghosts, and hell beings. Beyond that are the twelve nidanas, which are: (1) ignorance, (2) formations or impulses, (3) consciousness, (4) name and form, (5) the six realms of the senses, (6) contact, (7) sensation, (8) craving, (9) clinging, (10) becoming, (11) birth, and (12) old age and death.

NIRVANA (Skt.). See *samsara and nirvana*.

PADMASAMBHAVA. One of the eight aspects of Guru Rinpoche, a great teacher who helped to bring Buddhism to Tibet from

India in the eighth century. He is considered the father of Buddhism in Tibet and is revered by all Tibetan Buddhists. He hid many teachings, which are called terma, in various places in Tibet, to be discovered for the use of future practitioners. See also *Guru Rinpoche*.

PANDITA VERSUS KUSULU. Pandita is a Sanskrit word that simply means "scholar." It is the source of the word "pundit" in English. The pandita tradition in Indian and Tibetan Buddhism emphasizes the importance of scholarly work, reading and studying texts as the basis for one's understanding. The kusulu tradition emphasizes meditation practice without a great deal of scholarly analysis involved. However, this dichotomy is somewhat deceiving, as the union of practice and study is necessary for realization. Some texts in the tradition of mahamudra meditation stress that the practice of direct valid cognition, or direct perception and understanding without confusion, is divided into two styles of practice. One is called the analytical meditation of a pandita, and the other is called the meditation of a kusulu or yogi. Here, pandita style means the use of examination or analysis. This is the analytical direct observation of a pandita in which you are observing specific characteristics or things. The other aspect, the meditation of a kusulu or yogi, is very simple and direct, without the usage of directed or analytically oriented observation.

PARAMITA (Skt., literally "gone to the other shore"). The paramitas are the transcendent actions or virtues practiced by a bodhisattva. The six paramitas are generosity, discipline, patience, exertion, meditation, and knowledge (prajna). The paramitas differ from ordinary activities or virtues in that they are all based on realization free from ego-clinging. The author contrasts them in this book with the confused activity of the nidanas, which further embroil us in samsara, or the painful confusion of everyday existence.

PRAJNA (Skt.). "Transcendent knowledge" or "perfect knowledge," it is the sixth paramita. It is called "transcendent" because it sees through the veils of dualistic confusion. Prajna is like the eyes and the other five paramitas are like the limbs of bodhisattva activity. Prajna can also mean wisdom, understanding, or discrimination. At its most developed level it means seeing things as they are from a nondualistic point of view.

SAMAYASATTVA. See *samayasattva and jnanasattva.*

SAMAYASATTVA AND JNANASATTVA. The samayasattva and the jnanasattva are two basic principles or aspects of visualization practice in the vajrayana. Samaya literally means "vow" or "bondage." Sattva means "being" or "body." The samayasattva is the practitioner's visualization of a deity, and it expresses his or her connection with the teacher and the teachings. Jnanasattva means "wisdom being" or "wisdom body," and it represents the wisdom and sanity of the lineage and the teachings descending or entering into your visualization and blessing it, or giving it a sense of power and wisdom. This is all without a nontheistic context. That is to say, although the practitioner visualizes the jnanasattva in front of him- or herself and then descending or joining in union with the samayasattva, nevertheless, the practitioner understands that there is no actual independent entity. In fact, the union of the samayasattva and the jnanasattva represents the fundamental unity of experience, beyond this and that.

SAMSARA (Skt.). See *samsara and nirvana.*

SAMSARA AND NIRVANA. Samsara is the vicious cycle of confused existence; the world of struggle and suffering that is based on ego-clinging, conflicting emotions, and habitual patterns. Its root cause is ignorance of our true nature, which is openness beyond the duality of self and other. Samsara is contrasted with nirvana, the state of enlightenment characterized by the cessation of ignorance and of the suffering of conditioned existence. The highest tantric teachings speak of the union of samsara and nirvana or their indivisibility.

SANGHA (Skt.). The community of Buddhist practitioners. The sangha includes both the monastic sangha, the community of monks and nuns, as well as the lay sangha. The sangha is one of the Three Jewels, or the three aspects of Buddhist practice that should be respected and revered. The other two are the Buddha, or the teacher; and the dharma, or the teachings of Buddhism themselves.

SHIKANTAZA. A Japanese term, used mainly in the Soto school of Zen, which may refer to a state of meditative realization or to the practice of meditation that leads to that experience. Chögyam Trungpa described shikantaza as the union of calm and insight, two fundamental aspects of the sitting practice of meditation. He had great respect for the Zen tradition and also for shikantaza meditation.

SHILA (Skt.; discipline). Shila is one of the six paramitas or transcendent actions of a bodhisattva. It also is used to refer more generally to the practitioner's discipline and conduct. Chögyam Trungpa frequently talks about shila in terms of particular aspects of conduct, such as telling the truth, and being generous to others. See also *paramita*.

SHUNYATA (Skt., literally "emptiness"). A completely open and unbounded clarity of mind characterized by groundlessness and freedom from all conceptual frameworks. It could be called "openness" since "emptiness" can convey the mistaken notion of a state of voidness or blankness. In fact, shunyata is inseparable from compassion and all other awakened qualities. Attaining some understanding and experience of shunyata on the mahayana path involves a realization of the ultimate truth. The vajrayana is then a natural development, returning to the relative truth in its powerful and brilliant form, leading to the realization of mahamudra.

SIX YOGAS OF NAROPA. See the footnote on page 114 in chapter 9. See also *tummo*.

TANTRA. A synonym for vajrayana, one of the three great vehicles, or stages on the path, of Tibetan Buddhism. Tantra literally means continuity. It may refer to vajrayana texts as well as to the systems of meditation they describe.

TATHAGATAGARBHA (Skt.). Tathagata is an epithet of the Buddha, which means "he who has gone beyond." Garbha means "womb" or "essence." Tathagatagarbha is Sanskrit for buddha nature, the enlightened basic nature of all beings, which is a central theme of many of the mahayana schools of Buddhism. See also *buddha nature*.

THREE POISONS. See *klesha*.

TIBETAN BOOK OF THE DEAD, THE (Tib., *Bardo Thödol*, "Book of Liberation in the Bardo through Hearing"). A famous Tibetan tantric text on working with death and dying and the after-death state. Chögyam Trunga worked on a translation of *The Tibetan Book of the Dead* that makes these teachings much more available to Western readers, through the explanation of their psychological significance. The origin of these teachings can be traced to Padmasambhava and his consort, Yeshe Tsogyal. It was later discovered as a terma or treasure text by Karma Lingpa, in the fourteenth century. Intensively studied in Tibet, both academically and during retreat practice, the text is often read aloud to dying persons to help them attain realization within the bardo, the state after death. The lineage that Chögyam Trungpa belonged to, the Trungpa lineage, as well as the lineage of the Surmang Kagyu, associated with his monastery in Tibet, had a strong connection with these teachings.

TILOPA (988–1069 CE). A renowned teacher of vajrayana Buddhism in India in the eleventh century. His most famous disciple was Naropa, who through his student Marpa introduced Tilopa's teachings into Tibet.

TRIKAYA (Skt., the three kayas or bodies of enlightenment). See the footnote on page 216 in chapter 17.

TUMMO (Tib.; Skt., chandali; fierce, wrathful). A term in vajrayana Buddhism for psychic heat generated and experienced through inner disciplines of meditation that focus on synchronizing body and mind. This inner heat burns up obstacles and confusion. See also the footnote on page 114 in chapter 9.

VAJRA (Skt.; Tib., dorje, literally "adamantine" or having the qualities of a diamond). In the vajrayana, vajra refers to the basic indestructible nature of wisdom and enlightenment. A vajra is also a tantric ritual scepter representing a thunderbolt, the scepter of the king of the gods, Indra.

VAJRAYANA (Skt., literally "the diamond way" or the "indestructible vehicle"). Vajrayana is the third of the three great yanas, or stages on the path, of Tibetan Buddhism. It is synonymous with tantra.

Sources

The following list provides the primary source (or sources) for each chapter of the book. In many cases, material from the questions and answers in one talk was used in several chapters. These secondary sources are not specified for each chapter. I have abbreviated the three main seminars as WSM (Work, Sex, Money) 1970, WSM 1971, and WSM 1972. Material from WSM 1971, talk 6, and WSM 1972, talk 3, was incorporated into other chapters, but neither was the main source of a chapter.

Chapter 1, "The Sacred Society": WSM 1971, talk 1
Chapter 2, "Meditation and Daily Life": WSM 1972, talk 2
Chapter 3, "The Myth of Happiness": WSM 1972, talk 1
Chapter 4, "Simplicity and Awareness": WSM 1970, talk 2
Chapter 5, "Overcoming Obstacles to Work": WSM 1971, talk 5
Chapter 6, "The Nowness of Work": WSM 1971, talk 3
Chapter 7, "Creativity and Chaos": WSM 1971, talk 4
Chapter 8, "Communication": WSM 1971, talk 8
Chapter 9, "The Flame of Love": WSM 1970, talk 1
Chapter 10, "Pure Passion": WSM 1970, talk 1
Chapter 11, "Family Karma": WSM 1971, talks 7 and 2
Chapter 12, "The Question of Money": WSM 1970, talk 3
Chapter 13, "The Karma of Money": WSM 1971, talk 7

Chapter 14, "Business Ethics": talk to the Ratna Society, a group
of Buddhist businesspeople, July 22, 1979

Chapter 15, "Regarding Money as Mother's Milk": talk to the
Ratna Society, June 19, 1981

Chapter 16, "Karma": WSM 1971, talk 2

Chapter 17, "Panoramic Awareness": WSM 1971, talk 9

Further Readings and Resources

Further Reading

The first book by Chögyam Trungpa published in North America was *Meditation in Action* (Shambhala Publications, 1969). It remains a classic on meditation and the conduct of everyday life based on the bodhisattva ideal of helping others and placing their needs above one's own.

Chögyam Trungpa's teaching on the Shambhala path of warriorship looks at how to bring sanity, celebration, and kindness into one's life and how to help build an enlightened society based on the principles of gentleness and fearlessness. These teachings, as they apply to overcoming fear and hesitation in our lives, are available in the recently published *Smile at Fear: Awakening the True Heart of Bravery* (Shambhala Publications, 2009). Other volumes include *Shambhala: The Sacred Path of the Warrior* (Shambhala Publications, 1984) and *Great Eastern Sun: The Wisdom of Shambhala* (Shambhala Publications, 1999). In addition, *Shambhala: The Sacred Path of the Warrior Book and Card Set* (Shambhala Publications, 2004) provides a small handbook and a group of slogan cards that can be used to contemplate these teachings on working with oneself and others.

Ocean of Dharma: The Everyday Wisdom of Chögyam Trungpa (Shambhala Publications, 2008) presents 365 short, inspirational quotations from the work of Chögyam Trungpa. Additional discussion of the practice of meditation and an in-depth treatment of mindfulness and awareness (shamatha and vipashyana) meditation is provided by Chögyam Trungpa in *The Path Is the Goal: A Basic Handbook of Buddhist Meditation* (Shambhala Publications, 1995). Cultivating loving-kindness and compassion toward all beings is at the root of Chögyam Trungpa's approach to working with others. *Training the Mind and Cultivating Loving-Kindness* (Shambhala Publications, 1993) presents fifty-nine slogans, or aphorisms related to meditation practice, that show a practical path to making friends with oneself and developing compassion for others.

The Sanity We Are Born With: A Buddhist Approach to Psychology* (Shambhala Publications, 2005) is an excellent overview of Chögyam Trungpa's writings on the Buddhist view of mind, the practice of meditation, and the application of the Buddhist teachings to psychology and solving psychological and human problems of self-doubt, depression, and neurosis. For readers interested in an overview of the Buddhist path, the following volumes are recommended: *Cutting Through Spiritual Materialism* (Shambhala Publications, 1973), *The Myth of Freedom and the Way of Meditation* (Shambhala Publications, 1976), and *The Essential Chögyam Trungpa* (Shambhala Publications, 2000).

Chögyam Trungpa's teachings on applying a meditative approach to art and being artful in everyday life are presented in *True Perception: The Path of Dharma Art* (Shambhala Publications, 2008).

Resources

Ocean of Dharma Quotes of the Week brings you the teachings of Chögyam Trungpa Rinpoche. An e-mail is sent out several times each week containing a quote selected by Carolyn Rose Gimian from Chögyam Trungpa's extensive teachings. Quotations of material may be from unpublished material, forthcoming publications, or previously published sources. To enroll go to Oceanof Dharma.com.

For information regarding meditation instruction, please visit the Web site of Shambhala International at www.shamb hala.org. This Web site contains information about the more than one hundred centers affiliated with Shambhala.

The Chögyam Trungpa Legacy Project was established to help preserve, disseminate, and expand Chögyam Trungpa's legacy. The Legacy Project supports the preservation, propagation, and publication of Trungpa Rinpoche's dharma teachings. This includes plans for the creation of a comprehensive virtual archive and learning community. For information, go to Chog yamTrungpa.com.

For publications from Vajradhatu Publications and Kalapa Recordings, including both books and audiovisual materials, go to www.shambhalamedia.org.

For information about the archive of the author's work, please contact the Shambhala Archives: archives@shambhala.org.

A Biography of Chögyam Trungpa

The Venerable Chögyam Trungpa Rinpoche was born in the province of Kham in eastern Tibet in 1940. When he was just thirteen months old, Chögyam Trungpa was recognized as a major tulku, or incarnate teacher. According to Tibetan tradition, an enlightened teacher is capable, based on his or her vow of compassion, of reincarnating in human form over a succession of generations. Before dying, such a teacher may leave a letter or other clues to the whereabouts of the next incarnation. Later, students and other realized teachers look through these clues and, based on those plus a careful examination of dreams and visions, conduct searches to discover and recognize the successor. Thus, particular lines of teaching are formed, in some cases extending over many centuries. Chögyam Trungpa was the eleventh in the teaching lineage known as the Trungpa Tulkus.

Once young tulkus are recognized, they enter a period of intensive training in the theory and practice of the Buddhist teachings. Trungpa Rinpoche, after being enthroned as supreme abbot of Surmang Dütsi Tel Monastery and governor of Surmang District, began a period of training that would last eighteen years, until his departure from Tibet in 1959. As a Kagyü tulku, his training was based on the systematic practice of meditation and on refined theoretical understanding of Buddhist philosophy. One of the four great lineages of Tibet, the Kagyü is known as the practicing (or practice) lineage.

At the age of eight, Trungpa Rinpoche received ordination as a novice monk. Following this, he engaged in intensive study and practice of the traditional monastic disciplines, including traditional Tibetan poetry and monastic dance. His primary teachers were Jamgön Kongtrül of Sechen and Khenpo Gangshar—leading teachers in the Nyingma and Kagyü lineages. In 1958, at the age of eighteen, Trungpa Rinpoche completed his studies, receiving the degrees of kyorpön (doctor of divinity) and khenpo (master of studies). He also received full monastic ordination.

The late fifties were a time of great upheaval in Tibet. As it became clear that the Chinese communists intended to take over the country by force, many people, both monastic and lay, fled the country. Trungpa Rinpoche spent many harrowing months trekking over the Himalayas (described later in his book *Born in Tibet*). After narrowly escaping capture by the Chinese, he at last reached India in 1959. While in India, Trungpa Rinpoche was appointed to serve as spiritual advisor to the Young Lamas Home School in Delhi, India. He served in this capacity from 1959 to 1963.

Trungpa Rinpoche's opportunity to emigrate to the West came when he received a Spaulding sponsorship to attend Oxford University. At Oxford he studied comparative religion, philosophy, history, and fine arts. He also studied Japanese flower arranging, receiving a degree from the Sogetsu School. While in England, Trungpa Rinpoche began to instruct Western students in the dharma, and in 1967 he founded the Samye Ling Meditation Center in Dumfriesshire, Scotland. During this period, he also published his first two books, both in English: *Born in Tibet* (1966) and *Meditation in Action* (1969).

In 1968 Trungpa Rinpoche traveled to Bhutan, where he entered into a solitary meditation retreat. While on retreat, Rinpoche received a pivotal terma text for all of his teaching in the West, "The Sadhana of Mahamudra," a text that documents the spiritual degeneration of modern times and its antidote, genuine spirituality that leads to the experience of naked and luminous mind. This retreat marked a pivotal change in his approach to teaching. Soon after returning to England, he became a layperson, putting aside his monastic robes and dressing in ordinary Western attire. In 1970 he married a young Englishwoman, Diana Pybus, and together they left Scotland and moved to North America. Many of his early students and his Tibetan colleagues found these changes shocking and upsetting. However, he expressed a conviction that in order for the dharma to take root in the West, it needed to be taught free from cultural trappings and religious fascination.

During the seventies, America was in a period of political and cultural ferment. It was a time of fascination with the East. Nevertheless, almost from the moment he arrived in America, Trungpa Rinpoche drew many students to him who were seriously interested in the Buddhist teachings and the practice of meditation. However, he severely criticized the materialistic approach to spirituality that was also quite prevalent, describing it as a "spiritual supermarket." In his lectures, and in his books *Cutting Through Spiritual Materialism* (1973) and *The Myth of Freedom* (1976), he pointed to the simplicity and directness of the practice of sitting meditation as the way to cut through such distortions of the spiritual journey.

During his seventeen years of teaching in North America, Trungpa Rinpoche developed a reputation as a dynamic and controversial teacher. He was a pioneer, one of the first Tibetan Buddhist teachers in North America, preceding by some years and indeed facilitating the later visits by His Holiness the Karmapa, His Holiness Khyentse Rinpoche, His Holiness the Dalai Lama, and many others. In the United States, he found a spiritual kinship with many Zen masters who were already teaching Buddhist meditation. In the very early days, he particularly connected with Suzuki Roshi, the founder of Zen Center in San

Francisco. In later years he was close with Kobun Chino Roshi and Bill Kwong Roshi in Northern California; with Maezumi Roshi, the founder of the Los Angeles Zen Center; and with Eido Roshi, abbot of the New York Zendo Shobo-ji.

Fluent in the English language, Chögyam Trungpa was one of the first Tibetan Buddhist teachers who could speak to Western students directly, without the aid of a translator. Traveling extensively throughout North America and Europe, he gave thousands of talks and hundred of seminars. He established major centers in Vermont, Colorado, and Nova Scotia, as well as many smaller meditation and study centers in cities throughout North America and Europe. Vajradhatu was formed in 1973 as the central administrative body of this network.

In 1974 Trungpa Rinpoche founded the Naropa Institute (now Naropa University), which became the first and only accredited Buddhist-inspired university in North America. He lectured extensively at the institute, and his book *Journey without Goal* (1981) is based on a course he taught there. In 1976 he established the Shambhala Training program, a series of seminars that present a nonsectarian path of spiritual warriorship grounded in the practice of sitting meditation. His book *Shambhala: The Sacred Path of the Warrior* (1984) gives an overview of the Shambhala teachings.

In 1976 Trungpa Rinpoche appointed Ösel Tendzin (Thomas F. Rich) as his Vajra Regent, or dharma heir. Ösel Tendzin worked closely with Trungpa Rinpoche in the administration of Vajradhatu and Shambhala Training. He taught extensively from 1976 until his death in 1990 and is the author of *Buddha in the Palm of Your Hand*.

Trungpa Rinpoche was also active in the field of translation. Working with Francesca Fremantle, he rendered a new translation of *The Tibetan Book of the Dead*, which was published in 1975. Later he formed the Nalanda Translation Committee in order to translate texts and liturgies for his own students as well as to make important texts available publicly.

In 1979 Trungpa Rinpoche conducted a ceremony empowering his eldest son, Ösel Rangdröl Mukpo, as his successor in the Shambhala lineage. At that time he gave him the title of Sawang ("Earth Lord").

Trungpa Rinpoche was also known for his interest in the arts and particularly for his insights into the relationship between contemplative discipline and the artistic process. Two books published since his death—*The Art of Calligraphy* (1994) and *Dharma Art* (1996) (a new edition appeared in 2008 under the title *True Perception: The Path of Dharma Art*)—present this aspect of his work. His own artwork included calligraphy, painting, flower arranging, poetry, playwriting, and environmental installations. In addition, at the Naropa Institute he created an educational atmosphere that attracted many leading artists and poets. The exploration of the creative process in light of contemplative training continues there as a provocative dialogue. Trungpa Rinpoche also published two books of poetry: *Mudra* (1972) and *First Thought Best Thought* (1983). In 1998 a retrospective compilation of his poetry, *Timely Rain*, was published.

Shortly before his death, in a meeting with Samuel Bercholz, the publisher of Shambhala Publications, Chögyam Trungpa expressed his interest in publishing 108 volumes of his teachings, to be called the Dharma Ocean Series. "Dharma Ocean" is the translation of Chögyam Trungpa's Tibetan teaching name, Chökyi Gyatso. The Dharma Ocean Series was to consist primarily of material edited to allow readers to encounter this rich array of teachings simply and directly rather than in an overly systematized or condensed form. In 1991 the first posthumous volume in the series, *Crazy Wisdom*, was published, and another seven volumes followed in the ensuing years. Starting in 2008, Rinpoche's senior editors, his widow Diana J. Mukpo, and Shambhala Publications all agreed to expand the understanding of the Dharma Ocean Series to include all of Chögyam Trungpa's work. Plans continue for many future volumes of his teachings to be published.

Trungpa Rinpoche's published books represent only a fraction of the rich legacy of his teachings. During his seventeen years of teaching in North America, he crafted the structures necessary to provide his students with thorough, systematic training in the dharma. From introductory talks and courses to advanced group retreat practices, these programs emphasized a balance of study and practice, of intellect and intuition. *Trungpa* by Fabrice Midal, a French biography (forthcoming in English translation), details the many forms of training that Chögyam Trungpa developed. *Dragon Thunder: My Life with Chögyam Trungpa* is the story of Rinpoche's life as told by Diana Mukpo. This also provides insight into the many forms that he crafted for Buddhism in North America.

In addition to his extensive teachings in the Buddhist tradition, Trungpa Rinpoche also placed great emphasis on the Shambhala teachings, which stress the importance of meditation in action, synchronizing mind and body, and training oneself to approach obstacles or challenges in everyday life with the courageous attitude of a warrior, without anger. The goal of creating an enlightened society is fundamental to the Shambhala teachings. According to the Shambhala approach, the realization of an enlightened society comes not purely through outer activity, such as community or political involvement, but from appreciation of the senses and the sacred dimension of day-to-day life. A second volume of these teachings, entitled *Great Eastern Sun*, was published in 1999. The final volume of these teachings, *Smile at Fear: Awakening the True Heart of Bravery*, was published in 2009.

Chögyam Trungpa died in 1987, at the age of forty-seven. By the time of his death, he was known not only as Rinpoche ("Precious Jewel") but also as Vajracharya ("Vajra Holder") and as Vidyadhara ("Wisdom Holder") for his role as a master of the vajrayana, or tantric teachings of Buddhism. As a holder of the Shambhala teachings, he had also received the titles of Dorje Dradül ("Indestructible Warrior") and Sakyong ("Earth

Protector"). He is survived by his wife, Diana Judith Mukpo, and five sons. His eldest son, the Sawang Ösel Rangdröl Mukpo, succeeds him as the spiritual head of Vajradhatu. Acknowledging the importance of the Shambhala teachings to his father's work, the Sawang changed the name of the umbrella organization to Shambhala, with Vajradhatu remaining one of its major divisions. In 1995 the Sawang received the Shambhala title of Sakyong like his father before him and was also confirmed as an incarnation of the great ecumenical teacher Mipham Rinpoche.

Trungpa Rinpoche is widely acknowledged as a pivotal figure in introducing the buddhadharma to the Western world. He joined his great appreciation for Western culture with his deep understanding of his own tradition. This led to a revolutionary approach to teaching the dharma, in which the most ancient and profound teachings were presented in a thoroughly contemporary way. Trungpa Rinpoche was known for his fearless proclamation of the dharma: free from hesitation, true to the purity of the tradition, and utterly fresh. May these teachings take root and flourish for the benefit of all sentient beings.

Index

dharma teachings, 7, 153, 215
dhyanas (meditative states), 100–101,
    199
diamonds, buying and selling, 158, 159
discipline
    in approach to money, 171–72
    in business, need for, 92–93, 178–79
    obstacles to, 179–81
    and spiritual practice, 138–39,
        182–83
discriminating awareness, 183–86
dualism, 9, 169, 173, 211–12

Eckhart, Meister, 199–200
ego
    and goal-oriented behaviors,
        72–73, 93, 95–97, 99–100, 162
    materialism and, 13–16, 42 43
    obstacles/pain from, 39 41, 51,
        67–68, 173
    and positive thinking, 208–9
    role in pursuing spiritual path, 215
    self-maintenance of, 13–15
    and the selling of dharma, 153
    simple, transforming into wis-
        dom, 173–74, 215
    sources of, 40, 113–14
    true self-confidence vs., 89, 105–6
egolessness, 110–11, 207, 210–12. *See
    also* bodhisattva precepts;
    spiritual pathway
emotions, passions (kleshas). *See also*
    ego
    ambition and compassion, 162
    and ego power, 14–15
    power of, 116
    and working through karma, 202
eternalism, 185, 209
evil, 50–51, 69, 152

family relationships
    and discipline, 138–39
    healthy marriage, 143–44
    as karmic situation, 140–41

open communications, 142–43
openness and flexibility, 140
relationship with children, 137–38
in traditional Tibetan society,
    134–35
true passion and, 123, 124
as two-way learning process,
    138–39
in Western society, 135–36
fear
    as barrier to true passion, 124–25
    of creativity, 42
    ego and, 14, 34, 40–41
    and karma, 140, 209
    of the void, 113, 124–25
    and work attitudes, 86, 90
feminine/masculine principles, 106–7,
    130–33
freedom, true, 27–28, 110, 125–26
Fremantle, Francesca, 246
friendship
    in business relations, 184, 195–96
    with offspring, 140
    and sexual communication, 107,
        143–44
frivolity, frivolousness
    in sexual relations, 103, 105
    towards money, 155–56
    towards work, 56
    transforming, 57–58

Gandhi, Mahatma, 160
generosity, real
    and commitment in marriage,
        144–46
    and good communication, 143–44
    of parents towards children,
        137–38
    and sexual communication, 108
    as stagnation, 129
    in work situations, 66–68
gift giving, 168, 176
goal-driven behaviors. *See also* ego;
    spiritual materialism